CONTEMPORARY LAW SERIES

PETER A. BELL

JEFFREY O'CONNELL

Accidental Justice

The Dilemmas
of Tort Law

Yale University Press   New Haven and London

Set in Sabon type by à la page, New Haven, Connecticut.
Printed in the United States of America.

Library of Congress Cataloging-in-Publication Data

Bell, Peter A., 1945–
    Accidental justice : the dilemmas of tort law / Peter A. Bell and Jeffrey O'Connell.
        p. cm. — (Contemporary law series)
    Includes bibliographical references and index.
    ISBN 0-300-06257-5 (cloth: alk. paper)
    1. Torts—United States. 2. Accident law—United States.
    I. O'Connell, Jeffrey, 1928– . II. Title. III. Series.
    KF1250.B4 1997
    346.7303—dc20
    [347.3063]   96-36656

A catalogue record for this book is available from the British Library.

The paper in this book meets the guidelines for permanence and durability of the Committee on Production Guidelines for Book Longevity of the Council on Library Resources.

10   9   8   7   6   5   4   3   2   1

To Dylan and Eamon Duke and Virginia Mae O'Connell, the future; and to William Henry and Natalie Barry Bell, the foundation

CONTENTS

PREFACE

We have tried not to slant this book toward our own individual (and sometimes differing) opinions. As least we have not proselytized nearly as strongly as each of us has done in our individual writings. Rather, we have jointly sought to present and explain, reasonably fully, a spectrum of our own and other viewpoints under one cover. Thus, although we have not presented matters that we judged to be clearly wrong, we have included presentations of viewpoints with which one or both of us may disagree. We have further presumed on the whole that the proponents of divergent opinions are sincere in those views. This reflects not only our judgment but our belief that the merits of ideas are normally better understood free from attacks on the integrity of those presenting them. We have nonetheless tried to alert the reader to the interests of both tort law's adherents and its critics in their debates. In that connection, obviously it is not always easy to discern the extent to which various positions are the product of self-interest as opposed to conviction.

We gratefully acknowledge Thomas E. O'Connell, President Emeritus, Berkshire Community College, for his perceptive help in reading and suggesting changes in the manuscript; Ruy Garcia-Zamor, University of Virginia School of Law Class of 1997, and Andrea Heinbach, Leah Krause, Erin Markey, and Chris Dalton, Syracuse University College of Law Classes of 1993 and 1994, for their able research assistance; and the secretarial staff at both universities for their expert assistance, especially Susan Pitts at Virginia and Lynn M. Oatman at Syracuse. Finally, we are much indebted to Dan Heaton of Yale University Press for his meticulous and deft editorial efforts.

The best-selling author Stephen King would find himself quite at home in the world of tort law. It is replete with horror stories. The stories are not all blood and guts—poisoned towns, incinerated motorists, mangled babies. In fact, much of the horror of tort law that Americans have heard about recently has come from legal machinery run amok. The stories are familiar: a drunk falls in front of a subway train and emerges with a $9 million judgment against the transit authority; a heart attack victim takes Sears and Roebuck to court for producing an overly difficult pull-start on its power mower; a criminal intruder recovers thousands of dollars after falling through a school skylight; a woman wins a huge judgment against McDonald's after being scalded by coffee spilled from a container while she tried to add cream and sugar.

More recently, books, articles, and full-page advertisements have trumpeted an even louder note of woe. Tort law, it is argued, imposes a hidden tax on the goods and services we all consume, a tax that adds significantly to the price of some products. Moreover, thanks to tort law, some valuable products are never developed, useful producers go out of—or never go into—business, and America's competitive edge further erodes.

Although there is considerable debate about tort law's responsibility for the foregoing catastrophes, there is none at all about the basic and continual horror story, told repeatedly in tort cases. Tort law, after all, is the law that determines the circumstances in which persons or businesses will be judged responsible to pay money to compensate other persons for their injuries. Its story is often one of bodies maimed, of spirits scarred or broken, and of lives extinguished. These have ever been life's tragedies from which we have always tried to protect ourselves.

Tort law purports to turn its corrective eye toward these events when there is at least an allegedly external cause. Birth defects devastate whole lives and families. But tort law is for the most part initially passive. It stays out of the nursery until someone singles out the maker of a drug, like thalidomide, as having improperly provided a drug to expectant mothers that ultimately caused those defects. Millions of people, a Harvard study suggests, leave hospitals needlessly injured, dying, or dead as a result of their stay. Tort law isn't normally activated until someone points to specific improper medical care, rather than just to some disease or trauma, as the cause of that condition.

Today's horror stories echo those involving tort since at least the beginning of the Industrial Revolution. According to one theory of legal history, in medieval times, when accidental injuries inflicted by strangers were much less common, tort law lined up on the side of the victim. If someone directly injured a person by his actions, the injured person was entitled to bring a tort lawsuit and recover money damages. Proof of wrongdoing was unnecessary: "If a man assaults me, and I lift up my staff to defend myself, and in lifting it up hit another, an action for claim lies by that person and yet I did a lawful thing. And the reason . . . is because he that was damaged ought to be recompensed."[1]

Paradoxically, when accidental injuries proliferated during the Industrial Revolution, tort law's protection beat a retreat. Victims of railroads and the other awkwardly developing industries of the times found that tort law now insisted they could not recover compensation for injuries unless they first proved that the injurer had acted unreasonably. Why the change? According to traditional legal theory, to protect the nineteenth century's burgeoning entrepreneurial activity.

A tension had arisen that continues to play out in tort law today: between the desire, on the one hand, to compensate injured people and to deter injury-causing conduct and the fear, on the other, of discouraging useful activities.

That tension has made itself felt in successive waves of tort litigation for more than 150 years. The first wave involved the workers of the United States' infant industries, brushed aside almost as rudely in the tort system as they were in the socioeconomic system. The labor reform movements around the turn of the century were reflected in increasing (but erratic) tort success by injured workers, and, ultimately, by the creation of workers' compensation systems. Workers' compensation removed worker injuries from tort law and allowed for their reparation (at significantly reduced dollar levels) without any need for the worker to prove his employer at fault.

Other classes of injuries encountered similar early resistance in tort law. Like workplace accidents, a second great wave—automobile accidents—tended to expose tort litigation as slow, expensive, erratic, and often inequitable in its process of compensating the injured. The result has been pressure to turn to no-fault schemes, which—like workers' compensation—would bypass tort litigation. Automobile accident law already has no-fault elements in about a third of the states.

When automobile accidents led to claims against the manufacturer of the car, such products liability tort suits, along with those for medical malpractice, became the dramatic tort wave of the modern era. Unlike typical car crash injuries, which give rise to lawsuits between ordinary citizens, these injuries threatened the livelihoods of influential institutions and persons—product manufacturers and health care providers—whose activities often led to injury.

Not surprisingly, efforts are afoot at federal and state levels to curb especially medical malpractice and products liability tort litigation. With respect to these kinds of accidents, the ever-increasing financial stakes have raised the decibel levels in the arguments between adherents and critics of the present tort system.

That cacophony has approached the level of a victim's scream with the newest wave of tort lawsuits, those involving injuries—including diseases like cancer—purportedly stemming from toxins in the environment. A logical outgrowth of the environmental movement of the past twenty years, mass toxic tort lawsuits have paraded an even grimmer set of horrors onto the torts stage. Such suits confront us with stealthy but deadly maladies on a massive scale—and threaten the destruction of entire industries, sometimes victimized, it is argued, by greedy lawyers grossly exaggerating clients' condition. They also show woefully slow and inequitable, awesomely expensive and unpleasant tort machinery chewing away on both victim and those accused of causing the victim's condition.

This book is the story of these horrors, of tort law's response to them, and of tort law's paradoxical role in both avoiding—and creating—other horrors in its often clumsy effort to correct the first horror thrust onto the lives of victims of accidents and ailments.[2]

ACCIDENTAL JUSTICE

CHAPTER ONE

How Tort Law Works

Horrors visit us all. They come any day. Howard Young and his family were visited on a Tuesday.

It was an unremarkable Tuesday for most people, even for most other suburban lawyers rising early to dress and breakfast with minds on the 8:12 or the 8:23 train into the city. Not so for Howard Young. Tension crackled throughout his modest suburban home with the fitfulness and compressed fury of an electronic bug zapper. Upstairs, Howard's wife, Nicole, changed two-year-old Laura, who showed little of her customary playfulness. Elissa, eight, dressed attentively in her brightly bordered bedroom, with barely a nod at the Yamaha keyboard that usually lured her from the morning schedule.

Howard was the source of the storm clouds darkening the family's moods. He had been a smashing success at every academic endeavor set before him, but at thirty-one Howard was feeling the approach of failure. It wasn't there yet. He didn't really see it. Nonetheless, the apprehension was familiar—and palpable. Although failure had never actually touched Howard, its threat had haunted much of his uncluttered life—from Little League baseball and school recitals through the seemingly endless tests of college and law school right up to the state bar exam and his first six months as an associate at Plimpton, Beane and Ballantine, nearly five years ago.

Failure loomed again this Tuesday: Howard feared that he might lose his big case and maybe even his job. An irascible, unpredictable judge awaited him at court. Howard had convinced his law firm to take on the discrimination case, and he had invested thousands of working hours and tens of thousands of the firm's dollars in it, and now the judge seemed ready to throw it out. Howard well understood how his firm would view the dismissal of such a costly suit, particularly in this time of declining revenues. And he was all too aware that Plimpton, Beane had begun selective downsizing, beginning with "less productive" associates.

Do a bad job in court, Howard told himself, and your carefully built pyramid of success could sink into the sand.

But first he had to fix breakfast for Laura and Elissa. Elissa's lunch had to be packed, coffee brewed, the dog fed. The morning ritual and his children's arrival in the kitchen brought Howard emotionally back to them, and before the morning's parting, the Youngs exchanged warm if hurried embraces all around.

After those farewells, Howard Young's Tuesday wound ever tighter until it unraveled completely. On the train into the city, he wrote, crossed out, and wrote more notes on a smudged legal pad. The scribbles were more hasty and turned more scribbly as he neared the station's imposing halls. The march to his office, last-minute arrangements with his secretary, and cab ride to court with his clients and senior partner were a background blur as Howard's mind continued to race through his case's legal labyrinth, looking for the exit.

Things went as badly as he had feared. The judge arrived straight from hell. He was abusive, disdainful—and he dismissed the case. Howard was trampled. In the numb haze that surrounded him after the judge's curt ruling, Howard saw himself tending to his clients, coolly discussing the judge's misconduct and the grounds for appeal with the senior partner, and, back in his office, meticulously filing all the notes, cases, and other relevant documents on a forever afternoon. On the two occasions when he had to go out of his office, he perceived in the averted eyes of other lawyers his own growing invisibility. He couldn't make himself leave the office early. He grasped at routine to keep him afloat.

When leaving finally seemed permissible, no destination offered. His mind, firing off random, disconnected thoughts, insisted that he could not go home. He stopped at a bar. He drank, slowly, solemnly, alone. Gradually, his mind relaxed its sputtering and resumed more comfortable patterns of thought. He would not go home that night because he could not look as painfully into the depths of his own inadequacy as the presence of his dependents would require. He called Nicole and explained. She was concerned. He reassured her; he would stay overnight uptown with his law school roommate.

Howard returned to his small table. He ate occasionally the free hors d'oeuvres and gazed at the changing clientele. When Howard left the bar he actually felt better.

But it quickly became apparent that he was not better at negotiating the hard realities of the world. That world insisted, despite his slow imbibing and his perfunctory eating, that he was drunk. It set out to prove its point with a series of rolling sidewalks, sharply angled curbs, and indecipherable signs. Howard finally located the subway station, but he stumbled and twisted his ankle as he struggled down stairs to the uptown platform.

Feeling unsteady and a little nauseated, Howard leaned heavily against a girder. He tried to quiet his racing heart and heavy breathing, so as not to attract attention from the half-dozen people nearby on the platform. He waited. He waited so long that he began to worry that the subway had short-circuited. Twice he thought he heard the train coming, but nothing materialized. Howard worried more.

When he finally heard train sounds in the tunnel, Howard tottered to the platform edge and tried to see down the track. He saw only darkness. Cautiously, he put a foot closer to the edge. In so doing, he pushed on his twisted ankle. He felt sudden pain, lost his balance, and fell. Howard landed hard, on his back, in the middle of the track. He looked up, hurt and surprised. The people on the platform seemed far away, and so uninterested that Howard almost forgot he was in any danger. People looked at him, then looked away.

Howard's forgetfulness lasted only a few moments. In that time, the faint tunnel noises he had heard grew into a real train, racing into the station. Transfixed by his impending doom, Howard did no more than cover his face when the sudden shriek of brakes signaled the train driver's panic. The train knocked Howard against the side wall, then struck him again and dragged him thirty-five feet before coming to a stop. Horror had arrived.

Howard Young did not die.[1] At times, he wished he had. His spinal cord severed, Howard never regained the use of his legs. Burned about the head and upper body by contact with the electrified third rail, he remained horribly scarred even after a series of painful skin grafts to rebuild his face. Comatose for three days as a result of brain injuries, Howard awoke to a life of significantly diminished mental capacities. He could no longer concentrate for extended periods. His prized ability to pick up complex concepts quickly and easily had been replaced with a sluggish, groping tenacity, but he could manage only limited understanding of anything complex.

Remarkably, there was no damage to Howard's emotional faculties. That was a mixed blessing. He could feel the love of his family and friends and the encouragement of the doctors, nurses, and rehabilitation counselors who dominated his life for the next four months. But he could also feel the sadness and desperation of Nicole and his young daughters as they struggled to adjust to a world without his physical and emotional support. For a long time, little Laura was afraid of him, disfigured as he was. Elissa found herself in a new role, which she described to a friend in a time of frustration as being a "maid." Nicole, in effect now a single parent with three children, entered the exhausting world of constant obligation. Howard had little to give back to anyone emotionally, struggling as he was to cope with his feeling of complete inadequacy, his pain, and the role of the disabled that had been thrust on him.

Financially, the Youngs' situation was not as desperate in the first year after the accident as it might have been. Things were certainly tight, though. In spite of Howard's unusually good health insurance, provided through his law firm, the Youngs still had to pay nearly $40,000 from their savings for their share of the medical, rehabilitation, and maintenance expenses. That nearly exhausted their financial reserves, but their standard of living remained about the same because the law firm voluntarily paid Howard's full $150,000 salary for a year after the injury.

Nicole, however, was acutely aware that once that year's grace ended, the bottom would fall out. Howard, like most people, had no disability insurance to replace the loss of income for longer than six months.[2] It was clear that he could never return to the legal profession and that it would be a long time before he could hold any sort of job outside the home. Social Security disability insurance payments would replace only about $20,000 of his income. Nicole might be able to find work as an editor or technical writer, but the $20,000–25,000 from such a job would be reduced by $7,000–12,000 for child and home health care. Their net incomes could not possibly pay for the medical procedures and rehabilitation recommended by Howard's doctor for the next five years. Poverty loomed.

Financial help with the consequences of accidents sometimes comes from the law of accidents: tort law. Even in accidents that at first blush seem the victim's fault—like Howard Young's—further investigation may reveal circumstances that permit the victim to gain at least partial compensation for his injuries.[3]

For the victim of an accident, embarking on a tort lawsuit is no simple matter, however. If someone is having a baby, Dy-Dee Diaper Service learns of it through obstetricians or hospitals, and the company solicits business by mailing forms and information about diapers well before the baby's birth. No such system exists for accident victims. In fact, any lawyer trying to employ such a system would violate her state's rules of professional conduct.

This doesn't mean that lawyers who commonly represent injured persons fade into invisibility. Advertising—as well as attitudes toward it—has changed radically in the past twenty years. Lawyers once regarded it as undignified and improper to advertise their services. A lawyer, after all, was a professional; professionals' services differed from consumer products like children's cereals, triple-track windshield wipers, and personal-care beautifiers. The public should be informed of such services in a dignified manner, at most a listing in the Yellow Pages.

Lawyers' attitudes, like the times, have changed. These changes have been particularly pronounced among lawyers who regularly represent the injured in tort lawsuits—the plaintiffs' torts bar. Perhaps these lawyers, more than most, need advertising to reach potential clients. The clientele of such lawyers are the Nicole and Howard Youngs of the world, although usually less well educated and certainly less legally sophisticated than the Youngs.

Such clients are not like the businesses that provide the work for most lawyers. Unaccustomed to using lawyers, these clients don't have regular access to a network that can tell them what lawyers do and which lawyers are good. Often they won't have any idea that a lawyer could be helpful to them in their situation. So the plaintiffs' lawyer has reached out to make injury victims aware of her useful services and also of her advantages over other lawyers.

Most persons with valid tort claims, however, still do not seek out a lawyer. Recent studies indicate that fewer than one in five victims of another's negligence claim for compensation. A higher ratio of those injured in road and workplace accidents may claim, but even there, fewer than half do so.[4]

That Howard and Nicole Young did make a claim was a product of circumstance and luck. Howard was, after all, a lawyer. That meant that many of his closest friends were lawyers. Among them was Jack Wilkes, the law school roommate he was on his way to visit when he was crushed by the train. Jack happened to be one of those friends whom horror does not drive away. Jack also happened to be curious. In the course of his visits to Howard at the hospital and at his suburban home, Jack became quite interested in finding out exactly what had happened at the subway station. He had Howard's somewhat hazy recollections of the events, but Jack wanted to know more, to figure out why the train did not stop, why no one had helped his fallen friend.

What Jack found out, simply by knowing what and whom to ask, led Howard and Nicole to a tort lawyer. Jack knew that the Transit Authority police would have written a report about the accident that nearly killed Howard Young. Jack knew to call the Transit

Authority's office of legal counsel. From them, he learned that anyone injured in a subway accident could receive a copy of the accident report simply by requesting it in writing. Jack drafted such a
letter and had Howard sign it; within four weeks, a copy of the
report came back.

The report confirmed the basic events much as Howard remembered them. Witnesses on the platform recalled that Howard had
been unsteady in his movements, obviously drunk, and leaning
against a girder until the time he moved forward to look for the
train. Witnesses reported that Howard had lain on the track from
one to three minutes between the time he fell and the time he was
struck. The report named five people who had been standing near
enough to Howard to have possibly helped him after he fell.

Most interesting, the report indicated, through the statements of
witnesses and based on observations, including the screech of brakes,
that the train may have been going faster than permitted by Transit
Authority guidelines. The report also contained a statement from
the train's motorman that he had been trying to make up time lost
due to a malfunctioning door; he had not seen Howard on the
tracks when he first entered the station because he had turned away
to close the cab door, which was ajar.

Nicole did not know what to make of the report, and Howard
could not pay attention to it long enough to draw significant infer-
ences. Jack, however, read the report as a clear signal that Howard's
injury was not simply the result of his drunken foolishness. It was
also the product of the unreasonable actions and inactions—the
negligence—of other people. Jack suggested to Howard and Nicole
that they might find the financial help they desperately needed in a
tort lawsuit against those who could have prevented Howard's
injuries if they had only acted with reasonable care.

Finding a lawyer was not the pin-the-tail-on-the-donkey process
for Howard and Nicole that it is for most injury victims who finally
decide to consult one. They did not have to rely on the Yellow Pages,
the subway or TV ads, or some second cousin's one-shot experience
with a lawyer (perhaps on something as unrelated as a real estate

closing). Although Howard was too embarrassed to let anyone in his old firm know that he might bring a lawsuit for injuries that were so obviously his own fault, Jack had no qualms about asking litigator friends for recommendations. Wary of the reputation of plaintiffs' lawyers as sharks, Jack especially requested his friends to recommend a lawyer who would treat Howard and Nicole as full human beings, as well as be able to extract as much money as possible out of those who shared responsibility for Howard's injuries.

The plaintiffs' lawyer whom the suffering Youngs finally visited in May, nearly eight months after the accident, was Pamela Jane Cowcroft. P.J., as she was known, was a thirty-six-year-old partner in a ten-lawyer suburban law firm that specialized in representing injured persons making workers' compensation and tort claims.

P.J. had been introduced to the excitement of trying cases in her second year of law school. In mock trial competitions there, and in nine years of law practice thereafter, P.J. had developed and tried nearly fifty cases. She found that law came alive in the context of people's injury claims. Merely mediocre at the doctrinal regurgitation and theoretical dabbling that law school exams required, P.J. excelled at fitting her clients' injury stories into the pigeonholes that tort law demanded. She superbly communicated with juries about the wrongdoings of others and their effects on her clients.

It didn't cost the Youngs a penny up front to talk with P.J. about their possible claim. In fact, P.J. made it clear to them from the outset that they would not have to pay anything out of their increasingly empty pockets for her legal help. She had already read the accident report sent her by Jack Wilkes. She listened attentively to the Youngs as they told her what had happened on the night of the accident and what had happened to their lives as a result. P.J. told the Youngs that she and her associate would need to do a little more checking on the matter and that she would let them know in a week whether she would take their case.

During that week, P. J. Cowcroft and her law firm went through a decision-making process unique to personal injury lawyers. Most lawyers, when approached by a client seeking representation, need only decide whether the potential client can pay their bills. Although these lawyers may believe that they should indicate the likely outcome to the client, they often are financially indifferent to that outcome. But they do tell the client what he can expect to pay for representation. The plaintiffs' personal injury lawyer, by contrast, must quickly make careful, reliable predictions about the likely outcome of her client's case. She has to make that forecast skillfully, because if the client loses, the lawyer will not be paid. And even if the client wins, the amount recovered may not be enough to justify her time and effort.

Plaintiffs' tort lawyers represent injured persons on a contingency fee basis; the lawyer's receipt of her fee depends entirely on the client's receipt of money for his injuries. Accordingly, P.J. and the other lawyers in her firm had to quickly and carefully examine the Youngs' situation, through the eyes of the judge and jury who might eventually decide the merits of their case, and through the eyes of the potential defendants or their insurers who would decide whether and in what amount to offer a settlement.

That P.J.'s firm gives this sort of hard look at a client's situation before agreeing to represent him is one of the major implications of the contingency fee system by which the injured receive representation in tort cases. The contingency fee method has plaintiffs' lawyers act as gatekeepers for the tort system. An injured person whose claim has insufficient merit will not—or should not—get his foot in the tort law door because he will be unable to find a reputable lawyer to represent him. The lawyer is said to put her money where her mouth is.

The correlative of the contingency fee method is that adequate legal representation can be available regardless of income. A person injured under circumstances that probably will entitle him to sufficient compensation will be able to get a lawyer to represent him if he wants one. This is so even though lawyers representing a client on a contingency fee basis are supposed to charge that client for the costs of bringing such a suit. These costs do not include attorneys' fees but do include such expensive items as photocopying, the fees of expert witnesses, the high price of obtaining information in formal legal proceedings before a trial, and attorneys' travel. But most injured people who lose a tort lawsuit will not have enough money to cover these expenses, which can range from less than a thousand dollars in simple matters to more than a million dollars in complicated litigation. So most of the time, lawyers simply do not collect for such expenses if the case is lost.

Like all free lunches, the contingency fee system does have costs. Prime among them is the size of the lawyer's fee when the injury victim is finally compensated. Typically, the lawyer takes 25–40 percent of that payment in fees, a percentage agreed to at the outset by lawyer and client. P. J. Cowcroft would take back to her firm $33,000 or more out of every $100,000 a defendant paid the Youngs. She would admit that settling or winning tort cases for persons seriously injured, like Howard Young, results in lucrative fees for her and her firm. She would argue, however, that such is the price injury victims must pay for the security of ready access to legal help provided by the contingency fee: a system that pays lawyers nothing when their client loses a case must pay them a handsome amount when the client wins. Otherwise, capable lawyers would have insufficient incentive to practice personal injury law.

These same economic considerations also mean that the contingency fee closes the door to the courts for many people even if they have valid tort claims. Many plaintiffs' tort lawyers will not represent a claimant in a products liability or medical malpractice case— the two most common kinds of litigated tort cases—unless the client has injury claims worth more than $100,000. The costs, in lawyers' time and litigation expenses, are simply too great for it to be financially worthwhile. This means that many persons with significant but not crushing injuries will not be able to get a lawyer, even if the law would eventually grant them compensation.

Moreover, it means that entities that often find themselves as defendants in tort lawsuits—such as major businesses and insurance companies—can influence the access of injured persons to the tort system. To the extent that such defendants can make a tort lawsuit time-consuming and expensive, they can reduce the number of persons who will be able to sue them. The more time and money a plaintiffs' lawyer must lay out to win a tort suit, the greater the injury a person must suffer before a plaintiffs' lawyer can afford to represent him.

Many people, however, like Howard Young and his family, have been so tragically injured that if they can be successful in a tort claim, they undoubtedly will receive enough money to make it worthwhile for a capable plaintiffs' law firm to put its resources into the case. In the Youngs' case, the decision comes down to the two basic questions that faced P. J. Cowcroft's firm: what are the chances that the Youngs will be successful in their legal claim, and will the person or persons against whom they succeed be able to pay the amount awarded by the court?

To answer these questions, P.J. first had to determine which persons or entities might be liable for the Youngs' injuries. She identified them as (1) the witnesses who stood on the subway platform after Howard fell, (2) the driver of the train, and (3) the Transit Authority. P.J. discarded other possible defendants as not worth suing. (The bar that had served Howard Young had gone bankrupt and hadn't carried insurance.)

She then had to determine what the Youngs' "causes of action" might be. That meant identifying the rules of tort law that each defendant might have violated, and under which a court would hold him or it liable to pay compensation. Likewise, it meant identifying the injuries to each of the four Youngs that a court would find deserving of compensation.

P.J. readily identified the broken tort rules as being in the category of negligence. Simply put, negligence law essentially requires someone who acts unreasonably to compensate persons who are thereby injured. In the Youngs' case, P.J. prepared to write a short formal document, called a complaint, to be given to (or "served on") each of the potentially liable persons and entities and then presented to the court if a lawsuit were formally started.

The complaint might say the witnesses acted unreasonably by not reaching down to offer Howard a hand or other assistance that would have moved him off the tracks out of danger's way. It would probably say that the train driver acted unreasonably by driving too fast, by not watching the tracks carefully enough, and by not applying the brakes soon enough. It probably would not accuse the Transit Authority itself of doing anything unreasonable, but would assert, rather, that the Authority should compensate the Youngs because of its special employment relationship with the negligent driver.

P.J. would recognize that the Youngs' chances of success against the five or more witnesses were slim indeed, since in most situations tort law does not require bystanders to assist someone in danger, even if it would be reasonable to do so. Nevertheless, she was prepared to push hard to convince judges that tort law, in situations like Howard Young's, had already decided that such witnesses could be liable to an injured person if they do not take reasonable steps to help him out of his danger. She was even prepared to try to convince judges that such a decision would be the most appropriate rule for tort law, even if it had not been previously clearly set forth as the rule. In other words, she might use Howard's case "to set precedent."

In such manner, tort plaintiffs and their lawyers constantly pressure courts to examine anew the legal rules that determine whether an injured person will receive compensation. Where a person has serious injuries, plaintiffs' lawyers have the incentive to be very creative in the view of law they present. That constant, creative pressure has made tort law extremely dynamic—some complain overly dynamic—during the past half century.

P.J. would also recognize, however, that the legal claims on which the Youngs had the best chance of success were the claims of negligence—unreasonable behavior—on the part of the subway train driver, who had been speeding and not looking where he was going. Even with a seriously injured plaintiff and a probably successful legal claim for liability P.J. and her firm would not be ready to represent the Youngs. Their fee was valuable to them only if the claim would succeed against a person or entity that could actually pay the compensation due.

This "deep pocket" is the object of the plaintiffs' tort lawyer's continual search and attention. Tort law responds to claims of injury and responsibility by delineating the circumstances in which certain injuring parties are judged legally responsible for a plaintiff's injuries and are ordered to compensate that injured person. It does not help a plaintiff to win a substantial tort judgment against a defendant who cannot pay.

Frequently, this means that it does no good to sue the most obvious wrongdoer. A subway train driver cannot possibly pay his share of Howard Young's injuries. Neither could most people. The owner who doesn't control his easily angered dog can't. The football coach whose player is paralyzed because the coach didn't teach him the correct impact protection can't. The painter whose bucket falls on someone can't, either.

As a result, the plaintiffs' tort lawyer must often see beyond the obvious defendant to secure compensation for her client and income for herself. It is second nature for her to look for responsible parties with deep pockets. When there has been a rape on campus, the victim's lawyer rarely will focus her attention on the rapist. He probably hasn't been caught. Even if caught, he probably has no money. Instead the lawyer's attention will turn almost automatically to the university, a deep pocket, and she will examine whether it took reasonable steps to prevent rapes. If not, the university may pay for the victim's injuries. Of course, if the rapist *were* found and did have sufficient assets, he, not the university, would ultimately be responsible for payment.

The search for the deep pocket most commonly proceeds down one of two avenues. The lawyer needs to find either a legally responsible defendant who has liability insurance or a defendant, such as a corporation, with substantial financial resources of its own. Pursuit down each of these avenues has led to some unusual twists and turns in the development of tort law.

Most Americans know a little about liability insurance. Most commonly, it is bought as part of a package of car insurance or homeowner's insurance. The insurance company agrees to pay compensation, up to a specified limit, for injuries related to use of the policy owner's car or home. Millions of ordinary Americans have it. So do most businesses and other institutions.

In the case of Howard and Nicole Young, however, would most of the individual wrongdoers have liability insurance that would pay for Howard's injuries? The inactive witnesses might have homeowner's insurance, but would that extend to injuries they negligently cause because of their subway behavior? The train driver might have similar insurance coverage, but it clearly won't cover injuries he causes in his work. P. J. Cowcroft can always hope that one of those subway bystanders turns out to be a junk bonds mogul. She won't, however, invest her time and resources in the Youngs' tort lawsuit if all she has are such insubstantial hopes.

So where's the party with the deep pockets? Over there, behind the driver: the Transit Authority. Naming the Transit Authority as a defendant would be so obvious to P. J. Cowcroft that she wouldn't even stop to consider why an entity that may not have done anything wrong—after all, it explicitly prohibited the kind of speeding and inattention that made the driver a wrongdoer—should be legally responsible for the Youngs' injuries.

If asked, however, P.J. would refer to the legal doctrine of "vicarious liability." This means that a person or entity is sometimes legally responsible for the consequences of other people's wrongdoing. That responsibility is not imposed because this party has done anything wrong itself, as the university in the rape situation mentioned previously may have. It is imposed because there is a special relationship between the wrongdoer and the party being held liable vicariously.

Vicarious liability most commonly provides a deep-pocket defendant when the wrongdoer is an employee of that defendant. The law requires the employee's injury-causing actions to have been within the scope of his employment. So the platform bystanders' employers would not be vicariously liable. The subway driver was clearly working for the Transit Authority at the time of the accident. If a court should decide that he were liable to the Youngs, it undoubtedly would also hold the Transit Authority liable, vicariously.

Given the high percentage of employed persons in our society, this legal doctrine of vicarious liability provides the deep pocket otherwise missing in many serious accidents. Increasing existence of deep pockets markedly increases in turn the number of tort suits that can be brought by injured persons. The vicarious liability doctrine is so old and well-settled in tort law that it is almost never questioned. Basically, it stems from the notion that an employer who benefits from his employees' activities ought as well to bear the burden of those activities when they go awry. Without the rule, thousands of injuries caused by others' wrongdoing would go uncompensated, because they could never make it to court.

Settled on her possible defendants and on the legal bases for a decision in the Youngs' favor, P. J. Cowcroft and her firm still have one final *t* to cross before deciding to represent the Youngs. They need to precisely assess the dimensions of the Youngs' injuries. Their prime interest in making that assessment is to determine just what injuries the law will recognize as deserving of monetary compensation. They want to know just what money damages the Youngs will get from tort law.

Tort damages stem from the underlying premise that the victim of another's tortious conduct should receive money damages in an amount that will put him in the same situation he would have been in had the accident never happened. The plaintiff, in other words, should be fully compensated for his injuries.[5]

This foundational premise cannot be taken literally. No one, certainly not lawyers and judges, can put Howard Young back into the world as he was before he was run over by the subway train. What this underlying premise of tort damages really means is that a jury (or a judge sitting alone in a case where neither side requests a jury) will be asked to examine the plaintiff's life as it is now and is expected to be in the future. They will compare it to the plaintiff's life as it was and was expected to have been in the absence of the injury. Then they will award the plaintiff a sum of money that fairly represents how much worse off he is and will be as a result of the accident.

With respect to some items of damages, this task is not all that daunting. Hospitals and medical and rehabilitative personnel charge finite amounts for their services. A judge or jury (called fact finders) need only be able to compute the "past medical costs" component of a plaintiff's damages. Other parts of the damage assessment task, however, are dauntingly difficult. For example, the fact finder, often with the aid of expert witnesses, must try to figure what income the plaintiff would have earned in his life if uninjured, and subtract from it any lifetime income he is expected to earn in his life after the injury. Much more speculatively, the fact finder must assess the value of the pain, the mental suffering, and the decrease in life's joys that the plaintiff has experienced and will experience. His family's emotional loss will also be assessed. Then, the judge or jury must determine an amount of money that fairly represents these intangible injuries.

Tort law engages in this sort of agonizingly detailed evaluation of the unevaluable for every injured person who succeeds on a claim that some defendant is liable for his injuries. If Howard Young's tort lawsuit goes to trial, P. J. Cowcroft will present extremely detailed evidence about what happened to him. Officials from his law firm will testify about the quality of his work and his prospects as a lawyer. Experts will testify about the likely earnings of a lawyer with those prospects. Medical experts will testify about the likely progress of his physical condition during the remainder of his life. They will also testify about the kind of pain associated with his injuries, the treatments he has undergone and those he is expected to undergo. Psychological experts may testify about Howard's mental condition and about the distress generally suffered by persons with similar injuries. His family, his friends, and Howard himself will testify about the difference between what he and his life were like before the accident and what they are now. P.J. will probably hire specialists to produce a videotape of a typical day in Howard's life. And the defendants may produce their own experts of myriad sorts to testify about the same matters or in other ways try to minimize the horror of what happened to Howard.

Having put Howard Young's past, present, and future life and condition under a microscope in this fashion, a jury of six to twelve will deliberate among themselves and, most likely, award a lump sum of money to the plaintiff.[6] This purports to represent full compensation for his injuries. Everyone involved recognizes that this is a highly individualized, highly uncertain, and highly cumbersome and complicated process. But it is also a process with an intense focus on the realities of the injured person.

Having previewed that process, and having moderate confidence in the probable range of damage awards, P. J. Cowcroft and her partners finally decide to represent the Youngs. They also decide to initiate a lawsuit against the Transit Authority, the driver, and the five platform witnesses. Next, P.J. will write up the formal complaint, confer with the Youngs and have them sign it, file it with a court, and formally serve it on the defendants.

A tort defense attorney will become involved in the case very soon thereafter. Unlike the plaintiffs' tort attorney, the defense lawyer has little say in whether a case will be brought or not. Neither he nor his client has the luxury of saying "forget it" after a careful evaluation of the circumstances surrounding an injury.

The defense attorney does have one important luxury denied his counterpart. Win or lose, he gets paid. Most tort defense attorneys are paid either on the basis of what they normally charge for each hour they work or perhaps on the basis of a previously negotiated retainer. With payment by retainer, a lawyer or law firm agrees to represent an entity in all (or in a certain number) of cases in which that entity is sued, in return for a flat fee or a per case fee.

As with the contingency fee, this method of payment has significant implications for the conduct of tort lawsuits. On the plaintiff's side, every day that a suit proceeds without payment is a day when compensation the plaintiff may need has not arrived; it is also a day for which his attorney has worked without pay. On the defense side, every day that a suit proceeds without payment may well be a day that even a clearly liable defendant has access to the money that tort law may eventually exact. For every day of work a defense attorney on any hourly fee puts into the case, he is paid. So long as his client doesn't care about speedy resolution of the suit, the defense lawyer certainly doesn't care.

Indeed, not only may the defendant not care, he may even prefer delay, given the difficulties it creates for the plaintiff and the plaintiff's attorney. The defendant may care very much, however, about the costs of defending the suit. The defendant's lawyer is paid for his work. The defendant also pays the expenses of the litigation as they occur. Even if a defendant and his attorney believe that they will not be held liable under tort law—that they will win the case—they understand that it *is* going to cost a substantial amount of money to win. As a result, a defendant often finds it appealing to consider paying *some* money to the plaintiff in settlement of a suit rather than continue to run up its defense costs beyond what it will cost to settle.

Set against this implication—that the tort system may encourage payment of marginal (maybe even meritless) claims—is the long-term interest that major defense players in tort litigation have in *not* giving money to plaintiffs with weak or meritless cases. Because plaintiffs and their lawyers need to find defendants with deep pockets for their tort claims, insurance companies and businesses often are involved in tort litigation as defendants. Insurers and businesses know that they are much less likely to be sued if they have a reputation for not settling cases easily and for being eager to defend tort suits all the way to trial. If a potential defendant has such a reputation, plaintiffs' attorneys like P. J. Cowcroft will believe that *their* expenses to obtain payment will be high, certainly much higher than if they could obtain a quick settlement. Therefore, plaintiffs' attorneys will need to be much tougher doormen, and will likely refuse to represent plaintiffs with low chances of winning or with less substantial injuries.

Because many tort defendants are such repeat players in the tort system—parties who defend many suits—it can be, and often is, in their best interest to spend more money to defend and win a tort suit than they would have paid by coming to an early settlement. Such defendants' willingness to fight claims hard will discourage other plaintiffs from filing suits, especially if they involve small damage claims or claims of very questionable merit.

Such efforts to defeat the pursuit of a claim would not operate in the case of the Youngs and P. J. Cowcroft. P.J. had properly concluded that there was considerable merit to the Youngs' claims and that their damages, if they won, would be quite high. Absent a substantial settlement offer from the Transit Authority, which looked like the only defendant with enough money to make such an offer, the case would proceed toward a trial.

The way the tort system decides a case such as the Youngs' has many complicated aspects, three of which especially influence ideas about the values and problems of tort law in the United States today. Tort lawsuits are decided very slowly; they cost a lot to decide; and they are decided to a considerable extent by juries. The parties to the Youngs' case would experience all three aspects.

By the time the lawsuit was filed on behalf of the Youngs against the Transit Authority and other defendants, nearly a year had passed since Howard's injury. Meanwhile, the Youngs' financial well-being was slipping away. On the accident anniversary, Plimpton, Beane and Ballantine stopped paying Howard's $150,000-a-year salary. Nicole's income, after deductions for child and home health care, provided about $9,000. Howard's $20,000 from Social Security insurance provided their only other source of income.

Some of their medical expenses were still covered by the health insurance Howard had had at the law firm. The mortgage payments on their home did not go down. Food and utility expenses were higher than before the accident, because Howard needed a special diet and a constantly warm house. It became quite clear that the Youngs would have to sell their home and move to subsidized housing. There was no other way they could afford to sustain Howard at the minimal levels of medical care and rehabilitation ordered by his doctors. Medicaid would pay for some of that, but certainly not all. The Youngs' only financial hope was their tort lawsuit, and they needed that financial help quickly.

No such luck. Tort suits proceed slowly; and they proceed *excruciatingly* slowly when the deep pocket involved, like the Transit Authority, doesn't even have the incentive of daily lawyers' fees to push it to seek a prompt settlement. For example, consider the case of Milton Rivera, who was twenty-nine when he was struck by a subway train that was alleged to have been negligently driven. Had Milton lived, he would have been thirty-seven by the time a jury awarded him $1.87 million. He would have been forty at the time New York's highest court reversed that verdict and ordered another trial.[7] Settlements can come faster, but it's a mistake to count on it. Lawyers on both sides are notorious for waiting until the eve of trial to settle tort cases. The families of seven Chicago-area residents who died in highly publicized incidents in which they swallowed cyanide-laced Tylenol capsules finally settled their tort claims against the capsules' manufacturer nine years after those families had lost a spouse, a parent, or a child.[8] That delay was hardly surprising in a court system in which the *average* tort case is not tried until six years after it was filed.[9]

In nine years, Elissa and Laura Young will have spent most of their lives in poverty. In nine years, without adequate medical care and rehabilitation, Howard Young's future, to say nothing of his life, could be gone.

No improvement is in sight for tort cases. Budget cuts on state and federal levels mean that fewer judicial and court resources exist, relative to the number of cases being brought to court. Vermont actually suspended all civil jury trials for a substantial time a few years ago because the state had run out of money to pay juries. The mammoth machinery of criminal justice, with its mandatory speedy trials, expands constantly, leaving courts less and less time to spend on civil matters, including tort cases.

Likewise, there does not seem to be much prospect for a reduction in the costs of litigating tort cases. As society advances more deeply into the so-called Technology Age, litigators increasingly use expensive expert witnesses to allow jurors to understand what was done right—or wrong—with respect to accidents. For example, in Howard Young's case, each side will probably make use of accident reconstruction experts to determine, among other things, whether the train would have hit Howard anyway had the driver been proceeding carefully. Lawyers increasingly use experts to prove just what injuries a plaintiff suffered. Discovery—the name given a lawsuit's complicated formal processes for unearthing relevant information from opposing parties' witnesses and documents—has become more, not less, time-consuming and extensive. And computers allow the generation of ever-increasing amounts of paperwork in tort litigation, as in everything else.

When combined with the costs of legal representation, these factors assure that tort lawsuits regularly entail huge costs to conduct. In the average tort suit, where a plaintiff receives compensation, he gets only 46 percent of the total amount of money expended—and that does not include court costs to the public.[10]

At the end—at least the first end—of this long and expensive process sits the jury. Juries decide tort cases. Ordinary people compose juries. Each jury is made up of people different from those of any other jury. No lawyer knows before trial who will be on the jury that decides his case.

Even though few tort lawsuits go to trial, the jury's position as the ultimate decider has tremendous significance for all who venture or are dragged into the tort system. It means that often it can be quite difficult to predict the results in any one case. Predictability though, does not completely disappear: seasoned litigators develop quite good senses of which cases are winners and which are losers. Litigators can be aided in their efforts to predict a range of damage awards by companies that compile and categorize jury verdicts by locale, type of case, and type of injury. Nevertheless, no particular jury has a decision-making past that litigators can use to aid their predictions.

Similarly, the jury as decision maker means that there will be considerable inconsistency in damages awarded in tort cases and even in some liability decisions. In one striking example, five different juries heard exactly the same evidence in a multiplaintiff Texas asbestos case. Required to reach several conclusions about specific issues in the cases, the juries came back with substantially different answers.[11] Instances abound in which commentators have accused juries of treating essentially similar injuries quite differently in terms of the amounts of damages awarded to the injured parties. For example, Yale law professor Peter Schuck recently excoriated a Bronx jury for awarding $9.3 million to a plaintiff who lost his left arm when struck by a subway train after falling on the tracks while intoxicated. His criticism was based on a newspaper report that previous awards for that sort of injury had ranged between $1.25 and $1.5 million.[12] Given the daunting task of damage assessment that most juries face, with little judicial guidance, such notable inconsistencies will continue.

While endemic, such unpredictability and inconsistencies are not without some checks. Trial and appellate judges have the authority to throw out or modify jury awards that are clearly against the weight of the evidence or are so extreme as to be outside a range of reasonableness. In fact, within three months of the jury verdict a judge set aside the $9 million award that Professor Schuck found "clearly excessive."[13] Such checks can provide some protection against fears that juries will disregard tort rules and injury realities whenever the sight of a maimed plaintiff tugs at their heartstrings.

Whatever its faults, adherents of tort law urge that the jury grounds it firmly in the community. Juries, by definition, are not expert in a case's often complicated factual issues. For example, in the Youngs' case, the jury will not know much about the technical aspects of driving trains, such as appropriate speeds and safety precautions. Accordingly, those who are expert in the complicated facts will have to make their understandings intelligible to ordinary people. Elite technocrats can strongly influence tort decisions if they can make their expertise comprehensible to the community, but they cannot control those decisions. Moreover, the jury's determinations about what happened are likely to be strongly influenced by its sense of the justice of the situation. That forces each side in a tort case, it is argued, to think about and present evidence with a concern for feelings about justice, as well as a concern for the specific tort rules involved. Finally, the jury is relatively immune from the influences of institutionalized interest groups. State legislatures, on the other hand, whose determinations mightily affect tort law's general rules, *can* be lobbied by interested groups. Those groups can also make campaign contributions to and target information to judges. But they cannot do much deliberately to influence the decision of any particular jury, which exists only for the life of a single trial.

Thus, with a jury potentially in front of them, a temporarily "free" lawyer at their side, and severely injured lives behind and ahead of them, Howard, Nicole, Laura, and Elissa Young move through the courthouse doors into the tort system. Their experience will give us a fuller understanding of what tort law in America aims to achieve and what in fact it accomplishes.

CHAPTER TWO

Legal Rules That Bend, Not Break

If Howard Young and his family were able to see the whole of the tort legal world into which they were entering with their lawsuit—the Goodyear blimp view, say—it would look like a giant labyrinth. From the start, the tort plaintiff (or claimant) has to make choices about what paths—what legal claims—he will pursue. The plaintiff will need to have, or to discover, certain information to allow him to move forward along that path toward compensatory damages. The plaintiff's opponent, the defendant, will be constantly inclined to raise or point to legal and factual obstacles, any of which may terminate—or at the least diminish—the value of the plaintiff's lawsuit, perhaps very early in the labyrinthine quest, or perhaps very late, when compensation seems in sight.

The paths and obstacles making up this legal labyrinth are the product of choices. Those choices, predominantly those made by judges on the supreme courts of the fifty states, constitute what we commonly refer to as tort law.

Tort law, like the law of contracts or property, is a part of the common law. That means it is made primarily by judges rather than legislatures. Judges normally do not actively seek the opportunity to make a lot of new tort law. They don't list it among their New Year's resolutions. The government doesn't assign them the job of remodeling tort law. Judges simply happen to be there when people come to complain about having been wronged. Judges are the professionals assigned by society to resolve disputes among people, including those disputes which we classify as torts. When the injured person says, "They owe me money because they injured me," and the alleged wrongdoers say, "We don't owe him a cent," judges have to decide the legal outcome of the dispute. A judge can end up adding an increment to the common law of torts when she decides that in a given injury situation, a certain result—usually the payment or nonpayment of money damages—is authorized or necessary.

Each of these decisions is law. It is a decision that in these particular circumstances defendants will or will not have to pay compensation of some sort. A decision takes its place as part of the common law because other judges can look to it and other precedent—previous judicial decisions in similar cases—for guidance in trying to decide similar disputes. Because no two cases are exactly the same, judges will generalize from prior decisions in attempting to determine the law that governs the case before them. To assist this process, judges—commonly in cases that have been appealed—produce written opinions explaining why they reach a certain result. Such opinions usually justify decisions as the product of the application of general rules to particular situations. In this way—the resolution of particular disputes, accompanied by written opinions—the common law has grown over the centuries, applying rules, finely tuned by application in dispute after dispute, to the changing circumstances of our world.

The tort lawsuit filed by Howard Young and his family against the Transit Authority and the other defendants was assigned randomly to Judge Constance Small, one of the many judges in the state trial court for tort (and other) cases. Like many of her judicial colleagues, Judge Small did well academically in law school, although not well enough to be selected for the law review (the law school's scholarly publication, edited by its top students). She had worked for several years after law school as a government lawyer—in her case, for the city's civil law office—before joining a medium-sized, politically well-connected law firm in her thirties. After a decade of business litigation work at the firm and consistent political work for the area's dominant political party, Ms. Small had been nominated as the party candidate for a judgeship. She had been elected handily. Although she had rarely worked on tort cases as a lawyer, Judge Small had already presided over more than a dozen such trials in her five years as a judge by the time the Youngs' case was assigned to her.

The legal decisions which Judge Small would have to make in the case of *Young v. City Transit Authority* involved the three kinds of issues that are the most debated parts of tort law: (1) What behavior makes one legally responsible for another's—or one's own—injuries? (2) What kind of causal link must exist between such behavior and the injury? and (3) Just what injuries (or losses caused by the misconduct) will be compensated, and to what extent? These legal issues inspire different responses from decision makers not only in transportation accident cases like Howard Young's but also in the kinds of cases that increasingly attract tort law's headlines, when the plaintiff's claim is based on injuries allegedly resulting from poor medical care, from defective products, or from exposure to toxic substances in the environment. Resolution of the three kinds of issues listed above constitutes the heart of tort law.

As in other states, two levels of appellate judges would be available to review decisions of a trial judge. Before tort law, in the person of Judge Small and state appellate judges, even begins to work on the Youngs' claims, a very basic decision about those claims has already been made. That is the decision to permit *any* injured persons at all to go to court with tort claims. In other words, the social decision to have tort law at all.

If Howard Young had been the conductor on the subway train the night of his accident and had been injured in the sudden lurch of an uncontrolled emergency stop, he would not have been able to bring a tort lawsuit against the train driver or the Transit Authority. The conductor, if he wanted to make a claim for monetary compensation for his injuries, would have had to seek that compensation within the state's workers' compensation system. Like all the administrative systems set up to provide compensation for injuries, workers' compensation provides a somewhat easier route to such compensation than does tort law. For example, like most other administrative systems, it allows the worker to receive compensation regardless of whether he can prove anyone guilty of wrongdoing. Like the other systems, workers' compensation takes some things away from potential tort plaintiffs as well. Most importantly, it offers the injury victim who succeeds in securing compensation a lot less money than does tort law (providing less than full wage loss and nothing for pain and suffering, for example).

Judge Small would probably think it pretty silly to speculate about the Youngs' ability to bring their tort compensation claims to a court, with its constitutionally selected judge and jury. She'd no doubt point out that tort law has been around forever—or so it seems to lawyers. She would acknowledge that the workers' compensation law takes a substantial number of personal injury claims out of the tort system. But she would point out that although workers' compensation swept the nation early in this century, the number of tort lawsuits filed each year is at a record level and continually increasing.[1]

Judge Small would have to concede, if pushed, that another significant chunk of personal injury claims was carved out of the tort system by the passage of no-fault statutes governing injuries from automobile accidents in about a third of the states in the 1970s. While even those states generally permit auto accident victims with serious injuries to make tort claims, efforts continue to expand the coverage of no-fault plans, both to the rest of the nation and to more instances of injury.

More significantly, perhaps unknown to Judge Small, there are forces at work in the United States quite eager to dismantle and perhaps extinguish tort law. Several leading iconoclastic scholars have advocated abolishing tort law, either in favor of more streamlined, coordinated administrative compensation for injured persons or in favor of contractual arrangements between potential injurers and potential victims.[2] America's businesses, insurers, and medical professionals—those most often forced by tort law to pay money—have become increasingly receptive to ideas hostile to the tort system as more and larger tort claims have been brought successfully against them. They have seen to it that the workings of the tort system have become a matter of public debate, fueled by full-page ads in major newspapers and magazines and the creation of organizations solely to "reform" tort law.

So far, the political response to the notion of tort reform has been considerable, though the rhetoric has sometimes outstripped the action. Beginning with the first medical malpractice "crisis" of the mid-1970s, state legislatures enacted changes that made it harder for injured persons to win tort suits or capped the money damages they could collect. Such restrictions, which often extended beyond medical malpractice, have continued to be enacted in most states, at varying rates and to varying extent. Beginning with the Reagan and Bush administrations, proposals surfaced in Congress to restrict tort law throughout the nation. Federal attention initially focused on tort lawsuits involving defective products—so-called products liability suits. However, by the time a newly Republican Congress considered the first significant such legislation in 1995, the antitort mood was sufficiently strong that other broad areas of tort litigation were included in the proposed restrictions.

Even more wholesale legislative challenges to the tort system have taken place on both federal and state levels in the past two decades, but only with respect to particular classes of injury. Federal legislation sought to carve certain vaccine-related injuries out of the tort system, consigning them to special administrative systems. State laws occasionally did the same with respect to children catastrophically injured at birth.

Other efforts to deal with the modern personal injury world have similarly sought to carve certain kinds of injuries or injuries resulting from certain activities completely out of the tort system. Of course, when the injuries being carved out are all those resulting from auto accidents, or, as has been discussed recently in New York, all injuries resulting from medical treatment, even such piecemeal changes may radically reduce tort law's domain.

And although the call for abandonment of *all* tort law for personal injury seems somewhat far-fetched, the call to abandon it in automobile accident, medical malpractice, and products liability cases—the cases which constitute the majority of tort litigation—is much less so. The time may be coming soon when even Judge Small will not so blithely assume that tort law is the way to deal with the injury problems involving the Youngs and the Transit Authority.

Until then, however, decisions must be made. First among them involves the standard of behavior that tort law demands of citizens. Actually, unlike criminal law, tort law doesn't *demand* any behavior of us. It does say, however, that if we behave in certain defined ways, and someone is injured because of that behavior, we will have to pay money to compensate that person for his injuries.

The major debate about this standard of behavior in tort law over the centuries has been whether or not the law should order such compensation only when the defendant has done something "wrong." *Wrong* within tort law has long been defined as causing another's injury intentionally, recklessly, or negligently. Although plenty of judicial decisions refine just what those terms mean, they all denote that a defendant behaved in a way he shouldn't have.

The principal competing view has been that the law should order a defendant to compensate an injured person with money when the defendant's actions caused that person's injury, regardless of whether the defendant acted badly in any way. Tort law calls liability in such instances "strict liability." The traditional history of tort law, recently challenged, tells us that strict liability was the dominant standard until about the middle of the nineteenth century.[3] Since then, all agree, fault—especially negligence—has reigned as the general determinant of tort liability.

For a person to be found negligent, and thus liable to pay money damages for the injuries caused, a court must determine that he acted unreasonably. Courts often phrase this standard slightly differently, finding the defendant liable where he did not act as a reasonable, prudent person would have or where he acted or failed to act so as to create an unreasonable risk of harm. According to Howard Young, the operator of the subway train that ran him down acted negligently because a reasonable operator would (1) not have been speeding or (2) would have paid more attention to events in front of him or (3) would have applied the brakes sooner and more effectively. The five witnesses negligently failed to act, Howard would argue, because reasonable people in that situation would have taken the steps necessary to rescue him from his fall onto the tracks before the train arrived.

Not surprisingly, there is much law—there are, that is, many judicial decisions—about the circumstances in which it is proper for someone to be judged negligent. Tort law says that in a certain set of circumstances, it is permissible for a jury to have concluded that the defendant was negligent. In most such situations, the law also implies that it also would have been permissible if the jury had not found the defendant negligent. Rarely does the law say the circumstances were such that the jury *had* to decide the defendant was negligent, although it sometimes happens, such as when his actions also clearly violated a statute or governmental regulation (against speeding, for example). In other words, tort law is clear that people have to act reasonably but not so clear about *exactly* what it means to act reasonably in a given case. The judicial decisions tend to delineate a range of behavior that could be found to be unreasonable but also could be found to be reasonable. When a defendant's behavior falls into that range, the judges turn the decision about whether the defendant was negligent over to the jury. Lawyers get guidance about what behavior within that range generally will be found unreasonable and what will not by watching what juries decide in many cases.

Nevertheless, that guidance is fuzzy. It must be. In saying that it will not require a defendant, unless he has acted negligently, to compensate an injured person, tort law promises to examine in detail the individual circumstances of any accident. Sometimes, it will be obvious that certain behavior—for example, driving while intoxicated—is unreasonable. Often, it will not be obvious, and the determination will hinge on slight variations in the circumstances. For example, it might not be unreasonable to drive while intoxicated if the driver is only a little intoxicated and he is taking his child to the hospital, a child who became seriously injured after the driver had already had a few drinks. But it might be unreasonable to drive even then if the driver's neighbor was right next door, sober, and would have taken the child to the hospital if asked.

There is much greater certainty about liability if negligence is replaced by strict liability as the basic standard for tort liability. Nevertheless, tort law has for the most part opted to retain the minimum fault requirement of negligence. Some areas of strict liability exist, but they are limited areas. Tort law, in the midst of its general adoption of negligence, retained strict liability for persons and companies that engage in "ultrahazardous" or "abnormally dangerous" activities. If the Transit Authority had been using explosives to construct a new subway tunnel and Howard Young had been injured as a result of one of its explosions, the Authority would be automatically liable for his injuries even if everyone agreed that the Transit Authority had behaved reasonably in all respects. However, because the law requires that the activity in question be very, very hazardous and that it be an activity in which few people engage, there are not many injury situations to which this form of strict liability applies.

The other area of strict liability, which developed more recently in tort law, pertains to the manufacture of a product that has a defect. Liability in this area often turns on whether the product that caused the plaintiff's injury is different, in a dangerous way, from the other products of the manufacturer that are supposed to be the same. A common example of such situations arises when someone is injured by a Coca-Cola bottle. Either the Coke has something in it that hurts or sickens the consumer, or the bottle breaks in an injurious way. The injured consumer, to win a tort suit against Coca-Cola, need only prove that the bottle or its contents was not the same as all the other bottles of Coke that the company made. Since other Cokes do not contain foreign substances or other Coke bottles do not shatter when picked up firmly, Coca-Cola will be held liable even if it brings in twenty technicians to testify how extraordinarily careful Coke has been in the bottling process.

This limited area of strict liability for injuries caused by manufactured products is quite different from the "strict products liability," which seemed poised twenty-five years ago to create quite a large section of strict liability in tort law. Led by innovative judges and scholars, tort law in the 1960s developed what was deemed to be an expanded doctrine of strict liability for defective products. Those leaders advocated the new doctrine because they saw a need for the costs of injuries resulting from products to be spread more fully across all those products' consumers, rather than concentrated on injured persons. They thought that a business that profited from the manufacture and sale of a product should also bear the costs of the injuries that resulted from the product, even if the business had not behaved badly. Those widely shared philosophies soon ran up against the reality of a world of injury in which people got hurt in their interactions with cars, bikes, drugs, perfumes, and a host of other products that were made and marketed just the way society wanted them to be. Following turbulent doctrinal periods in the 1970s and early 1980s, tort law has settled into products liability rules that use the words *strict liability,* but as a practical matter largely hold manufacturers liable only for products designed or marketed negligently.

As a result of all this, Howard Young, like any other injury victim, will not win his tort lawsuit against the driver, the Transit Authority, or the five witnesses unless he proves that they behaved negligently. Scholars continue to debate the merits of expanded strict liability versus negligence. The courts do not.

Howard Young's drunkenness poses a different, less clearly resolved issue with respect to the significance of behavior that falls below tort law's standards. Howard got stewed, and because of that, he fell onto the subway tracks. Tort law's negligence standard may provide a fuzzy guide in some situations, but it will be crystal clear in Howard's: any lawyer in America can tell you a jury will determine that he acted unreasonably. The difficult decision for tort law is what significance that determination should have for the plaintiff's chances to get compensation.

A quarter century ago, most tort law would have thrown Howard Young out of court without a penny. He would have been found to have been "contributorily negligent," which completely barred a plaintiff's claim for damages from a negligent defendant. Although that seemed fair enough to observers when the plaintiff had been very negligent in causing his own injury and the defendant somewhat less negligent, it bothered them and the courts much more when the plaintiff's negligence had been relatively slight. At first, tort law bent in response to that concern through the creation of complicated, situation-specific exceptions to the rule that a plaintiff at fault lost completely. After years of such incremental modification of tort law, there occurred a relatively rapid movement throughout the nation, predominantly through new state legislation, to adopt the doctrine of "comparative fault." That doctrine requires a fact finder—usually the jury—to allocate percentage shares of fault for the plaintiff's injuries to each of the parties responsible for the accident, including to the plaintiff himself.

For example, in Howard Young's case, a jury might conclude that everyone involved in his accident—the driver, the witnesses, and Howard himself—had acted negligently, and that Howard's negligence amounted to 50 percent of the contributing fault, the driver's 35 percent, and the witnesses' only 15 percent. The jury might also conclude that Howard had suffered $4 million in damages. In those states, like Howard's, which adopted the "pure" form of comparative fault, the court would simply subtract from the plaintiff's damages an amount equal to his assessed percentage of fault. In Howard's case, he would receive $2 million, paid by the driver (actually, the Transit Authority) and the witnesses in proportion to their respective fault. In some other states, which have adopted a "modified" form of comparative fault, Howard might receive no money at all if he is found to be more negligent than the defendants. With respect to negligent plaintiffs like Howard, therefore, a choice in tort law can boil down to completely barring the claim of the plaintiff who bears more than half the responsibility for his injuries or just reducing his damages by the percentage of his fault. Nevertheless, the process by which a jury compares the fault of one party to an accident with the fault of several others has become quite familiar in the tort system. So familiar, in fact, that analysts paid almost no attention to it in discussing a recent notorious case in which an elderly woman won tort damages in a lawsuit against McDonald's because it served her a cup of scalding hot coffee at one of its drive-up windows, coffee that she subsequently spilled on her lap, causing severe burns. Although widespread media coverage portrayed the tort verdict as further erosion of national norms of self-responsibility, it largely ignored the fact that the jury in that case had decided that the plaintiff had been contributorily negligent and had reduced her damages by an amount equivalent to her contributory fault.[4]

Split as the states are on the question of what happens to the more-than-half-at-fault plaintiff, there is even greater uncertainty within tort law about how to deal with another kind of plaintiff's conduct that might arguably bar his claim against a negligent defendant. That kind of conduct is termed "assumption of the risk." As the term implies, it involves situations in which a plaintiff has either voluntarily encountered the risk of harm posed by the defendant's negligent conduct or has agreed expressly ahead of time not to hold the defendant liable for any negligent behavior. The former kind of assumption of the risk can arise at a baseball park to be used against the fan who is struck by a foul ball while sitting voluntarily in seats unprotected by any netting. Or it can come up in a factory, where an employee works with a machine from which the safety guard has been removed, and subsequently gets his hand caught in that machinery (and where workers' compensation law doesn't bar the claim because it's not the employer but the manufacturer of the machine who is being sued). Although baseball clubs almost always win the foul ball injury suits, courts increasingly are restricting the use of assumption of the risk as a defense in situations in which the plaintiff has acted reasonably in confronting the risk of harm and in situations, such as the workplace, in which there are societal pressures on the plaintiff to take the risk.

The advocates of a broad assumption-of-the-risk defense stress the need for the law to recognize individual autonomy: if people want to take chances in life with risky things or activities, the law has no business stopping them. If defendants are held liable even where the plaintiff has knowingly encountered the risk, the advocates say, then fear of liability will drive the defendants away from giving people the chance to take such risks. There won't be any more convertibles. Baseball stadiums will have protective plexiglass everywhere, so kids and grown-up kids will have to put away their mitts and watch the national pastime through a protective filter.

The argument becomes more heated when the law tries to deal with the second kind of assumption of the risk, involving express waivers of liability. These situations can arise almost anywhere: companies that offer scuba diving or parachuting lessons give their customers forms to sign, the signature being at the bottom of a promise that the consumer will not hold the company responsible for any injuries its actions might inflict on her. Such clauses often show up in residential leases, where tenants absolve the landlord of any responsibility for his negligent behavior. They are beginning to show up in health clinics and may become more prevalent in the provision of medical services generally.

Courts have struggled with whether to accept these clauses as effective to bar a plaintiff's claim. They, and tort law, find themselves torn between the contractual belief that a deal is a deal and the humanitarian belief that a defendant should not get away with negligently injuring someone just because it was able to convince him to sign away his rights before he may have had any good idea that he would be the victim of the defendant's misbehavior. Advocates of individual autonomy have railed at courts for refusing to hold plaintiffs to their signed waivers in cases in which it was obtained in return for the provision of some important service, like housing.[5] These advocates would argue that regular subway passengers like Howard might, when buying a season pass, be able to sign agreements giving up their right to sue the Transit Authority for injuries they suffer in the subways in return for reduced fares. Waivers should be honored by the courts, the autonomy advocates say, because they allow the people that tort law supposedly protects to choose whether they want that protection or want other advantages (in this case, lower fares) in exchange for giving up protection against tort damages.

Whatever struggles go on in tort law over the basic standards for liability and over the implications of plaintiff's negligent or risk-assuming conduct can pale next to the battles about what kinds of causal relations between a defendant's negligence and a plaintiff's injury are necessary before the courts will order payment of tort damages. This causal battleground is present in its simplest form in Howard Young's tort case. In its more complicated forms, the causal battleground pushes tort law toward a very different and unfamiliar perspective on responsibility for injuries.

It is a basic requirement of tort law that the plaintiff must prove that the defendant's negligence, or other culpable conduct, probably caused his injury. In Howard Young's case, this issue will come up because the Transit Authority and driver will claim, at least with respect to a finding that the operator was negligent in driving the train too fast, that Howard would have been injured regardless of such negligence. In other words, the two defendants will say that because the operator could not see Howard on the tracks until the train was partway into the station, the driver would have been unable to stop in time to avoid hitting Howard even if he had been operating the train with reasonable care.

Such arguments force courts and juries to examine how the world would have been different if certain circumstances had not existed. The question whether a plaintiff would have been injured even if the defendant had not been negligent can be very difficult to resolve. Both P. J. Cowcroft, the Youngs' lawyer, and the defense lawyers will expend considerable time and effort to pin down, as much as possible, such relevant facts as: (1) just how fast the train was going when it entered the station; (2) at what exact point a reasonably alert operator would have seen Howard lying on the tracks; and (3) precisely how would such factors as the subway train's braking equipment and the condition of the tracks affect how quickly the train would stop once the need for emergency braking became apparent. Each side would be inclined to hire accident reconstruction experts, who would testify, on the basis of such facts, about how long it would have taken the train to stop had the driver been acting reasonably the night of Howard's accident. Although determining whether causation actually exists can thus be factually complicated, the law itself is clear that the plaintiff must prove that the defendant's conduct in fact caused his injury.

That clarity evaporates in other kinds of tort cases, kinds that have increased markedly in the past fifteen years. These cases involve plaintiffs who can't prove that a defendant's negligence probably—more likely than not—caused their injuries because either (1) there are two or more defendants whose actions are equally likely to have caused the plaintiff's injuries, or (2) there is no way for the plaintiff to prove that a particular injury came from the defendant's negligence rather than from some other source that also causes that kind of injury. Both kinds of cases have forced tort law to reevaluate its traditional rules requiring injury victims to prove a specific individualized causal link between their particular injuries and the particular negligence of the defendant.

Modern tort law initially encountered and was changed by the first kind of causal problem in cases involving women who developed a particular cancer as a result of the negligent marketing of the drug diethylstilbestrol (DES) to their mothers during pregnancy. Because of the unusual kind of cancer from which they suffered these plaintiffs—DES daughters—generally had no trouble proving that they were injured because of their exposure *in utero* to DES. The manufacturers of DES clearly provided a faulty product to pregnant women. The plaintiffs' causation problems came up because nearly three hundred companies had manufactured DES for pregnant women during the 1940s and 1950s. Because their mothers had taken DES twenty or more years before the daughters developed cancer, because prescription records often did not exist, and because DES pills from one manufacturer often resembled those from another, the plaintiffs in many cases could not identify which manufacturer's DES caused their injuries.

Most courts have responded to this problem by dismissing the claims of plaintiffs who cannot identify the manufacturer whose DES their mothers took. They have been unwilling to change traditional rules in a way that could result in a defendant paying compensation for an injury that its faulty product did not cause. Other courts have ruled that defendant manufacturers will be liable, unless they can prove their DES couldn't have been responsible for this plaintiff's injury, but only for that share of a plaintiff's damages proportional to the manufacturer's share of the DES market.[6] They have been unwilling to allow manufacturers whose faulty products quite clearly injured many people to escape tort responsibility for those injuries simply because the nature of the manufacturing and distribution process and the long-latency period for plaintiffs' injuries made it impossible for plaintiffs to accomplish the traditional tort task of linking up a particular injury with a particular faulty product of a particular defendant. Interestingly, even among those courts which have accepted market-share liability rules, only one has been willing to establish a rule that could result in a defendant's being held liable even when it can prove that its DES was not the drug that injured this particular plaintiff.[7] The law is reluctant to move so far from its roots of individual responsibility.

That reluctance has become starkly apparent in the second kind of causal problem cases with which tort law has been asked to grapple in the past decade. Increased sensitivity to environmental toxins has led to a rash of suits by persons, many with some form of cancer, claiming that their serious illnesses were caused because the defendant negligently exposed them to a toxic substance. A typical such suit may result, for example, from the discovery of a leukemia "cluster"—an unexpectedly high number of children with leukemia in a particular locality. Should that discovery coincide with discovery that some local companies have contaminated the drinking water of that locality with a chemical known to cause leukemia-like cancers in laboratory animals, a tort lawsuit on behalf of the victims may follow. The families of the stricken children will be unusually lucky in litigation if they can prove that the children were exposed to substantial doses of the defendants' chemicals and that such exposure probably causes some leukemias. Their lawsuit will likely founder on causation's shoals because most childhood leukemias result from something other than exposure to such chemicals. While they might be able to prove that exposure to the defendants' chemicals does cause some people's leukemias, they may well be unable to prove that it is more likely than not (a greater than 50 percent chance) that such exposure caused any particular plaintiff's leukemia. Even among those chemicals that scientists agree are carcinogenic, very few contribute to more than a small increase in the total incidence of cancer in the population.

Although respected scholars have urged courts to move away from traditional more-likely-than-not causation rules in such cases, the courts have thus far refused to budge.[8] Courts may be willing to give a plaintiff partial compensation in situations, such as Howard Young's, where he negligently contributed to his own injuries. Nevertheless, they have been unwilling to abandon a philosophy of full compensation or no compensation to hold a defendant partially liable (for, say, 15 percent of the plaintiff's losses) where other causes contributed to more of the injuries like the plaintiff's in a given population than did the defendant's negligence.

But even in this no-budge area, tort law is bending. Many courts have allowed persons exposed to carcinogenic substances by a defendant's fault to recover some compensatory damages *before* they develop any cancer or other physical disease. Such plaintiffs have frequently been able to obtain money damages to pay for the increased monitoring costs of medical tests and doctors' examinations reasonably necessary to watch out for the kind of cancer that can result from such exposure. Some plaintiffs have been also able to get damages to compensate them for the emotional distress they suffer when they find out that they have been substantially dosed with a carcinogen. In other kinds of tort suits, usually involving medical misdiagnoses or mistreatments that increase the plaintiff's chances of illness—a mastectomy or the like—some courts have allowed a plaintiff to sue for his or her lost chance of life or good health. As a result, a plaintiff whose chances of surviving heart disease were reduced from 55 percent to 35 percent by a defendant's negligence would be able to recover 20 percent of the damages associated with untimely death.

A similar "bend" in tort law can be detected with regard to another set of legal rules that affect whether defendants will be held liable for their negligence: those associated with "failure to act" claims. This is the sort of claim that Howard Young made against the five witnesses to his accident. Even if Howard can prove that the witnesses could have helped him escape from the oncoming train without danger or significant difficulty to themselves, they will argue that tort law imposes no obligations on them to act affirmatively to protect others.

In general, tort law has promulgated that "no duty to rescue" philosophy for centuries. The basic rule is that no one will be held liable because he did not help save another person from imminent harm, even if a reasonable person would have so helped. Again, tort law, in spite of the carefully reasoned blandishments of law professors and the shrieks of popular outrage, has refused to budge from its basic commitment to this kind of individual autonomy.[9] The law seems willing to make people pay for injuries when they act unreasonably but seems unwilling to penalize such unreasonable inaction.

Nevertheless, judges are not totally insensitive to the moral failure inherent in passivity in the face of peril. They become as outraged as anyone else when they hear about a score of New York City spectators who supposedly watched but did not help a three-year-old who was being raped. As a result, the law bends. Liability is imposed if the person who unreasonably fails to protect another from an imminent harm has a "special relationship" with the victim. For example, a niece cannot abandon her aunt, nor can an innkeeper unreasonably fail to protect his guests. Liability is also imposed if the unreasonable nonactor had something to do with the plaintiff's failing to get help from another source. A bystander who attempts to aid the victim, thus encouraging other potential rescuers to retreat, but who then abandons the effort, has left the victim worse off than if he had done nothing. The more hostile the courts become to the failure-to-act rule, the more encompassing become these categories of exceptions.

But even expanded exceptions probably will not be enough to permit Howard Young to succeed on his claims against the five witnesses. They had no formal relationships with him. They had no hand in his being on the track. They do not seem to have undertaken in any way to help him. They may have behaved the worst of all the characters involved in Howard Young's accident, but they probably will bear no responsibility in the eyes of tort law.

Once the law decides on responsibility, it has gone only partway down the road of controversy. There remains the need to decide what sorts of plaintiffs' injuries negligent defendants must compensate. For better or worse, tort law translates the harm done to people's lives into money. Money breeds fights: in this instance, disputes are likely about how that translation of harm to money should occur.

For the most part, tort law has long been reconciled to paying the plaintiff who proves liability for the monetary costs his injuries impose on him. Without much fanfare, tort law orders defendants found liable for a plaintiff's injuries to pay for his past and future medical expenses. For Howard Young, this would mean that if he succeeds in proving that the subway driver's negligence caused his injuries, he would receive money for all the money he had paid for his care up to the time of trial and for all the money he is expected to have to pay in the future for such care, rehabilitation, special equipment, aides, and the like. Pursuant to the increasingly questioned "collateral source rule" of tort law, the defendant might have to pay Howard for all those expenses even where many of the expenses were already paid for by his health insurance.

There is also agreement that an injured plaintiff should be compensated for income lost as a result of his injuries. Most commonly, this has meant that the injured plaintiff recovers the difference between what he would have earned if not injured and what he earns, or could reasonably earn, now, following the accident. For

Howard Young, of course, lost earnings could be a massive component of his damage award, even discounted by his comparative fault. He was a young man earning $150,000 a year at the time of the accident. In spite of the bleak workday that led Howard to calamity, P. J. Cowcroft would probably be able to produce credible evidence indicating that Howard's income most likely would have increased substantially in future years as he progressed to more senior status at that or another law firm. Howard cannot work now. As a result, a jury might easily conclude that Howard was deprived of several million dollars in future earnings by the defendant's negligence. That figure will be adjusted somewhat by the application of hotly contested rules about how inflation, taxes, and interest income should affect lost earnings awards. Nevertheless, Howard would get a very large sum of money once his past and future medical expenses are added to these lost earnings. If Howard's case reaches the point where appropriate damages are considered, the Transit Authority would have been better off financially if there had been a dozen homeless persons on its tracks rather than one successful lawyer.

The most serious disputes about damages in tort law focus not so much on payments for money lost, or expected to be lost, by a plaintiff, but on the validity of payments for the plaintiff's noneconomic, or intangible, harms. The Youngs' lawsuit would bring many of those questions to the fore. Howard would seek recovery for his "pain and suffering." Nicole, Elissa, and Laura would seek damages for their loss of their husband or father's normal companionship, and possibly separately for their emotional distress because of his injuries. Judge Small, and probably appellate courts, if the case is appealed, will have to decide whether and how much monetary damages are appropriately given for such intangible kinds of injuries. She and the appellate courts will make that decision in an atmosphere of controversy toward tort compensation for noneconomic harms.

Tort law has long given physically injured persons money for the pain and suffering that accompanies their physical injuries. In following the prescription that tort damages aim to put an injured person back in the place of well-being he would have occupied in the absence of the defendant's negligence, the courts have regarded physical pain, despair, humiliation, and loss of life's pleasures from bodily injury as just as deserving of compensation as medical expenses. The law recognizes that no precise dollar value can be automatically put on such physical and psychological hurt. It also recognizes that giving victims money will not erase that hurt—a Howard Young frustrated and humiliated by his mind's dysfunctioning arguably just becomes a wealthier frustrated and humiliated man when he is compensated for such harm—although the money may allow an injured person to substitute some pleasures for those his injury took from him. In the face of decades of significant criticism, tort law has held firm to allowing such recoveries.

Tort law has flip-flopped like a captured mackerel, with about as much coherence, with respect to other damage claims for intangible injuries, particularly when those injuries have come about because an accident damaged relationships plaintiffs had with a physically injured person like a spouse or child. Tort law worked its way ever so slowly over the past fifty years toward recognition of claims solely for emotional distress. These steps were taken in cases where negligent drivers badly frightened people, where doctors erroneously told people they had terminal diseases, and in cases where a parent was devastated by the accidental killing or maiming of his or her child.

At first, fears of fabricated claims haunted the courts, so they required that such a plaintiff have some physical injury in addition to emotional distress. As the genuineness of claims became more apparent, the courts' fear became that the courts would be flooded with trivial claims, so the requirement became "serious emotional distress," with most states requiring some physical manifestation of the emotional upset as a guarantee of severity. Although courts learned eventually to live with the uncertainty of money damages for essentially psychological injuries, they never learned to live with the possibility that the emotional ripples from any accident would spread liability on and on to "unlimited liability." Accordingly, although most states will now permit a plaintiff to recover emotional distress damages when a close relative has been physically injured through the defendant's negligence, they limit that recovery to instances where the close relative—often a parent—actually observed the accidental injury take place. In Howard's home state, the only way Nicole, Elissa, or Laura could recover for their anguish at what happened to him would be if they had been on the subway platform that night *and* had also been at risk of being hit by the negligently driven subway.

Rules governing "loss of consortium"—loss of the companionship, love, and emotional support of another (including, in the case of spouses, sexual relations)—had been even more restrictive. It took more than half this century before courts were willing to recognize that a wife could recover damages for loss of her husband's consortium—recognition they had readily accorded the husband whose wife was seriously injured, since she was historically, after all, his property. To this day, the law less commonly recognizes such a claim by children when a parent is seriously injured, or by a parent when injury strikes the child. Under state law applicable in this case, Elissa and Laura would recover nothing for the sudden emotional void which the accident left in their home, probably the greatest loss a young child could experience. The rationale? Because there could be many children in any one family, granting the child damages for loss of consortium could lead to that dreaded unlimited liability. Besides, dollars supposedly can't replace a father's love and support (in contrast, it seems, to a wife's).

The above concern—that compensation for intangible injuries isn't really compensation at all—takes its place next to concerns about uncertainty and inconsistency in juries' awards of noneconomic damages. Together they have fueled a reaction not only against the limited steps courts have taken in the past quarter century to expand claims for such harm but also against traditional damages for pain and suffering. Critics claim that such damage awards take a large bite out of the nation's productive capacity. Because nobody normally pays money to insure themselves against the sorts of intangible harms for which tort law provides compensation, these critics say, the tort rules in this area impose a tax on goods and services in the country to give people something they don't really want to pay for. As a result, many of the recent efforts to reform tort law have advocated reductions in or elimination of damages for pain and suffering.[10] Many proposals and even some enactments would limit pain and suffering claims to no more than, say, $250,000.

Tort law's decisions about the issues that may come up in Howard Young's case and about the broader related issues discussed in this chapter represent many of the most crucial issues in debates about the content and direction of tort law today. Those issues, and competing proposals for their resolution, can be understood only with some understanding of tort law's place and purpose in our society. It is to those that we turn in the next chapters.

CHAPTER THREE

Helping the Needy or Greedy?

In the week after she and her family formally embarked on their voyage into the labyrinth of tort law, Howard Young's wife, Nicole, matter-of-factly watched televised coverage of hundreds of thousands of demonstrators who flooded Washington's Independence Mall to protest abortion law. Later that week, while entering a shopping mall near her home, Nicole unthinkingly accepted a flyer handed out by a small group of gay activists who were protesting, with chants and signs, the county's lack of a law prohibiting employment discrimination on the basis of sexual preference. Demonstrations like these were so common in Nicole's experience that they formed a kind of unheard background noise in her daily struggles to keep the loose ends of the Youngs' lives from unraveling further.

Nicole would have been amazed to learn that the same sorts of mass protests were going on against the laws that she and Howard were counting on to assuage their injuries. The demonstrators against tort law were not in or on the malls. They were in the halls—of Congress and state legislatures, as well as of justice and academe. Apart from occasional organized groups of doctors, they massed not in crowds but in coalitions: the Product Liability Coordinating Committee (PLCC), or the American Tort Reform Association (ATRA). They did not surge en masse to be heard with shouts and placards. They (or their lobbyists) walked in—well-dressed representatives, briefcases in hands—with carefully reasoned supporting documents protesting the injury that injury law was doing to them, and to America.

Although Nicole was unaware of this demonstration against the current state of the law, she would have understood its basic import as being the same as that of the mall demonstrations: "The law does wrong; the law hurts unfairly; change it!"

These demonstrations are going on all over the United States. The demand is for change, for serious "reform," of tort law. The demanders are individuals as well as groups, from leading aircraft designers like Bert Rutan to the PLCC, which claims membership of 700,000 firms. While *Time* magazine describes the 1990s as the "age of the self-tort crybaby," ATRA and its forty state tort-reform coalitions expand their already well-financed efforts to curtail litigation's "terrible toll on the U.S. economy." Following then–Vice President Dan Quayle's demands for federal restrictions on tort lawsuits, the Citizens for Civil Justice Reform coalesced to coordinate his efforts nationwide. President George Bush, in his crucial election-year State of the Union address in 1992, called for tort reform. Tort reform became a key item in the GOP Contract with America and part of presidential candidate Bob Dole's economic platform.

Many people might be puzzled, as might Nicole Young, by the strength and intensity of these demands. After all, tort law has been around for the life of the United States without exciting much attention outside the dusty circles of legal intellectual debate. Why the big fuss now?

There is no clear answer to that question. A higher percentage of injured people bring tort lawsuits than used to. The average amount defendants in such lawsuits pay out has gone up, too. But the more careful studies of these phenomena show that the rates of increase in suing and payouts for, say, medical malpractice and defective products have not been particularly remarkable across the board.[1] There *were* rather remarkable jumps in liability insurance costs in the mid-1970s in medicine and in the mid-1980s in most commercial areas. However, these two- or three-year blips seemed to become manageable fairly quickly.[2] Taking into account all systems of insurance (public and private health and disability coverages, for example), tort law does provide a greater percentage of the compensation paid for injury and illness now than it did a few years ago. However, that increase has hardly been radical—from about seven

percent in 1982 to about nine percent in 1990.[3] Increases in tort payments have been roughly paralleled by increases in workers' compensation payments and over the long haul were far outdistanced
by increases in social security payments.[4]

Regardless of the reasons for the uproar, it now comes more from
potential tort defendants—the nation's professional and business
elite—than from the scholars and occasional judges whose voices
once dominated tort law protest. This opens up the debate. There is
nothing like the prospect of real change to energize even the most
hermetic legal scholar. As a result, the spotlights brought to bear by
would-be reformers have illuminated many of the concerns about
tort law that have long troubled thoughtful observers.

There are many such concerns. Because tort law gives people
money for their injuries, critics and supporters alike have initially
focused attention on its compensatory function. There are charges
that tort compensates too little, too slowly, too capriciously, and
sometimes even too generously—the last leading, it is argued, to
many padded, fraudulent, and even fabricated claims. There are
countercharges that tort law is the only adequate source of compensation for injuries in all of society. Because tort law takes money
away from some of those who injure others, analysts also focus on
how well tort law works as a deterrent to unsafe behavior—as well
as on how much it works unintentionally as a deterrent to useful
behavior. Related to these concerns is the shared sense that it not
only takes injured people an exceedingly long time to navigate the
capricious tort system to conclusion but that their passage is exceedingly expensive for all concerned.

There are also widespread concerns that tort law may fail basic
tests of justice in that its results are too inconsistent and arbitrary;
it is rife with unfounded claims; it can punish defendants out of proportion to their fault and reward plaintiffs out of proportion to their
hurt; and it favors the rich to the detriment of the poor. So there are
simultaneous and inconsistent claims (1) that tort law may be one
of the few places where law sustains and reinforces human dignity

and individuality or (2) that it is another example of law's trampling on those values.

These same concerns underlie many of the decisions judges have to make about the particulars of tort law. For example, if Howard Young's lawsuit proceeds to a trial and verdict, tort law as applied by Judge Constance Small at some point will face the issue of what significance the law will attribute to Howard's behavior—his drunkenness, his stumbling approach to the tracks, and his lethargic behavior once he fell. If a jury decides that Howard had acted unreasonably and had thus contributed to his own injury, tort law could prohibit him from collecting any money damages for his injuries. Or it could ignore his contribution and award Howard full compensatory damages, assuming that it found the defendants otherwise liable. Or it could try to assess his share of responsibility proportionate to the defendants' share and reduce Howard's damages in proportion to the share of the total responsibility he bore. These decisions amount, respectively, to making a plaintiff's contributory fault a complete defense, to making it no defense at all, or to adopting a comparative fault system. Tort law has long been faced with these particular choices, and in fact, as suggested earlier, has almost completely shifted its general choice from contributory to comparative fault over the past thirty years.

If this issue had not already been decided by a higher court in the state or by the state legislature, as it has been in most states, Judge Small in deciding the issue would be asked to consider most of the areas of concern about tort law in general that were mentioned above. She would be asked whether it seemed fair to allow a plaintiff—not so much Howard in particular, but a plaintiff generally like him—to recover damages if he was partially responsible for his injury, or if it were fair to prohibit him from completely recovering. She, along with other judges, would in turn ask what relevance plaintiffs' needs for compensation—undiminished by their own faulty behavior—would have to her decision. Similarly, she would consider which of these possible tort rules would do the best job of deterring unsafe behavior: Would lessening or preventing a plaintiff's recovery weaken tort's deterrence of defendants' unsafe behavior? Is some reduction or prohibition of recovery necessary to discourage a plaintiff's own unsafe behavior? Does tort law have any real effect on people's behavior in these kinds of situations? If it does, which rule would achieve optimal deterrence? Judges like Judge Small would consider as well which legal rule would minimize the costs of deciding tort cases. After all, a comparative fault rule might be most fair, but it also might have three negative results: it might tie juries in knots; it might demand vastly more evidence; and it might radically increase the complexity of trials in that juries would not only have to decide whether the parties were at fault but calibrate their contrasting behavior. Ultimately, a judge would have to consider the importance of her choice (1) on the law's ability to understand more fully the situations with which it deals—in this case, accidents—and (2) on the law's ability to enhance the well-being of those exposed to accidents.

These controversies demand resolution. The particular controversies, such as the decision whether to treat Howard Young's behavior as a complete or partial defense or no defense at all, are continually resolved as tort law is made by judges and, occasionally, legislators in the fifty states. The more global controversies, such as whether tort law should exist, or be radically curtailed or expanded, will be resolved much more irregularly, quite probably in waves of legislative decisions like those that led to the near-universal legislative adoption of no-fault workers' compensation systems in the early 1900s or to the legislative adoption in about a third of states of automobile accident no-fault laws in the 1970s.

Whenever decision makers (whether judges or legislators) examine the merits of such controversies, they will look to see whether tort law, or particular choices about tort law, will contribute positively to the solution of the problems of accidental injury in our society. If thorough, that examination will proceed through the concerns we have identified as pertinent to aspects of tort law both as they apply to the individual case and to society's needs in general—

namely, compensation, deterrence, dispute-resolution costs, optimal insurance premium levels, justice, and the enhancement of human dignity and well-being. In order to understand or evaluate the merits of tort law generally or of its particular legal rules, we must examine how it and its rules achieve these objectives of tort law. In this chapter and succeeding ones, we shall do just that.

Compensation leaps out from among tort law's myriad objectives because it is often seen as tort law's one prime goal. For Howard Young, it was also probably its one prime attraction.

Initially, Howard had not even considered bringing a tort lawsuit after his accident. During the immediate aftermath, all his energies had gone into mere survival. But once it was clear to him he would live and that his physical condition had stabilized, Howard's life began to have space for self-assessment. What he saw crushed him. He saw the lines of fatigue and worry constantly crisscrossing Nicole's previously tranquil face. He saw the fear in his young daughters' eyes and the furtive looks of need that often came his way. He saw glimpses of his own future of dependency and rejection and of constant family struggle. Emotionally, Howard felt as though a constant weight lay across his chest, never allowing him a deep breath.

Raised in an era of resurgent individualism, in a nation and a family in which one took credit for one's own achievements and felt shamed by one's own failures, Howard felt first and most strongly intense anger at himself. Fear of failure? Indeed, the "failure" he had feared—with fear strong enough to drive him ever upward as a child, student, and lawyer—was like a cool breeze compared to this whiteout blizzard that his own stupidity had brought down on himself and all those he most cared about. Howard had learned young the habit of blaming someone when things went wrong. Now things had gone disastrously wrong. And he blamed himself—intensely.

When, more than six months after the accident, his friend Jack Wilkes mentioned the possibility that others also might have been responsible for Howard's injuries, Howard responded fiercely: "No way, man. *I* did it. I had this wonderful life. I had a great career. I was just too demented to notice, and I was the one who threw it all away!" Three months later, however, Howard had become more attuned to the financial calamity that was closing in on his family as his grace year of salary at the law firm drew to a close. He was then more willing to listen when friends, particularly Jack, and Howard's own family talked to him about the possibility of a tort suit. True, those friends, as well as Nicole and other adult family relatives, also placed much of the blame on Howard for the disaster— although not to his face. But they were less attached to that particular blame than he was. When presented with the information about the subway train driver's misbehavior and the bystanders' refusal to help the fallen Howard, friends and family directed a major part of their anger at those who could have helped Howard but hadn't, and at those who could have avoided harming him but didn't.

As time passed and Howard could see those close to him blaming others, he began to understand more fully that he could shift some of the responsibility for his ruined life. Not escape it: but shift—and thereby share it. He could also begin to acknowledge what Jack and others told him: that a tort suit might provide the only way out of financial distress for him and his family. Reluctant to flaunt his own inadequacy and irresponsibility in front of hostile lawyers, the public, judges, and jurors, but resigned to suffer whatever public indignities were necessary to keep the wolf from his family's door, Howard Young finally agreed to explore with P. J. Cowcroft the possibility of a tort suit. Once that psychological step was taken, he seemed to have little trouble in agreeing later to file a suit.

In examining tort law's contribution to the goal of compensating injured persons, we need to look beyond Howard Young and his family—but at the same time to keep them in our vision. What tort law may do to and for the Youngs will illuminate a corner of the personal injury world important to a sense of tort law's compensatory place in late twentieth-century America. Other perspectives need attention, too, such as the needs of other sick and injured people, as well as the rights and responsibilities of people and companies ultimately paying tort awards.

The Youngs' situation helps explain why society wants to compensate injured people as well as what that compensation entails. Our reaction to the Youngs' plight will be sympathy, perhaps empathy. Society would like to help them if it could. When the unfortunate Youngs appear in court, the judge and jury will feel a strong pull to provide help. If these impulses alone governed, the judge and jury in unison with tort law's rules—tort law's machinery—would simply translate each of the Youngs' suffering into money and award it to them.

As discussed in the previous chapter, that translation of suffering into money would entail the three kinds of suffering tort law compensates. Some of the suffering consists of money actually being drained out of the pockets of injured plaintiffs—expenses forced on them by the accident. This is *expense suffering.* Some of the Youngs' suffering would be seen as the loss of money which the Youngs would have had if Howard had not been injured. This is *lost expectancy suffering.* The translation of Howard's lost expectancy suffering—like that of his expense suffering—would be highly individualized. Tort law's machinery would reach its conclusion by focusing on the exact realities (and expected realities) of Howard's pre- and postaccident life. However, this latter translation would be much more difficult, because of the uncertainties inherent in identifying what might have been.

Even greater translation difficulties inhere in the third kind of suffering which tort law compensates: nonmonetary injuries, such as pain and suffering, emotional distress, loss of love and companionship, loss of enjoyment of life, and the like. This suffering is *intangible suffering.* A judge or jury would find it difficult to ascertain precisely what suffering really existed. They would find it equally difficult to translate that suffering into a particular dollar figure.

Although this sort of highly individualized attention to the suffering of the particular claimants dominates tort law's performance of its compensation function, it need not. The difficulty of tort law's machinery in translating lost expectancy suffering and intangible suffering could be mitigated by recharacterizing the suffering. Instead of discussing Howard's own lost expectancy suffering, tort law could characterize a plaintiff's injury in general terms as a lost or diminished ability of people to generally support themselves or their families.[5] By deciding only in general what level of income gave one the "ability to support" himself and his family, tort lawmakers could greatly simplify the translation of this kind of suffering into dollars—that is, it could order payment of the average weekly wage earned in the state. Similarly, if lawmakers characterized intangible suffering in categories—say, damage to a hand, foot, or eyesight— and attached fairly precise dollar values to each of those categories, the translation would be much simpler, while admittedly less tailored to the individual claimant's needs. Indeed, workers' compensation schemes are patterned this way.

Regardless of how the suffering of injured persons is characterized, its compensation also comprises three general kinds. Tort law's compensation for expense suffering and lost expectancy suffering usually is characterized by providing dollars to a plaintiff to make up for dollars lost. This is *replacement compensation*. Compensation for intangible suffering takes two forms. Tort law can provide dollars that would allow the injured person to buy some source of gratification which would substitute for the gratification taken from him by his injury. For example, if a component of Howard Young's suffering was distress at being unable to engage in strenuous physical activity, he might be able to use his tort-awarded dollars to buy exercise machinery that would permit him to get strenuous exercise even in his physically disabled state. This is *substitute compensation*. For suffering like Elissa Young's loss of her father's emotional support, which is of a sort not easily replaced, tort law provides money as much to comfort the plaintiff as to do anything else. Elissa may be able to use her compensation dollars to buy things that make her happier, but the dollars primarily are an official acknowledgment of and consolation for her suffering. This is *solace compensation*.

From the start, viewing tort law as a kind of attempt to help the needy has run into serious challenges. Tort law is not the equivalent of a social services campaign, or of the sort of spontaneous "helping out" that happens on city streets when passers-by give cash tidbits to needy street people. Tort law does not operate by doling out charitable financial aid from some governmental or private coffer. It operates by demanding other people or entities to pay the plaintiff. Victims of torts may be as needy as the homeless, but from defendants' perspectives tort law may resemble a mugging more than sweet charity. Money is given to a person who needs help, but it is forcibly extracted from someone else. One person's loss is made whole by imposing the financial equivalent of that loss on another. Tort law does not make injuries disappear. It transfers them, in a mutated form, to someone else. In helping some, tort law hurts others. In theory, it hurts those others as much as it helps the accidentally injured.

Accordingly, the compensation objective of tort law calls for reasons for compensation beyond a simple desire to help the needy. Frequently, lawmakers justify tort law's injury-shifting in terms of reducing the total amount of injury. They argue that compensating injured plaintiffs in tort cases in fact ameliorates the total amount of suffering in society because it spreads the intense suffering of the plaintiff over a larger group of people, namely those who share the defendant's tort liability costs, either as consumers of the defendant's goods or services (in the case of the Transit Authority, as fare payers to the defendant), or as members of the defendant's liability insurance pool. The theory is that it is better that many people suffer a small deprivation than that an individual suffer a major one. Society is better off, according to those attuned to tort law's compensatory role, if the City Transit Authority compensates the Youngs, because tort compensation will significantly alleviate, if not remove, the Youngs' suffering, while imposing little suffering on others. Supposedly, people will hardly notice the tiny increase in their taxes or in transit fares resulting from a court decision requiring payment of damages in the Youngs' case.

The economic argument for this shift in resources runs like this: as money received increases, each new dollar supposedly adds less value to its owner; so a dollar gained or lost by a person with a few dollars is supposed to be worth more to him than a dollar gained or lost by a person with hundreds of thousands of dollars. Such a theory purports to justify not only the progressive income tax but tort liability insurance, whereby a few dollars are extracted from everyone in normal physical and economic health, for whom the loss of a few dollars in insurance premiums or a higher transit fare is easily absorbed, and then redistributed to the few who suffer accidents and are consequently unlikely to be able to bear the resulting financial burden.

Most people seem to accept this goal—but many economists (especially those of a conservative bent) blanch at such naked redistribution of income, bottomed on their revulsion at the idea of comparing one person's large loss with many people's small losses. For the economist, such redistribution is based on a theory of *diminishing marginal utility,* with a concomitant use of *interpersonal utility comparisons.* (Unfortunately, that's the way economists talk.)

Economists who challenge such redistribution of income argue it this way: if people have different net incomes, whether induced by accidents or not, a transfer that equalizes income would not necessarily make things better than before the transfer. In their eyes the gain to the person paid is equal in the aggregate to the loss of those who pay. Even if one considers a one-on-one comparison of a very wealthy person to a very needy one, in some economists' eyes, if by a transfer, the well-off person loses his chance to buy a fifth antique chair so that the person rendered a quadriplegic can buy a wheelchair, there is in their view no way to scientifically establish that the former does not need his new chair just as acutely as the latter needs his. It seems at least as plausible under such a view to assume that people who work hard to make and keep money are on the average those who value money the most, so that no scientific basis exists for concluding that redistribution from the relatively affluent to the relatively needy is the better course for society. Even more does this view dispute taking from the average person (as an insurance premium payer) to give to others in need. (Of course this theory does not condemn voluntary gifts through charity.)

But supporters of compulsory redistribution return to the attack with the (perhaps unscientific but nevertheless persuasive—to them, at least) argument that social welfare *is* advanced when an insurance mechanism like tort liability can pay for injury losses. Such losses, if unreimbursed, can lead to lack of medical care, rehabilitation, and even subsistence wages. Those kinds of losses are in the realm of what perhaps the most famous economist of his time, Lord Keynes, called "absolute" losses. For Keynes, the needs for humans fall into two categories: "Those needs which are absolute in the sense that we feel them whatever the situation of our fellow human beings may be [such as the needs of the victim with quadriplegia] and those which are relative only in that their satisfaction lifts us above, makes us feel superior to, our fellows [such as those of the antique collector]."[6]

Granted that drawing the line between these categories is difficult, and granted that redistribution of income may perhaps be justified only for such absolute needs, aid in the form of assuring payment for medical services and wage loss of the seriously injured would seem to many clearly to fall within the category of absolute needs.

But even assuming the legitimacy of the goal of such redistribution of income based on comparing one person's large loss with many people's small loss, there is nonetheless grounds in the eyes of many to excoriate tort law for its failure to achieve its compensatory goal. Their criticism rests on several major grounds, which we'll simply list and then discuss. First, they say, tort law fails because it refuses to compensate most injured, sick, or needy people. Second, where it does compensate, tort law's payments contribute little to society's compensatory aims because those payments are not necessary to ease the truly significant suffering of most injured persons. Third, even where necessary, tort compensation is often excessive. Fourth, it provides that compensation not only in a dilatory and quixotic but in a regressive manner, favoring wealthier persons over poorer persons. Finally, the tort system's extravagant administrative costs make it the last vehicle society should choose to do the job of compensating its injured.[7] Let's take these up in order.

Many injured people are missing from tort's compensatory reach. Most obviously missing are the victims of personal tragedies who have no arguable claim to tort compensation. These include people who have strokes and heart attacks. They include those dying tragically with cancer or AIDS and those afflicted from the Gulf and Vietnam wars, debilitated by stress disorders. Among them are persons whose investments have turned to dust, whose businesses collapsed, along with the life's savings that began them, and whose jobs were swallowed by the latest over-any-minute-now recession or corporate downsizing. Even among those persons injured in an accident, many are hurt in ways that may never suggest another's responsibility. Nearly 40 percent of accidental injuries in the United States occur under such circumstances, as when a motorist collides with an abutment or a tree or other inanimate object.[8]

And even for injured persons who might arguably have a claim for tort compensation, tort law provides far less compensation than its legal rules suggest. Study after study has confirmed that only a small fraction of the accidentally injured ever make any kind of claim for compensation and that even fewer ever formally file a tort lawsuit. A recent Harvard study of medical malpractice in New York State estimated, consistent with earlier studies, that there were eight times as many incidents of patient injuries caused by malpractice as there were malpractice claims.[9] Comprehensive research into claims arising from accidental injuries in both the United States and in Great Britain reached similar conclusions: a very small percentage of injured persons—in the neighborhood of 10 percent—make any kind of claim for compensation from an injuring party or his insurer.[10] Even those who are inclined to make a claim often find that the party who injured them hasn't enough money to make a potential tort judgment worth much more than the paper it's printed on. Many other tort claimants simply don't win. They run into the dead ends that litter the tort labyrinth: the need to prove not only a defendant's fault but that a particular defendant's faulty conduct or product probably caused this particular injury; or, like Howard Young, they face the obstacle of one's own contributory fault. These losing plaintiffs are, after all, no less in need of compensation, or loss-spreading, than those who win tort lawsuits.

Moreover, having a good legal claim is no guarantee of full tort compensation. The P. J. Cowcrofts of the world often will not represent an injured person in a complicated case such as one for a defective product unless his damages are severe—worth, say, $100,000 or more. Once a tort suit has begun, a plaintiff will face many incentives to settle it for less than he probably would win at trial. The Youngs, for example, need money now to keep their house, to pay for health care and rehabilitation, and to keep some of the pieces of their lives together. The average tort lawsuit reaches trial years after it is filed. Facing financial needs that press them severely, and looking at an uncertain decision about liability, the Youngs will be sorely tempted to jump at any halfway reasonable settlement offer from the defendants. If the Youngs were able to, or required to, hang on to the bitter end of prolonged litigation—including additional lengthy appeals—the financial compensation they received would hardly erase the additional suffering they had to endure in taking so long to get it. Besides, they would have to give a third or more of whatever they got to P. J. Cowcroft.

In fairness, tort law never purported to be an all-encompassing compensation scheme. Those who admire tort law point out that the legal limitations on recovery and the practical difficulties inherent in navigating the tort labyrinth naturally push most injured persons toward other compensation sources, such as their own health and disability insurance. Accordingly, tort compensation is often reserved for one group of injured persons—those who are rather seriously injured by someone else's fault, at least in the case of those injured by medical malpractice or defective products. That group will obtain much closer to full compensation for all the injuries they have suffered than will injured persons who receive compensation from other sources. Nonetheless, tort law has no completely satisfactory answer to the question: why should society give preference in compensation to this group injured by faulty conduct or products, when that preference is not based on any greater need? Tort law's apologists can only reason that it compensates the needy whenever it locates sufficiently wealthy (or insured) defendants whose behavior makes it appropriate (as well as economically efficient) for the law to force them to compensate someone they injured.

Serious questions do exist, moreover, about whether most compensation provided by tort law is necessary. Many injured persons who bring tort claims have access to those other kinds of compensation, which to a considerable extent meet their most pressing needs. With respect to the category of suffering that tort law almost alone seeks to compensate—intangible pain and suffering—its compensation may likewise be unnecessary because arguably money can do little, if anything, to alleviate pain and suffering.

As to those other sources of compensation to which injured people in our society can turn instead of tort law for compensation, most people in the United States have some form of health insurance that will cover at least a substantial portion of their medical expenses. Persons with income loss can have access to private and public disability insurance, as well as workers' compensation, sick leave, and even welfare. (Admittedly, almost no alternative compensation sources exist for intangible injuries.)

The existence of these alternative sources of compensation has led some to suggest that tort compensation is not really necessary to take care of the most important components of people's injuries.[11] There is certainly no question that the overwhelming number of persons compensated for accidental injuries in the United States receive that compensation from sources other than tort law.[12]

Nevertheless, this does not mean that tort compensation is unnecessary where it can be obtained. The American Law Institute (ALI), a prestigious organization focusing on legal research and reform, recently took a hard look at the availability of other sources of compensation to injured and sick persons as well as at the adequacy of such compensation. It found that injury victims bear a substantial share of the burdens of their injuries all by themselves: overall, the study concluded, injury victims on average bear 38 percent of their own economic losses, even after figuring in all other compensatory sources.[13] Most of the costs borne by injury victims themselves are for lost income.

The place where tort compensation seems least necessary is for those injuries that occur in the workplace. Such injuries usually can be compensated by workers' compensation systems, which provide injured persons money for their medical costs and money to replace their lost wages. Four-fifths of injured workers who make workers' compensation claims receive, on average, about 90 percent of their lost wages. (On the other hand, it might be pointed out that the highest-paid 20 percent receive proportionately much less compensation because of limits on the total an injured person can receive—usually, as suggested earlier, only a percentage of the state's average weekly wage. Moreover, the most seriously injured workers, those with permanent injuries, likewise fare worst, because workers' compensation awards do not increase automatically with inflation and because awards for partial [as opposed to total] disability are keyed to outmoded schedules.[14])

Although workers' compensation on the whole seems to provide relatively good and speedy compensation to many injured persons, it does nothing for persons like Howard Young, who were not injured on the job. For that approximately 75 percent of the injured, nontort compensation must be found in the patchwork of private insurance and public benefit programs that operate in uneasy alliance to address personal injury compensation. Private insurance consists primarily of health insurance and disability insurance—with life insurance a major compensatory factor in regard to fatal injuries. The recent ALI report concluded that there are "large numbers of uninsured and underinsured" people in our society, lacking access to health insurance and receiving inadequate health care.[15] The report determined that even these large holes in access to health care looked tiny in comparison to the widespread lack of protection for wage losses due to injury payable from private disability insurance. The report found that even larger holes exist in the compensation offered by Social Security Disability and public assistance programs, to say nothing of the fact that some of the public assistance programs require the injury victim to lapse into a state of poverty before benefits become available.[16] The conclusions of the ALI report seem to be that tort law, with all its delays, expense, and fortuity, retains an important place in compensating persons even for economic loss alone. And tort law certainly plays the critical role insofar as compensation for intangible injuries is concerned. Virtually no other compensation source provides money for such suffering. Critics of tort's compensatory role point out, however, that giving people money for intangible injuries means throwing dollars at injuries that money can't cure. Therefore, even in this area tort compensation is controversial.

While this observation has considerable merit, it must be remembered that compensation for intangible suffering has two components: substitute compensation and solace compensation. The former may have real value as compensation, value that most people would recognize. Even if their pain cannot be removed, Elissa and Laura Young's lives might be improved by giving them dollars reflective of their emotional devastation. Those dollars could pay for high-quality child care, for alternative schooling, for vacation breaks from the stress of the Howard-dominated household, and for many other things that would brighten parts of their lives in both the short and long term. Even when one focuses on solace compensation alone—money provided as a comfort or consolation for one's hurt—it may be that even this limited official, tangible recognition of the importance of the family's loss and of the validity of their emotional reactions will have importance to their futures and to their abilities to deal with the appallingly difficult situation confronting them.

Even if necessary, tort compensation is excessive, its critics claim. There are two basic components to that charge. One component adds to the criticism of compensation for intangible injuries just discussed the assertion that tort law forces a kind of insurance against intangible injuries on people that they don't want to pay for. If Nicole Young had really wanted to receive money for her emotional upsets in the event her husband was accidentally physically and mentally disabled, presumably she would have sought emotional distress insurance. Her unwillingness to do that demonstrates, according to tort law's critics, that Nicole was unwilling to buy insurance for economic compensation for noneconomic or emotional harm at a price it would have cost (assuming that she could have found an insurance company willing to sell it at any price). This shows she didn't really want emotional distress insurance that tort law insists everyone have, according to this line of analysis, just as my unwillingness to pay $40,000-plus for a Mercedes-Benz shows that I don't *really* want it. But if tort law provides such compensation for the emotional injuries suffered by Nicole, Elissa, and Laura, then consumers will be forced to pay for it, because the defendants and their insurance companies who pay such damages will pass those costs on to the people who buy their products or services. Transit Authority passengers, for example, will have to pay at least a few cents more each week for the right that tort law gives them to collect money for their or their families' emotional harms in the event of an accident. On the other hand, as we have speculated, if the Transit Authority offered its riders lower weekly ticket package prices and separately sold emotional distress insurance at the price it cost the Authority to provide it, almost no one would buy it. In fact, almost no one now buys insurance to pay themselves for pain and suffering or any other form of intangible harm. From a purely compensatory viewpoint, therefore, tort compensation for intangible harms can be deemed excessive.[17]

The second component of the charge that tort law compensates excessively emanates from decades of research indicating that tort law pays relatively more in compensation for minor injuries than it does for major injuries, especially for automobile accidents. Persons with minor injuries on average receive a much higher percentage of their economic loss from a tort claim than do persons with serious injuries. From this data, some infer that tort law overcompensates minor injuries and undercompensates major injuries. Why?

A principal explanation offered to explain small-injury overcompensation focuses on the pain and suffering component of tort damages. That explanation notes that this component—present in every personal injury case—cannot confidently be translated into dollars and cents. The law is dealing with a commodity where there is no market. There is no ready referent by which to decide what an aching back is worth.

In this view, that quandary of trying to measure the unmeasurable has led to a pragmatic—albeit inherently flawed—solution. Quite often the starting point for bargaining over the value of pain and suffering is a multiple of the actual economic losses (what lawyers and insurance adjusters term *special damages,* or *specials*). To determine what to offer for pain and suffering (*general damages*), insurance adjusters often multiply by three, perhaps four, maybe more, the amount of the claimant's medical bills and wage loss.

Although this solution allows insurance adjusters greater clarity in deciding the dollar value of intangible injuries, it also offers claimants tremendous inducements to "pad" their claims, especially smaller claims. If general damages are determined by multiplying an accident victim's medical expenses, then the victim can profit by every dollar he spends on his medical care. For each medical dollar spent, the victim can expect three or four dollars more to compensate his pain and suffering. Moreover, because his health insurer is probably paying for all or most of his medical bills, there isn't much to dissuade the victim from pumping up those expenses. Those expenses are particularly easy to run up with the help of a cooperative doctor with whom an unethical lawyer may have a cozy referral relationship. "Don't skimp," urges the lawyer to an eager doctor already facing unrealistic limits on payment for his treatment of other patients imposed by Medicare, Medicaid, and private health insurers.

Nor is this kind of inflation of claims easy to detect. An insurance adjuster will find it hard to insist that medical treatment beyond a certain point is unnecessary, especially in a small auto accident or "slip and fall" case. After all, there has been an accident and a variety of arguably legitimate complaints about, say, "soft tissue" injuries—whiplash, for example—that are impossible to detect from X rays or any other objective evidence. Many point to evidence that this padding pervades the world of small auto claims.[18]

According to this explanation, smaller claims are seen as much more subject to padding or "the buildup" because it costs defendants and insurers more to litigate the claim than to pay it. On the other hand, as explained in Chapter 1, many defendants, and especially their insurers in tort lawsuits, are so-called repeat players—defendants who are often sued. Such defendants have a strong interest in not paying for "nuisance suits." After all, if the defendant gets a reputation for fighting claims even when it will cost them more to win than they might have paid out in a settlement, then injury victims and especially their lawyers will be much less likely to bring such small claims against that defendant in the future.

To this challenge, those who believe small claims are overcompensated respond by pointing to other phenomena at work. An insurance company may be especially inclined to pay early what might even seem an inflated value for a claim, as long as the dollar figure is relatively low, in the realization of how easy it will be for a claimant to further pad his claim. Additional inducement for an inclination to pay smaller claims with minimal deliberation may be the ability of the insured injurer to sue his own insurer for bad-faith refusal to settle a victim's claim that should have been promptly disposed of. Exposure to such potentially punitive bad-faith claims causes some insurers to be gun-shy about a general policy of recalcitrance in facing low-stakes claims. All this potential for "bother" may give smaller claimants disproportionate bargaining power with the insurance company. As a result, in small cases, an insurer may often pay far more than the claim might seem to be worth.

Conversely, though, these same intractable issues—evaluating who was at fault and the value of pain and suffering—work to the advantage of an insurer in large cases, ameliorating the risks of recalcitrance. In a big case, the injured victim's needs are likely to be pressing, with his sick leave or health insurance having (or about to) run out, assuming he has them at all—and, of course, many people in our society are without such coverage. Thus the victim cannot afford the risk of losing or even of a long delay in negotiating a claim. As a result, in large cases the claimant often gives in by accepting far less than his claim would seem to be worth. All this is reflected in the fact, as suggested earlier, that the claimant with large losses so often receives but a small proportion of his losses. This, in turn, means that, especially for (but not limited to) auto accident and slip-and-fall cases, those who suffer the most pain are the least likely to be paid for it.[19] In effect, then, if insurers are often overpaying small claims, they are corollarially underpaying large ones.

Another serious concern about tort law's compensation function has arisen from recent suggestions that, rather than helping the needy, tort law in fact favors the wealthy vis-à-vis the poor. For those who see tort law's compensatory aim as helping the needy or as spreading losses from those who cannot bear them very well to a broader group who can, such suggestions have proven particularly distressing.

Quite simply, tort law is alleged to be regressive because a major component of most tort awards consists of the plaintiff's lost income. Persons who are wealthy—those with high income before the accident—will collect far more than the relatively poor when damages are awarded for lost wages. Howard Young will get much more money if he wins his tort suit than would one of the mail clerks in his law firm who had gone through the same events and suffered exactly the same physical injuries. This would not be so troublesome if, as in other insurance areas, the insured had to pay more in to obtain this right to get more out of the system in the event he was injured. That is not so in tort law, the critics claim. The costs of tort awards are added to the prices of goods and services across the board, so that when the poor person pays for a subway ride or buys a ladder, he pays the same amount in tort insurance costs for it as does the wealthier person. If both suffer identical injuries from such a fall, however, the wealthier person will collect significantly more from such tort insurance. Furthermore, studies show that middle- and upper-income groups sue more often than do the poor—and certainly are in a much stronger position to hold out for a higher settlement than the poor. At any rate, the fact remains that tort law will retain regressive aspects in its compensation so long as it holds to a philosophy of compensating for full individual income loss, coupled with little if any differentiation in what people pay into the compensation pool.

Tort law's individualized compensation likewise explains in part its final major drawback in compensating for personal injuries. A plethora of studies have shown conclusively that the tort machinery gobbles up half or more of all the dollars that defendants pay in tort lawsuits. No one wants to compensate injured people with a bucket brigade of money that wastes every second bucket. So long as massive transaction costs—especially in lawyers' fees on both sides—continue to plague tort law, almost any alternative compensation system will look better in comparison. Any such system would be able to promise equal or greater benefits for injured people as well as lower costs for those who end up paying those benefits: a deal that can't be refused.

In the final analysis, though, tort law offers the potential of more complete compensation to almost any eligible injured person than society offers anywhere else. Tort law also holds out compensation to persons who might not find it elsewhere, short of retreat to a life at or below the poverty line. Nevertheless, critics raise serious questions about the compensatory worth of a relatively small but growing pocket of generous compensation that is hugely expensive to run, favors the less needy, and provides compensation on the basis of what happens to cause a person's need rather than on the basis of the need itself. One cannot be at all confident that tort law in general, or the particular tort rules that dominate 1990s law, well serve society's aims to help the needy and minimize societal pain.

CHAPTER FOUR

Making a Safer World

The immediate attraction of tort law for the Youngs—its compensatory function—would not by itself make it attractive to the rest of society. There are many other ways to compensate sick and injured persons, ways that would be faster, more certain, and less expensive for all concerned.

Tort law does more, however, than just compensate. Most conspicuously, it deters unsafe behavior. Just as the threat of criminal sanctions deters antisocial behavior, the threat of tort liability deters behavior that risks injury. Placing all or some of the costs associated with Howard Young's accident on the parties to the Youngs' lawsuit will reduce the chances that similar accidents will happen in the future.

That, at least, is how it works in theory. It is a theory at the very heart of tort law. Deterrence, along with compensation, has been one of the two main pillars on which tort law has been constructed for more than a half century.[1]

Recently, however, scholars, "reformers," and even some judges have expressed skepticism about whether tort awards have any significant deterrent value. Judge Constance Small, presiding over the Youngs' lawsuit, and other judges and legislators may well choose different tort rules if they were convinced that these skeptics are right. Certainly, for example, the case for awarding money to Nicole and her daughters for their suffering becomes much less compelling if such damages don't reduce the chances of similar emotional devastation in the future. Accordingly, all who participate in the tort process need an understanding of tort's deterrent role in theory and an appraisal of its effects in reality in order to decide how to advance the law's handling of accidental injuries.

The deterrent theory of tort is both simple and complex. You can hear the simple part from the lips of P. J. Cowcroft, the Youngs' lawyer, as she talks about the value of her work: "I'm the cop on the safety beat. There are a whole lot of people out there who don't want to walk the straight and narrow. There are drivers who want to speed; there are doctors who want to hurry to the next patient, or next task, or even to the golf course; and there are thousands of producers who want their production lines running faster and faster, and cheaper and cheaper. They say they try to be reasonably careful, and some may even think they are: but they aren't. They really want, more than anything, to get where they're going with a minimum of fuss.

"I'm the one who makes them fuss about safety."

Speaking with the moral conviction and bravado typical of the plaintiffs' personal injury lawyer, P.J. explains: "They know I'm out here. They know that if someone gets hurt by their carelessness, I'll haul their butts into court and make them pay for it, make them pay plenty."

Many people carry with them this image of tort law—the cop on the beat. It is a powerful image, hard to disregard. All of us have had personal experience with how we and others behave when a police officer is around. We drive more carefully—at least more slowly—when we see a police car. Even teenagers sometimes behave less antisocially when they see the police. Insofar as tort law resembles a police presence, people and companies who might behave carelessly are bound to act more safely when tort law is around.

One of the beauties of tort law, in the eyes of P. J. Cowcroft and other fans of its safety-enhancing potential, is that it is there constantly. With the aid of tort law, the safety police are as omnipresent as are the victims of accidents. Anyone who gets hurt may potentially enforce the tort law against those who hurt him. Moreover, tort liability isn't just a slap on the wrist. If unsafe behavior causes significant injuries, a careless actor can find himself staring at a several hundred thousand dollar sanction or more. When it comes to *severity* of sanction, at least—usually regarded as a key factor in assessing the deterrent effects of criminal law—tort law is said to have impressive clout with those potential injurers at whom its threat is directed.[2]

Tort law's deterrent power compares even more favorably with that of the criminal law when we compare those who feel their sting. One of the difficulties with criminal law as a sanction has always been that many criminals sense that they are very unlikely to be caught and have considerable difficulty imagining future punishment. Those subject to tort sanctions, on the other hand, often realize that they have a lot to lose from that sanction. (Admittedly, though, if they don't have a fair amount of money available themselves or through their insurance, they probably won't be sued.) Moreover, most of those actors with deep pockets sense there is a substantial chance they will be "caught" by tort law if their careless actions injure people significantly. Insofar as the sanctioned entities are businesses or insurance companies—a large share of the population against which tort law gets enforced—those whom tort law threatens are in the business of predicting future costs.

In its more complicated form, tort law as deterrent also appears as a regulator of the marketplace. As market regulator, tort law works in three principal ways to push or pull behavior in safer directions. First, it adds the costs of avoidable accidents to the cost-benefit analysis people commonly perform when choosing among alternative behaviors. Second, it makes dangerous products, services, and activities more expensive than their safer competitors, thus dampening demand for items that more often lead to injury. Finally, it encourages the development and use of safer ways of living. Moreover, says this complicated deterrent theory, tort law does all this "just right"—it is neither too lenient nor too harsh in its regulation of the market in safety.

Observers most clearly see tort law in its "market regulator" role when it forces people to take into account—to "internalize"—the health and safety consequences of the behavioral choices they make. Businesses and individuals constantly make choices about how they will behave, choices that affect the chances that they or others will be injured. Those choices range across a continuum from the very broad to the very narrow. At the broad end, for example, an entrepreneur may consider whether to begin an ultralight airplane business; a medical student whether to specialize in obstetrics; or a pharmaceutical company whether to produce vaccines. More narrowly, for example, the Transit Authority may consider whether to install speed reducers on the subway tracks leading into its stations; a homeowner whether to trim a large dead branch from a tree; a bar owner whether to stock a new kind of beer glass that does not break into sharp fragments on impact; or the pharmaceutical company whether to produce a live-virus (Sabin) or killed-virus (Salk) vaccine, with their differing risks.

In making these choices, actors typically try to figure out the relative costs and benefits accompanying available alternatives. Looking at expected benefits, the business gauges what the gross sales of its product or service will be, including the expected return from a differently fashioned product or service; the individual gauges how financially and emotionally rewarding it will be to deliver babies or how valuable it will be to improve his view by removing the dead branch. Looking at expected costs, the business must estimate research and development expenses, as well as the costs of raw materials, production, and marketing for the competing vaccines. Or it must assess how expensive in labor and materials it will be to install the speed reducers. The individual doctor-to-be will investigate the costs of office space, equipment, staff, hospital privileges, and information necessary to practice obstetrics satisfactorily. Or the homeowner will estimate the costs of tree limb removal.

Tort law helps to ensure that this common cost-benefit mode of decision making will maximize social welfare. It does this by forcing people to factor into their cost-benefit analysis the full expense of the accidental injuries that they may reasonably expect will be associated with one choice or another. If a business or individual chooses a course of conduct that increases the number and severity of injuries more than it otherwise benefits society, tort law will make it pay, relatively fully, for those injuries. Without tort law, the business or individual would not have to pay the same attention to the risks of injuries included in the alternatives it is examining.

Some examples may clarify this complicated side to the theory of tort as a deterrent. There are many steps the City Transit Authority could take to reduce or eliminate the chances that its subway trains will enter stations too fast. All of those steps—including the use of speed reducers, mentioned above—will cost the Transit Authority money, probably a significant sum. Concerned about the system's financial health, Transit Authority officials will be reluctant to spend money that has little if anything to do with keeping the trains running or keeping its riders happy. They will be reluctant, that is, unless they believe that spending such sums to reduce accidental injuries will save the Authority money in the long run. Tort law can provide those savings. The Transit Authority officials will know that if they do not take reasonable measures to prevent speeding—measures that will cost less to implement than the costs of the injuries that would otherwise occur—some of the persons injured by subway speeding will bring tort lawsuits against the Authority, which will drain a disproportionate amount of money from the agency's treasury. Faced with the opportunity to save the money that would otherwise leak out in tort settlements and judgments, Transit Authority officials will spend anything significantly less than that much money to avoid the accidents in the first place.

Similarly, tort law will deter a pharmaceutical company from marketing unreasonably unsafe products and will push the company to spend money reasonably to avoid injuries caused by those products. Waves of litigation about intrauterine devices (IUDs) will make producers of similar products examine more carefully the full range of adverse results that might be linked to that product well before they decide to put it on the market. Absent tort law, these companies would worry less, believing that effective "spin control" might defuse any objection to injuries from their product. They might expect to reduce harm to their company by claiming surprise, by cooperating openly with regulatory agencies examining the situation, and by withdrawing the product from the market with carefully orchestrated statements of great concern for their customers. Tort law, on the other hand, would not be so forgiving: it would make the company pay for the injuries it caused if the risks of its product outweigh its benefits.

Other pharmaceutical company choices can likewise be shaped by tort law's influence. As suggested, a vaccine manufacturer may face the choice between using two different vaccines for a given illness. One may be somewhat cheaper to produce, while the other may be less likely to produce undesirable side effects in vaccinated persons. If the demand for each type is the same, the company will produce the cheaper one. Even if it were inclined to use the costlier virus, to be more protective of consumers, the company would fear a competitor's use of the cheaper vaccine, thereby giving the competitor an advantage in either market share or profitability. Tort law can change that decision. It tells the company and its competitors that each should evaluate carefully the increase in injuries that can be expected to occur if it uses the cheaper vaccine rather than the safer one, because it will have to pay for many of those injuries if it was unreasonable to choose the less safe alternative. Basic tort doctrine would determine that decision to be unreasonable if it would have cost the company less to use the more expensive vaccine than the total costs of the injuries that the safer vaccine's use would have prevented.

This is not the only way in which tort law regulates the market in safety. In its second "market regulator" form, tort decreases injury in society by making injury-producing activities or goods more expensive than their safer competitors. If it is significant, that greater expense will nudge consumers away from risky products, services, and activities toward safer ones. If some obstetricians practice less safely than others, they can expect to face greater liability expenses than the others. Those additional expenses should require them to charge more for their obstetrical services than their safer colleagues.

Even if patients do not learn of the other doctors' better safety record, their lower costs should attract some patients from their more dangerous colleagues. In addition, even where consumers do not have a safer alternative, they will consume somewhat less of most goods, services, and activities as the price rises. Either way, there will be less demand for more dangerous parts of our lives. The result? Fewer accidents will occur.

Finally, tort law as market regulator may enhance safety in a positive, not just a negative, way. Tort law doesn't just dampen demand for unsafe goods and services. It may also increase demand for safer goods and services. In some instances, tort law may be the critical stimulant that leads to the development of safer products or processes. All goods, services, and activities carry with them risks of injury to consumers. Vaccines have side effects, often serious ones. Airplanes, including ultralight ones, crash. Bar glasses break, and so on.

Over time, tort law should encourage safety advances in these and other areas. Tort law does so most obviously where providers of goods and services are already subject to liability for their actions. If bars are being held liable for injuries received in bar fights among their drunken patrons—as they often are—and if a significant factor in many such injuries is cuts from broken glasses, then they may pay a fair amount of money for glasses that disintegrate into tiny cubes on impact rather than break into sharp shards.[3] Thanks to tort law, there should be a strong demand for products that reduce injuries.

That demand may exist, due to tort law, even where the products are safe enough to evade current liability. Researchers, inventors, and the like know that if they can discover a way to make safer goods, there should be a market for their inventions and discoveries. Providers of goods and services will want to buy these inventions and discoveries because they are cost effective—use of this "safer way" will enable them to avoid tort liability when accidents occur. Thus, investors could fund the researchers who developed a safer whooping cough vaccine, confident that if a safer vaccine were discovered, vaccine manufacturers would be pressured by tort law to adopt it.[4] If vaccine makers were already being held liable for some of the side effects of their particular vaccine, they would be inclined to switch to the new, safer version so long as it promised to cut their liability costs more than it added to their production costs. If they were not being held liable at the time of the new invention, they would soon realize the need to acquire it, because its existence as a safer alternative would make them liable in tort for the injuries they could have prevented by switching from the old, more danger-ous vaccine. Either way, tort law arguably creates a ready, certain market for safety advances.

Moreover, according to this more sophisticated economic theory of tort law as a deterrent, all these kinds of pressures away from dangerous and toward safe behavior take place with just the right amount of force. In other words, tort law provides accurate deter-rence. In economic theory, tort law holds just the right level of eco-nomic threat over the pocketbooks of those who behave in ways that risk injuring others.

How can tort law make that claim? When people consider deter-rence and law, they most often think about criminal law settings, where deterrence has been studied and debated all over the world for centuries. Despite the breadth and length of that debate, it con-tinues heatedly in the United States, particularly with respect to what sanctions provide appropriate deterrence for what misbehav-ior. Anyone familiar with those debates might be quite skeptical when confronting the claim that tort law deters with just the "right" effect.

Nevertheless, tort law does just that, in theory, when it is work-ing as designed. Tort law makes wrongdoers pay for exactly the injuries they carelessly cause. Should Howard Young and the mem-bers of his family win their lawsuits, each responsible participant in his tragic accident will pay his or its share of the money damages that a jury decides are equivalent to the injuries suffered. Being one of those responsible participants, Howard will pay his share, too, in the form of a proportionate reduction in the money he or his family receives. The jury will hear extensive evidence about the exact injuries that Howard, Nicole, Laura, and Elissa have suffered. Most likely, experts will testify in order to help the jury understand how those injuries might properly be valued in dollars. In the end, if the lawyers, the judge, and the jurors all perform their roles as the economic theory of tort law expects them to, the jury will assess damages that represent the full nature of the plaintiffs' injuries.

If persons unreasonably injured by others can make those others pay the full price of their injuries, then tort law threatens negligent actors with a "punishment" that is exactly equal to the injuries they cause. Of course, the threat is not equal to the risk, because the actors know that they will have to pay for their unreasonably risky behavior only if an accident actually happens and injuries result. But the higher the chance of injury—the riskier the behavior—the stronger the tort threat. The more serious the injury risked, the stronger the tort threat. For instance, to determine the expected annual cost of its failure to restrict some of its trains to the prescribed speed as they approach stations, the Transit Authority estimates how many people are likely to be injured by speeding trains and estimates how serious, on average, those injuries will be. The Authority will be able to quantify its estimate of injury seriousness by examining what plaintiffs with similar injuries have received in tort verdicts in the recent past. The Transit Authority will be under an incentive to multiply the number of injuries expected times the dollar equivalent of the average injury in order to understand the expected costs associated with its trains' speed of entry into stations. The result determines the deterrent threat posed by tort law. It is a threat equivalent to the expected injury costs associated with the Transit Authority's risky behavior.

This is, in theory at least, an accurate deterrent. If the actor could avoid some or all of that harm by modifying his behavior—by installing, for example, speed reducers on its tracks approaching stations—tort law gives him an incentive to do so, but only to the appropriate extent. The actor is not threatened by tort law so much that he will avoid accidental injuries at all costs. Tort law only threatens a monetary cost. So the actor will take the safety steps necessary to avoid or reduce his costs only if those steps can be taken more cheaply than the costs in accidents that will occur if he does not take the steps. Otherwise, it is not worth taking the safety steps. The actor would be spending more money to avoid accidents than he would spend if he just allowed them to happen.

For example, if the Transit Authority expects that its speeding-into-station trains will cause $10 million worth of injuries that would not have occurred had they been driven at a slower, more reasonable speed, and if it knows that speed reducers are the cheapest way to eliminate such accidents, it will install the speed reducers only if they can be installed for less than $10 million. If it would cost the Authority more than $10 million to install the speed reducers, it will not be deterred from proceeding as it had in the past and allowing the accidents to happen. So, tort theory tells us tort law will not overdeter—that is, force an actor to spend more money on safety steps than it is worth in injuries prevented. Tort law will not underdeter either—that is, encourage an actor to spend less on safety steps than the injuries such steps will prevent. It deters "just right."

Tort law's effects in reality may not resemble at all what this deterrent theory would predict. Respected scholars contend that in reality tort law has little or no effect in encouraging safety. Some see tort law as downright perverse: as, unintentionally, discouraging choices that would lead to greater overall safety.[5]

Most of the challenge to the theory that tort deters comes in the form of "countertheory": theoretical explanations of why tort law cannot be expected to deter unsafe behavior, at least not well. Countertheory comprises three main categories of reasons why tort won't deter: (1) the law's sanctions are not perceived to be particularly strong; (2) tort law does not communicate clearly what behavior will be sanctioned; and (3) much of the behavior that tort law will sanction is not susceptible to being changed by money sanctions. Recently, countertheory has refined a fourth critique—that tort law in many instances discourages innovation—which asserts that tort law's deterrent effects often have a negative impact on safety and social utility.

Weak sanctions. The principal reason why potential injurers don't perceive tort law's sanctions as severe, according to countertheory, is that most of them have liability insurance. From automobile and homeowner's insurance to malpractice and product insurance, liability insurance is commonplace for the activities that take place in late-twentieth-century America. P. J. Cowcroft's cop on the safety beat seems unlikely to make people behave more safely if the negligent actor knows that it is someone else—his insurer—who will be "arrested" for his wrongs. Likewise, tort law as market regulator seems unlikely to have much deterrent force if the accident costs of an actor's choices are borne by an insurance company, not by the actor himself.

A similar challenge to tort's deterrent power is illustrated by the Youngs' lawsuit. Several people share principal responsibility for the Youngs' injuries: Howard himself, the train driver, the City Transit Authority, and, at least arguably, the people on the platform who refused to help Howard up from the tracks. For tort law to deter appropriately, each of these persons should perceive it as a significant threat. Yet realistically, if the Youngs receive any monetary payments, almost all the money will come from the Transit Authority. The platform bystanders and the subway driver are unlikely to be wealthy enough to pay significant amounts of money to the Youngs. They are equally unlikely to have liability insurance that would pay for their negligence in this situation. The Transit Authority is the deep pocket. Therefore, tort law will probably have no effect on people intimately involved in Howard Young's accident. To them, therefore, it is not a deterrent.

Moreover, countertheory points out, even in those situations in which tort verdicts are most likely to deter actors from behaving unsafely, sanctions will not be perceived as particularly strong. Outside of automobile accidents, the overwhelming majority of persons who are injured by the negligence of another never bring a claim.

Even those who do bring a claim rarely are paid fully for their injuries. Most claims settle, with some compromise payment that is usually substantially discounted from what the plaintiff would receive from a favorable jury verdict. Even with respect to claims that are tried to a verdict, tort law may simply refuse to recognize many serious injuries—such as the emotional losses suffered by Elissa and Laura—as worthy of compensation. Other losses are seriously undervalued, either because artificial caps have been placed on the amounts plaintiffs can recover for their injuries or because the law artificially limits the injury factors for which money can be awarded, as is the case in many states with respect to the negligently caused death of a child. This combination of systematic underclaiming and undercompensating means that the financial threat that tort law poses even to large, uninsured entities is much smaller than the accident costs that its behavior can be expected to cause.

Finally, there are several areas in which tort law has been particularly active in which claims are not made and damages are not assessed against negligent actors until long after the actor behaved unreasonably. This happens frequently in two of the principal areas of modern tort litigation, medical malpractice and products liability. It happens most often in the growing number of toxic tort lawsuits, in which people seek damages for injuries they allege were caused by exposure to toxic substances in the environment. Machinery may break or otherwise injure users years after it is manufactured or designed in a flawed manner. Patients die years after doctors mistakenly diagnose or treat them. Asbestos workers develop asbestosis or cancer ten to twenty-five years after being wrongfully exposed to asbestos. Even in the run-of-the-mill tort case like Howard Young's, where injuries occur right away, the defendants probably will not be forced to pay damages for several years—remember, the average tort suit takes six years to reach trial. Accordingly, when actors look at the potential tort sanction for an unsafe behavior choice, they often see it as far off, even if it does occur. We are all familiar with the perceptual phenomenon that big things far away look small. Even a large tort sanction, far enough away, will look small to today's decision maker. ("I probably won't still be president of the company years from now when and if the company is sued.")

There are some responses to this countertheory view that tort sanctions will not deter because they are perceived as being small. First, many entities do not have liability insurance. Before the insurance "crisis" of the mid-1980s, some estimates were that a third or more of the commercial market for liability insurance was self-insured.[6] That crisis led to a further surge in self-insurance.[7] If 40 percent or more of the commercial activities in the country are self-insured, liability insurance is not blunting tort's deterrent effect for a substantial portion of the nation's potentially injurious activity.

A second response is that tort law can retain substantial deterrent power even for those activities that are insured. Insurance charges can go up as insurers' predictions about the expected liabilities of their customers go up. The individual or organization that behaves more safely should pay less for liability insurance than the less careful individual or organization. Over time, the difference in insurance payments should approximate the difference between the insureds in the amount of tort damages resulting from their behavior. Unfortunately, such a logical result depends on the insurance companies to make use of liability information in setting the rates of its individual insureds. That does happen to some extent: insurance companies have a very strong market incentive to identify and offer lower rates to safer actors because they can make substantial profit from insuring them even at those lower rates and because those safer actors will either switch insurance companies or self-insure if their greater care is not recognized. However, to a substantial extent, liability insurers do not charge rates based on the liability potential—including the liability experience—of individuals or companies. Just as automobile liability insurance lumps together all young unmarried males in setting their rates, regardless of their propensity to "party," their academic standing, or other indicators of social responsibility, so most liability insurance rates its insureds in groups, not individually. To some extent that occurs because insurers believe that it would cost them more to develop more individualized predictions of liability costs than they would be able to recoup in profits from those identifications. That assumption may be inaccurate. One study in Florida showed, for example, that the 4 percent of the doctors with two or more malpractice claims accounted for half the total payouts in malpractice cases during a twelve-year period. Nevertheless, even with this indicator of doctors' propensity to be judged liable, medical malpractice insurers in Florida did not base premiums on a doctor's past liability experience.[8] Of course, such insurers may have reasons to doubt past experience as necessarily closely correlated with future risks. After all, when insurers don't bet their money the way outsiders say they should, maybe they know something the outsiders don't. In any case, a substantial portion of the people and institutions buying liability insurance do not find the price of that insurance linked to a specific prediction of their liability costs. Nevertheless, their insurance premiums most likely will differ depending on the industry or other large group to which they belong.

Although this limited experience rating—setting insurance rates based on the safety experience of the insured group—may help reduce the total amount of certain dangerous activities by, for example, deterring entrants into the most dangerous industries, neither it nor more individualized experience rating promises that tort law will be a substantial deterrent force where liability insurance prevails. Changes in premiums based on a person or company's liability experiences usually take place gradually, on the basis of some averaging of payouts over several years, perhaps five or more. The tort sanction may operate through experience rating, but it will be perceived as even further away—and thus as even smaller—than the already long-delayed final liability judgment in the average tort case.

There is a third response to countertheory's portrayal of tort sanctions as weak. This response contrasts the admittedly serious underdeterrence caused by low claiming rates and undercompensation on the one hand with the firestorm of antitort activity generated in recent years by manufacturers, doctors, municipalities, and insurance companies on the other hand. As groups, these potential injurers may not be facing anywhere near the number of claims and amounts of damages they should be facing in order to match the market regulator theory of deterrence that is "just right." Nevertheless, these groups now act and sound more aware of, more frightened by, and more punished by tort sanctions than at any previous time. Such groups now emphasize (1) the extra deterrent effects that tort law creates unintentionally by the existence of large legal defense costs, (2) the uncertainty—in a world that may exaggerate uncertain risks—regarding what choices by sellers of goods and services create liability, (3) alleged overpayment of smaller claims and payment of false claims. But even granting all that, there seems little doubt that many risk-creating actors pay substantially less than the real costs of the accidents they cause. So even if tort law's sanctions should be even stronger than they are, the reactions of those groups most touched by tort sanctions indicate that these sanctions remain significant among those imposed by law to enhance safety in the United States.

Unclear communication. Countertheory's second category of reasons why tort law fails to work well as a deterrent has the central theme that tort law does not communicate clearly what behavior will be sanctioned. Because businesses and individuals cannot understand very well which behavior will subject them to tort liability and which will not, that sanction will at best only haphazardly lead them to choose safer behavior.

This unclear communication has several aspects. First, many individuals and some businesses simply do not know much, if anything, about tort rules. Bartenders, construction supervisors, airplane mechanics, and doctors have enough problems keeping up with their basic job requirements. They have little time or expertise to enable them to keep up with continually shifting legal rules. Car and truck drivers might have more time but are as ignorant of tort law as most people. Even if they do understand enough about the basic rules—for example, the principle that "if you act unreasonably and thereby hurt someone, you will have to pay for her injury," not to speak of the arena of strict product liability—the actors may not understand that their specific behavior is dangerous, and thus subject to sanction. Tort law has little power over the motorist who believes that 30 MPH is a safe speed for a particular snow-covered street or over the bar owner who either doesn't believe there will be fights in his bar or doesn't know that there are safer bar glasses on the market.

Second, even when individuals and businesses are aware of tort rules and reasonably savvy about the dangers of their own particular behavior, tort law may not provide enough detailed guidance about what behaviors will be sanctioned. Tort law essentially tells actors to behave reasonably. It also tells them that the reasonableness of their behavior will be determined by a jury of nonexperts some time after an accident has occurred. Doctors are among the most vociferous group of common tort defendants who claim that such vague tort rules leave them facing what feels more like a liability lottery than a rational determination about proper medical behavior. Product manufacturers, told by tort law that they will be liable if the expected accident costs associated with a particular product makeup or design are greater than its social benefits, often feel they are simply guessing about how a jury—by definition made up of nonexperts—will react to cost-benefit calculations.

Third, tort law may communicate unclearly because it leaves to guesswork what liability costs will be. Tort law tells individuals and businesses that they will be held liable for medical costs, earnings losses, and pain and suffering incurred by victims they injure through unreasonable behavior. If a potential defendant is to be able to factor in these expected liability costs in making decisions about appropriate levels of safety behavior, he needs some clarity about these costs. If he cannot know ahead of time the physical or financial characteristics of the persons likely to be injured, the actor will find it very hard to assess liability costs. Even if the actor knew something about the characteristics of the persons to whom he was risking injury, he would recognize that noneconomic awards—for the Youngs' suffering, for example—could vary tremendously depending very much on the character of the jurors selected in a trial and on their emotional reactions to the plaintiff. These factors make it hard for actors to predict the size of the tort sanction they face. Uncertain about the size of the sanction, they are likely to err in deciding how much to expend on safety. Indeed, paradoxically enough, even if a defendant could show that, based on a cut-and-dried cost-benefit ratio, it had decided that it was cheaper to pay for its victims injuries than to avoid them, a jury might well be so outraged at what it perceived as callous indifference to human suffering that, far from exonerating the defendant, it would pile on punitive damages in addition to a normal award.

Here, too, there are responses offered to countertheory. First, while ignorance of tort law remains a problem for some potential injurers, particularly individuals, the increases in tort-imposed costs and public attention to tort issues of the last decade have reduced and are continuing to reduce that ignorance. Educational programs about what steps to take to avoid tort liability are increasingly available to medical and business groups.

Second, the prevalence of liability insurance among the sorts of entities likely to have the hardest time deciphering tort law's commands can actually enhance deterrence where it is hindered by ignorance and uncertainty. Insurers are like a central clearinghouse for information about liability-causing accidents that are linked to particular industries or kinds of behavior. They are in the business of predicting accidents and the costs thereof. This combination of information and expertise can assist less sophisticated individuals and businesses to understand better what behaviors tort law sanctions, at what average costs. Although there are indications that insurers do not provide enough of this sort of advice, perhaps such information transfers will gradually increase, particularly as rising liability costs make it more worthwhile for insurers to help their customers make better safety choices.

Those entities large enough to self-insure may suffer less relatively in their ability to understand tort sanctions. Most of them have the incentive and the means to hire legal specialists to advise them about tort law's rules in their particular specialty. Moreover, even where that advice is not available, the prescription of reasonable behavior may itself provide at least general guidance to these larger entities. If they act with reasonable care to the best of their ability and judgment—which often will require consultation with the experts in their area of activity—they have a very good chance of avoiding liability. To win a tort suit, a relatively inexpert plaintiff and his lawyer will have to obtain evidence sufficient to convince a jury and appellate courts that the defendant's expert judgment was more likely than not erroneous. The plaintiff will have to do this in a setting in which the defendant will be represented by well-paid lawyers, who often have considerable expertise themselves with the particular behavioral choices alleged to have been unreasonable.

Finally, with respect to the liability costs of injuries that might be expected to result from actors' decisions, uncertainty is modified by the substantial experience with tort liability that is available for most activities. The Transit Authority surely has access to its own records, and probably those of other major transit authorities, for indications of the liability costs associated with train-passenger collisions and other accidents which result from speeding. If they do not, they have access to compilations of jury verdicts put together by various verdict reporting services for the types of injuries that can result from such accidents. Those individuals and businesses with liability insurance have access to similar information developed by insurance companies that handle so many liability claims. While no entity can confidently predict the actual costs associated with any one accident that might result from a decision about how to behave, the expected total costs of accidents may not be so difficult to ascertain.

Behavior not changeable. The third category of countertheory reasons why tort law deters poorly, if at all, focuses on the way unsafe behavior is likely to react to clear, strong threats of sanction from the tort system. There is something about much of the behavior being sanctioned, says countertheory, that makes it largely unresponsive to the threat of liability.

A principal reason for this unresponsiveness is that much unsafe behavior is nonconscious. Most of us have had the experience of being distracted while driving and know how easily our unreasonable driving behavior could have injured someone. Doctors report that such similar cases of distraction, of inadvertent misreading of labels and the like, are normal occurrences. Many accidents happen because people, even careful people, just can't be careful all the time. The threat of punishment will not change behavior when people are not consciously choosing their behavior.

Another human shortcoming that poses an obstacle to tort deterrence is the inability of people to process as real the small chance that an accident will occur from their unreasonable behavior. The driver of the train that crushed Howard Young had probably driven too fast into many stations during his career. Each time that he did so and no accident resulted, it reinforced his sense that his speeding did not lead to accidents. By the time he drove into Howard, he probably hadn't an inkling that he was risking injury by his behavior. So, too, the homeowner with a dead tree limb may simply not consider the small chance that it will fall on someone. It is not that either the driver or the homeowner would respond, if asked, that there is no chance the speeding or the failure to remove the dead limb would injure someone. In the everyday world in which no one is asking those questions, the very rare often becomes the nonexistent in normal human thought patterns. Tort liability for accidental injuries can optimally change the behavior only of those who recognize the chance that their behavior will injure others.

Organizational behavior also often influences individual behavior, resulting in similar barriers to effective tort deterrence. A manufacturing company's policy may honestly try to encourage careful attention to product safety in labeling, design, and manufacture. But such policies may be frustrated by middle managers with competing concerns for meeting quotas, short-term profits, and personal aggrandizement, and correspondingly little concern for hazardous decisions affecting the company's expenses only in the long run, when the managers may be elsewhere.

Related to the self-interest of organizational employees is another set of reasons for unresponsive behavior. One is that some people simply have too much at stake in their unsafe behavior to change it. The alcoholic doctor, the barely solvent bar owner and the late-for-the-game Dallas Cowboys fan all have in common a near-obsessive attachment to their unsafe behavior. They do not see as viable alternatives giving up medical practice, turning away some business and possibly alienating bar customers, or driving more carefully so as to arrive in the second quarter. The obverse of this high-stakes-in-unsafe-behavior applies when one has very low stakes in switching to safer behavior. Included among such persons and institutions are most individuals of modest means and most institutions in financial hot water. Tort law cannot effectively encourage them to make the possibly costly shift to safer behavior because they have virtually nothing to lose from the assessment of tort liability against them. They couldn't pay tort claims even if courts ordered them to.

Although there are responses to this category of countertheory as well, it must be acknowledged that tort sanctions will rarely have much direct deterrent effect on nonrational behavior and on relatively poor persons. Nonetheless, the *indirect* effect that the law may have should not be ignored, for it could amount to substantial deterrence of unsafe behavior. One of the more controversial common steps tort law takes in this regard is to hold persons or institutions liable in tort *in addition* to the person whose negligence most immediately and obviously caused the injuries complained of. The Transit Authority will be held vicariously liable for its driver's speeding, for example. A bar may be held liable for the driving or fighting of one of its patrons. In this way, tort law can reduce the amount of unsafe behavior that occurs even from nonrational behavior. Tort law gives employers strong incentives to screen out drivers and other workers whose nonrational behavior is often dangerous. Tort law may not be able to get through to someone once he has had a few drinks, but it can get through to the bar and its employees who are serving the drinks to discourage them from increasing a situation's dangers.

Moreover, tort law encourages entities to make changes in the safety environment to take into account human failings in the processing of information and the carrying out of safety commands. Aware that its employees will not succeed completely in stopping patron drunkenness, bars can take steps to monitor driving by patrons leaving the bar—for example, by requiring drivers to check their keys with an employee when they arrive. Similarly, as also suggested earlier, the Transit Authority can turn to the installation of speed reducers on the approaches to subway stations if it judges that its driver training and screening programs will not sufficiently deter speeding.

Finally, even if an individual or entity's behavioral resistance to tort sanctions cannot be circumvented, tort law can help reduce the amount of unsafe behavior. Take, for example, dangerous driving—the tortious behavior most often mentioned to illustrate nonrational, can't-process-dangers, high-stakes behavior. Tort law keeps insurance rates for the drivers most likely to exhibit that kind of behavior—teenage males—quite high. Fewer such drivers are on the road because of tort law. Disproportionally represented in that group kept off the road by costly insurance can be persons of modest means, those identified above as otherwise least susceptible to direct tort sanctions. (Although admittedly many may simply drive while illegally uninsured.) In like manner, if tort law makes trucking companies pay for the negligent driving of its truckers, those companies will end up with higher costs than competitors. If the competitors are safer trucking companies, customers will increasingly turn there, because they can charge lower prices. If the competitors are railroads, airplanes, or boats, customers will increasingly turn there. Because of the competitive disadvantage imposed by tort law misbehavior on dangerous activity, there will be less danger created.

Thus human and organizational difficulties in responding to the threat of tort sanctions must not always be seen as frustrating tort law's direct deterrent effect. Insurance companies recognize that nonrational driving behavior can be made more safe. That's one of the reasons they often reduce premiums for people who have taken a driver's training course, where instructors teach about how to avoid dangerous situations and how to reduce the chances of one's own nonrational dangerous behavior ("take frequent breaks on long trips," "pull over and sleep if you feel drowsy," and so on). Many manufacturers have responded to the increasing menace of tort judgments by reorganizing their product safety efforts. Hospitals have increasingly pursued systems that will reduce the chance of error: for example, many require at least two people to check that medication being administered is in fact that which was prescribed. In short, tort-prone behavior patterns *can* be modified. Tort law can provide an incentive for those modification efforts.

Discouraging innovation. The final thrust of countertheory portrays tort law more negatively. Instead of tort law as a tired old relic, ineffectually trying to flag down dangerous behavior from its front-porch rocker, this wing of countertheory presents an image of tort law as a somewhat out-of-control watchdog whose vicious barking keeps at bay many of the innovators whose fuller participation in society would improve everyone's life and, at the same time, reduce the dangers that the watchdog was supposed to be protecting against in the first place.

Tort law, in this picture, has its own unintended safety-reducing effects. Best known, perhaps, are the claims that doctors engage in "defensive medicine"—practices that they consider medically unnecessary but legally prudent. All in all, they result in the socially useless expenditure of money. By definition such costly practices don't reduce the chance of injury. Moreover, these defensive practices increase the cost of health care for everyone. Many people will thus be able to afford less health care with further ill effects.

But tort law not only encourages wasteful expenditures, according to countertheory, it affirmatively hampers by suppressing innovation. The theory is that companies begin to develop useful new products, many of which would be much less dangerous than those they would replace, but then are discouraged from marketing these products by the fear that they will be held liable should unforeseen injuries result from the product's use. The companies fear unknown effects of their own products, and they fear irrational second-guessing of their decisions by jurors whose anticompany and antinovelty passions are inflamed by the sight of a horribly injured individual. Thus, countertheorists claim, safer substitutes for asbestos were developed but never marketed. Thus intrauterine devices, which are the safest form of birth control for some women, have been largely driven from the market. Thus work in America on other new methods of contraception has virtually stopped.

Thus makers of "head-up" display panels, which allow airplane pilots to see vital information without looking down from the windshield, have refused to install them on small planes. This last example illustrates the theorists' belief that tort law favors old dangers that people are used to (the need for the pilot to look away from where the plane is going in order to see vital instruments) over new dangers (possible vision obstruction by the head-up display). Because jurors are unfamiliar with the danger, they are more likely to determine that creation of the new dangers was faulty, even if that action led to greater overall safety than familiar but even more dangerous methods. That same concern has led to criticism of tort law's assault against manufacturers of disposable cigarette lighters on the grounds that successful litigation will force people back to the use of even more dangerous matches.[9]

Another way that tort law can overdeter stems from expanded rights of discovery, whereby one side in litigation can force the other to disgorge pertinent evidence before trial, including, say, a defendant's documents related to the development of an allegedly offending product. Fearful that any possibly negative comment in a written memo can be inflated all out of proportion or otherwise taken out of context before an impressionable lay jury, a company's engineers, scientists, and other technical personnel may well refrain from committing problems to writing while designing a product. They will choose instead to rely on more ephemeral but less helpful oral communication—subject as the latter are to being misunderstood, misinterpreted, just plain forgotten, or otherwise overlooked or disregarded. Hardly helpful in trying to get the bugs out of a new product.

A final way in which tort law can perversely encourage unsafe behavior pertains to products or conditions that cause accidents and that could, if unchanged, cause more accidents. Even with the means to make the product or condition safer, a potential tort defendant may not make the change because he fears that an injured person will use the change as evidence in a tort suit that the defendant was at fault in not changing the product or condition earlier.

Judges and legislators who make tort law must be sensitive, then, to the unintended effects of their decisions. That sensitivity must include awareness that forcing a safety measure on a particular activity may reduce one kind of accidental injury yet increase another kind. For example, one of the major arguments put forth by social workers and psychotherapists who want to avoid liability for the injurious actions of their clients is that the threat of this sort of liability would cause them to reduce significantly their willingness to counsel dangerous patients. They believe that the resulting reduction in therapeutic counseling available to people who are dangerously mentally ill would lead to significantly more injuries than would be avoided by imposing liability on therapists who allegedly failed to report patients' confidential disclosures and thus to prevent those patients from injuring others.

Moreover, tort law decision makers need to be sensitive to what legal rules mean in practice. A shortcoming of personal injury litigation's incentive to safer practices is the inevitable focus on the plight of the (often tragically) injured individual before the court. For example, a defendant obstetrician may claim that his actions in supplying limited amounts of oxygen to a baby were not negligent—even though more oxygen might have prevented the baby's blindness—because supplying more oxygen would have increased the risks of brain damage. But it is *this* blind baby who is in front of the jury, not some hypothetical brain-damaged baby in another case. In the emotional context of the particular case, sensible but hypothetical arguments on behalf of the defendant obstetrician may well fall on deaf ears.

Nevertheless, although the countertheorists provide valuable insights into possible undesired effects of tort law on safety, their estimates of the law's dire effects may be exaggerated. There are, for example, no reliable measures of the amount of defensive medicine that takes place in the United States. Clearly, medical personnel and hospitals take some steps, some of which they do not think medically necessary, in order to prevent tort lawsuits. What has not been well studied is whether these steps as a whole do in fact make medical practice safer.[10] Some—perhaps much—of what countertheorists refer to as defensive medicine provides excellent evidence that tort law can at least force changes in behavior, even granting that some defensive medicine may indeed be wasteful.

Even where there is "wasteful" defensive medicine, tort law may be less the culprit than countertheorists believe. Medical professionals may misperceive what safety measures tort law demands. In other words, just as poor television reception may result more because of problems with the receiver or intermediate transmitters, "poor" tort law signals may be the result of inadequacies in the transmission or manner of receiving tort law's messages. The basic tort standards for medicine are said to be fairly clear: doctors have only to practice medicine the way a respectable group of their colleagues would practice. In situations where it is clear to *either* a judge or a jury that some respectable segment of the medical profession believes a procedure to be unnecessary, a doctor sued for not performing that procedure will likely get a verdict in his favor. If doctors are receiving just the opposite message—that in order to win a tort lawsuit they need to perform defensive measures that the medical community clearly understands to be unnecessary—then theorists presumably need to pay as much attention to the people and institutions that translate the law for medical professionals as to the law itself.

Countertheory's related concern that tort-imposed costs will limit poorer people's access to health care likewise can be seen as exaggerated. Malpractice costs, tort proponents argue, amount to a small fraction of the health care provider's average expenses (about 1 percent of total health care costs). It hardly adds enough to medical charges, for example, to make a typical patient who otherwise would get medical help in a serious situation forgo it (though access, in some situations—for example, to obstetrical care for poor rural and inner-city mothers—may well be affected). For the citizen of modest means, it is the astronomical cost of health care itself that blocks access, not the additional (comparatively small) tort costs.

As with defensive medicine, no one has succeeded in evaluating tort law's threat to technological advances that would improve quality of life and safety. On their face, tort rules should not pose a threat to valuable innovation. A new product that would replace a more dangerous one, such as asbestos, would not subject its manufacturer to tort liability unless the product was ruled to be unreasonably dangerous—unless, that is, the new product's expected social costs were found to have outweighed its expected social benefits. Most countertheorists who have focused on tort's detrimental effect on innovation have produced primarily anecdotal evidence to support their claims. Careful researchers have found many of these anecdotes to be of doubtful value. For example, when U.S. Senate staff investigated the claim that Monsanto had given up on a promising substitute for asbestos because of fears of the irrational tort system, they found that the Environmental Protection Agency had looked at the company's own studies of the product and had concluded that those studies offered "reasonable support" for a conclusion that the substitute caused cancer. According to work done recently under the auspices of the Brookings Institution, researchers have reached mixed conclusions about whether tort law negatively impacted on useful innovation, depending, apparently, on the nature of the industry investigated.[11] (It might be noted that the codirector of that study—Peter Huber—was the leading countertheorist espousing the view that tort law seriously interferes with innovation. His own evidence in that respect has been disputed as excessively anecdotal.[12])

The final response—to the oft-expressed concern that tort law deters potential defendants from fixing dangerous conditions for fear that their changes will be used against them as evidence that they had previously been negligent—likewise acknowledges the reality of the concern but questions its magnitude. Most states do not allow a plaintiff to introduce evidence of subsequent repairs or changes in a product or condition in her tort suit. In those states that do allow such evidence, any risk of liability for the accident that happened can be outweighed by the risk of additional accidents and even more certain liability if the dangerous aspect is not changed (granted that those avoided injuries are hypothetical, unlike the reality of the injury of the claimant in front of the jury). Moreover, if a particular defendant knows how to change his product for the safer, it seems likely that others in the industry will, too. Not only will they gain a competitive advantage by making the change, but their efforts also seem likely to come to the attention of a plaintiff with a competent lawyer. In short, the legal protection extended to such changes and the myriad forces operating in favor of the change in states without such legal protections cast doubt for some that producers often maintain dangerous products in order to avoid tort liability.

All this theory should make Judge Small's head hurt. She knows that the debate about the validity of the deterrent theories of tort law is no trifling matter, particularly with regard to the law that would apply to the Youngs' case.

Everyone agrees that the tort system is expensive to operate. Almost everyone agrees that the law's compensation function could be performed more quickly and cheaply through some sort of loss insurance (like health coverage) or administrative compensation system (like workers' compensation). Moreover, there is a major category of injuries—pain and suffering, for example—for which money damages may provide little real compensation. Full-scale assaults on tort law in general and on its compensation for pain and suffering injuries in particular have been launched in legislatures and courts recently. Those assaults are much more likely to succeed if decision makers believe tort damages have little or no deterrent impact on the amount of accidental injury in our society.

Certainly Judge Small and appellate judges will be much less likely to interpret the law to allow Nicole and her children to sue for their emotional devastation if they don't think those payments will make for a safer transit system. Judge Small, who actually has to make legal decisions in the face of the competing theories about deterrence, might well react: "That's nice, but where are the data? Where's the evidence about whether tort law deters or not?"

Although the validity of deterrent theory is clearly pertinent to the direction of tort law, and though countertheory has made many converts, there still are no definitive answers. The evidence is equivocal. Fair-minded interpreters, looking at the same phenomena, reach different conclusions.[13] The most concentrated effort to examine deterrence effects across the major areas of tort litigation, originally sponsored by the prestigious American Law Institute (made up of eminent judges, lawyers, and law professors), concluded that the overall evidence was "mixed," both with respect to the behavior-changing effects of tort liability and with respect to whether those changes enhanced safety.[14] That review found the evidence strongest in favor of deterrence with regard to automobile accidents. A concurrent comprehensive study of medical malpractice in New York State led its Harvard director to conclude that tort law had been a valuable stimulant to "broad-based improvements in the institutional environment and procedures through which medical care is provided."[15] Evidence for deterrence seems weakest in the area of environmentally induced harms.

Leaving Judge Small to deal with the daunting uncertainty that exists about tort law's safety-enhancing effects, many of today's tort reformers press a different, yet related, challenge to tort law. Just as they can point to other devices—for example, no-fault systems, such as workers' compensation—that could compensate injured persons better than tort law, such reformers point to a host of other actors and factors that they consider much likelier than tort law to have significant safety-enhancing effects. Thus, they say, even if tort law does deter, its deterrent force is relatively unnecessary and not worth its high cost.

Again, the simplest example involves unsafe driving. Among the conscious—and thus more deterrable—dangerous driving behaviors, speeding, drunk driving, and failure to obey traffic signals stand out as the most dangerous. If a driver on the verge of engaging in one of those behaviors were asked, "Is there anything bad that might happen to you if you do that?" he most likely would reply, "I might get hurt" or "The police might pull me over." The driver, like most people, would identify the police—the criminal law—or fear of injury to himself—self-preservation—as the major actor and major factor that would deter him from his proposed dangerous behavior. People drive safely first because they are worried about their own well-being and second because they are worried that the criminal law will punish them, via tickets, fines, or, in the case of drunk driving, imprisonment.

(But if the real cop on the beat might appear a much more effective deterrent against unsafe behavior in this illustration than does the figurative cop, tort law, the criminal law plays almost no deterrent role in other classes of accident—medical malpractice, defective products, workplace hazards, and environmental toxins.)

Given the good chance of eluding apprehension in the course of risky driving, self-preservation is probably the more significant factor in encouraging safe driving. It applies to almost all aspects of motor vehicle operation that also create injury risks to others, except perhaps for car-pedestrian accident risks. And self-preservation instincts probably explain, much more powerfully than potential tort sanctions or any other factor, safe behavior in several areas other than driving, such as flying airplanes and maintenance of home or work premises. Nevertheless, self-preservation fails as an incentive to safety in most risky behavior situations in medical care, product manufacture, environmental discharge, and workplace production, where the wrongful actor is not normally at risk of injury. In those areas, however, another actor and another factor are often seen as diluting the need for tort sanctions. Government regulatory agencies, it is said, present detailed behavioral guides for many product manufacturers and workplace operators, for most environmental dischargers, and increasingly for health care providers. Thus, it is argued, by providing clear behavior guides forged by experts, threatening prompt and varied sanctions—some uninsurable—and empowered with the ability to intervene *before* an accident happens, government regulation promises much in the way of safety enhancement that tort law has been unable to deliver.

Unfortunately, regulation itself often fails to deliver in practice the deterrent to unsafe behavior that it promises in theory. Unlike tort law, regulation cannot cover as many of the hazards to which people are exposed. Unlike tort, with its army of potential enforcers— all potential accident victims, coupled with their lawyers—regulatory agencies often lack sufficient personnel to determine rules, detect violations, and enforce sanctions. The staid American Law Institute pointed out, with respect to the Occupational Safety and Health Administration (OSHA)—the government's main regulator of workplace safety—that "the average-sized firm or job site is less likely to see an OSHA inspector than to witness the passage of Halley's comet."[16] Furthermore, unlike tort law, with its substantial damage awards to seriously injured plaintiffs, regulatory fines are often inadequate to encourage correction of safety violations. And unlike tort law, with its private prosecution of cases and decision making by jurors chosen randomly from communities throughout the United States, agencies have been notoriously subject to "capture" by the industries they are supposed to regulate. Thus when the American Law Institute compiled all the empirical studies it could find of agency regulatory performance in the health and safety area, it concluded that the potential for constructive administrative agency action had "rarely been realized."[17]

Even when a regulatory body has the resources and the will to deter unsafe behavior, tort law may still have a role, as a complement to agency action. Tort lawsuits can alert regulators to possible safety problems. The extensive investigation of injurious products and actions that goes on in tort discovery can produce information for the regulatory process. For example, the Environmental Protection Agency was also led to its decision to ban asbestos use by the information developed in the wave of asbestos products liability lawsuits of the 1980s.[18]

Considerable skepticism has also greeted any claim that individual and organizational morality obviates much of the need for tort liability. This impetus ostensibly provided by morality to avoid dangerous behavior has perhaps its most obvious application to injuries caused in the course of health care, particularly by doctors. These individual actors' work objective is to help and protect their patients/clients. Surely, it is argued, that will drive them to behave safely more than the threat that they will be sued. Similar moral concerns may operate for drivers in school zones and for people who work for governmental or private institutions, including the officials of the Transit Authority.

As with regulation, however, tort law may act as an important complement to morality as an inducement to safe behavior. With respect to the accident that crushed Howard Young, for example, tort law may be an important vehicle for invoking moral judgments about safety. The Transit Authority officials who make judgments about safety expenditures will learn about Howard's injury through an accident report. As is the case with many different kinds of accidents, careful reports of subway accidents are probably in part at least inspired by the organization's awareness of the possibility that accident victims will file claims for compensation. In the subway, in the hospital, at the country club swimming pool, and in most other areas, the threat of compensation claims can cause organizations to make and keep detailed records of the accidents that occur. It is the making and processing of those records that often gives organizations enough understanding of the dangers associated with their patterns of behavior to make a moral judgment in favor of greater safety. (On the other hand, fear of litigation may also cause records to be altered or even destroyed.)

A final actor often mentioned as more of an incentive to safety than tort liability is the market. People prefer goods and services that are safe to those that are less safe. Often they are willing to pay more for goods or services that promise to expose them to less injury. Moreover, providers of goods and services recognize the importance of preserving a reputation for safety if they are to compete generally for buyers.

Although it might make tort deterrence almost irrelevant in a world of perfect information, the market has an incomplete role in the safety world, where people may often have little reliable information about the safety of the goods and services they consume. Few educated people are aware even of how their car—a big-ticket purchase sure to attract a large measure of their attention—fared on the National Highway and Traffic Safety Administration crash tests, or how it rates in accident data compiled from a central repository of insurance company reports about accidents. Fewer still have any idea of the number of malpractice claims filed against their physician or hospital. If people do not know basic information about the safety of the products or services that are more clearly related to safety and health than any other goods or services they make use of, then there seems less reason to believe they can make effective judgments about the safety of other goods and services. In such settings, the market seems unlikely to play an optimal role in encouraging providers to behave more safely.

At the end, Judge Small must be left with her headache. The theory about how tort law encourages just the right level of safe behavior in the society sounds fine, but it doesn't look quite so imposing once riddled with the potshots from countertheory and once its foundations are shown to have, at best, only modest empirical support.

Giving up on the deterrent potential of tort law—acknowledging it doesn't do much to discourage unreasonably dangerous behavior—

would have profound implications for the shape and future of tort law. Scholars and judges have not reached that point of surrender. Given the confused state of deterrence theory and the paucity of good empirical evidence, that restraint is probably inevitable. In fact, recent examinations of the question, and much of the theory and evidence discussed in this chapter, suggest that the more accurate and perhaps profitable inquiries to make about deterrence are those that focus on particular areas of induced injury. One might hypothesize, for example, that tort law does not deter negligent automobile driving very well or very importantly, because of the dominance of nonrational behavior in causing accidents, because of the prevalence of liability insurance, and because of the already-strong deterrence of criminal law and self-preservation. (That logic might help explain the public's relative receptivity to no-fault auto laws.) On the other hand, tort law—or at least some variant—might operate much more effectively as a deterrent in products-related injuries, where there is more rational choice for and against safety, in an environment in which the producers frequently self-insure and in which they may have relatively good information about expected liability costs and about the dangers associated with the choices before them. Health care–related injuries may entail many of the same considerations. (And yet, to indicate the complexity of tort law and insurance, a recent study suggests that deterrence is *best* achieved by tort law in the area of auto accidents.[19])

Countertheorists have raised serious questions about the deterrent value of tort that were not being articulated so clearly a decade ago. At the same time, empirical research on these questions is more prevalent, and there are several studies that purport to provide researchers models of how and how not to proceed. Even so, one wonders whether these studies will really answer the riddles posed in this chapter. For now, Judge Small and her judicial colleagues, as well as legislators, must wade through a bog of uncertainty.

CHAPTER FIVE

Flawed Transactions

Howard and Nicole Young can be excused for having little sympathy for Judge Constance Small's painful confusion about whether tort law makes their world safer. "These payments are going to help us out at a time when we need a lot of help," they would assert. Besides, even if there are many confusing factors getting in the way of the pure deterrence that tort theory promises, simple logic tells us that the Transit Authority is going to do whatever works financially to make their trains run more carefully if it gets socked for a few big tort judgments. "Who cares," the Youngs would say, "if the compensation and deterrence accomplishments of tort law aren't as clear or strong as legal theorists thought?"

The resounding answer that echoes through courtrooms, legislative chambers, classrooms, and the letters-to-the-editor sections of newspapers is that we all should care. We should care because we are all forced to buy some of whatever good the tort system is doing. Our groceries cost us more because their producers and distributors pay significant sums to insure against tort liability. A similar hidden tax attaches to visits to the doctor, public playgrounds, drinks at a local tavern, and virtually every other product and service we buy. Like any consumers, we don't want to pay very much for something unless it is very useful to us. We are particularly concerned that we get something very useful from the tort system, because that system can be very expensive to operate (despite its relatively small share of costs compared to, say, all health care).

In short, Howard and Nicole's lawyer friends would explain to them, the great cost of deciding tort claims is what makes us demand that tort law produce great benefits. In the face of uncertainty about the compensation and deterrence benefits tort law provides, observers understandably scrutinize the costs involved in using tort law to resolve disputes about accidents.

That the tort system is grossly expensive to operate becomes quickly apparent to even the casual observer. Considerably less apparent is what that high cost says about the role tort law should play in our society's response to accidents and some ailments.

How expensive is the tort system? Well, it may cost $300 billion a year. Or, maybe $152 billion or maybe much less.[1] Estimates of tort law's annual costs sometimes seem to vary inversely to the estimator's appraisal of the law's worth. Regardless, it is clear that a lot of money is being spent on the conduct of the tort system.

Even if analysts could be confident—which they cannot be—about how big the sum of expenditures is, these total cost figures provide little understanding of the cost problems of the tort system. It is a little like knowing that a city spent $730,000 on snow removal one winter. That seems like a lot, but to make useful judgments on the figure's appropriateness, an observer would want to know what city it was—one would react differently to that expense for Syracuse, New York, than for Charlottesville, Virginia—because one would instinctively recognize the need to know how much snow was being removed. Beyond that, the observer would want to know how often and how promptly snow was removed, what the cost was per snow removal truck, and the like. So, too, before informed judgments can be attempted about the costs of the tort system, one needs some idea of how many accidental injuries and negligently caused injuries occur annually in the United States, to say nothing of how many claims for compensation are made, how much time and money it takes to resolve those claims, what benefits come out of those claim resolutions, what is costly about the claims resolution process, and much more. Knowing that the tort system costs much makes us interested in finding out more about those costs, but surely does not tell us much about whether those costs are too high, reasonable, or bargain-basement.

Fortunately, recent research provides a useful sketch of the costs of typical tort lawsuits in various substantive areas relative to the compensation that those lawsuits provide people like the Youngs. The research confirms that those costs typically are extremely high. Usually referred to as transaction costs—because they are associated with the "transaction" of deciding what, if any, money should be transferred from alleged injurers to the injured—these operating expenses of the tort system typically are as great as or greater than the amount of compensation actually received by injured claimants.

Studies in the 1980s indicated that in automobile accident tort cases—which accounted for about half of all tort filings in 1985 and were decreasing relative to other kinds of tort cases—the average plaintiff received 52 cents out of every dollar spent on her case. The rest of the dollar went primarily to the plaintiff's legal fees and expenses (24 cents) and the defendant's legal fees and expenses (13 cents). Various other expenses—including the value of the time spent by plaintiffs and defendants and the value of the court's and insurance company's claims-processing efforts—ate up the rest of the dollar.[2]

Transaction costs consumed even more of the defense dollars in other more complicated kinds of accident cases. In accidents involving medical care or manufactured products, for example, the average plaintiff received only 43 cents out of every dollar spent on the case. With a smaller percentage going to the plaintiff, their contingent legal fees and expenses were smaller as a share of each dollar than in auto accident cases, equaling 20 cents. With these reductions in those portions of the pie, it follows that spending for defense legal fees and expenses in these generally more complicated cases was significantly larger, at 18 cents per dollar. So, too, the other expenses consumed much more in nonauto cases: 20 cents on the dollar. All by itself, the value of defendants' own time taken by the lawsuit accounted for 12 cents of each dollar spent.

Sketchier, but no more comforting, information exists about transaction costs in the even more complicated category of cases often known as toxic tort cases. Those cases—described by RAND researchers as potentially explosive in number—characteristically involve large numbers of persons exposed to allegedly toxic substances who manifest or expect to manifest illness long after that exposure. Information gathered from early waves of the asbestos cases showed that only 37 cents of each dollar spent on the typical case went to the plaintiff. In those most complicated high-stakes cases, a much higher share of each dollar, also 37 cents, was paid for defendants' legal fees and expenses, while plaintiffs' legal fees and expenses took 26 cents on average. The unique characteristics of asbestos litigation—along with the gathering of transaction cost data early in the life of its wave of lawsuits—make judgments uncertain about how typical these costs will be in other mass toxic tort cases.

High transaction costs—typical throughout tort litigation—will significantly reduce the Youngs' potential compensation. Suppose they are successful in their claims, at least those against the Transit Authority. That success may come in the form of settlement—the overwhelming majority of tort lawsuits are settled—or in the form of a verdict after trial. Suppose also that the Youngs, in total, obtain $1.5 million through their suits. That sum is not inconceivable, even though Howard was substantially responsible for his injuries, given the huge wage losses suffered by Howard and the severe emotional harms suffered by him and his family.

Before the Youngs spend any of even that sharply reduced estimate of their total injuries, about $500,000 will disappear. P. J. Cowcroft will take at least a third for her firm's contingency fee and the expenses involved in plaintiffs' side of the litigation. That would leave the Youngs with $1 million. Nor do those transaction costs take account of what the Transit Authority and the other defendants spent in fighting the claim.

Moreover, even these transaction costs don't reflect the social costs inherent in the long delay and uncertainty between injury and compensation that is characteristic of tort claims. One study estimated that 65 percent of claimants in even the simplest kind of tort lawsuits, involving automobile accidents, failed to collect compensation from liability insurance within six months of their accidents, not to speak of 45 percent of seriously injured traffic accident victims who never collect anything from such insurance.[3] In more complex cases, particularly those, like the Youngs', involving serious injuries, even fewer are paid and it takes an average of two years or more for financial help to arrive through the tort system. The fact that the most seriously injured tort claimants typically settle their claims for substantially less than even their economic loss provides telling evidence of the impact of delay and uncertainty for people whose hopes for holding onto a semblance of life as they knew it or for rehabilitating themselves may depend on prompt financial aid.[4]

The implications of this data seem staggering at first blush. If a charity with administrative costs as great as the tort system approached even the most generous Americans, those citizens would dismiss the organization derisively. A health or life insurance company that returned only half of its customers' payouts in benefits would be a target of investigation. If either the charity or the insurer took as long to pay out these relatively stingy benefits as does the tort system, its administrators would either be jailed or hit with punitive damages. The costs and delay that infect tort law seem to demand that it join the hypothetically atrocious charity and insurer in society's wastebasket. Any system for compensating accident victims would seem to be better than this one.

That conclusion seems even more compelling in light of the much lower transaction costs of other American systems for compensating the sick and injured. The workers' compensation systems present in every state to provide compensation for injuries that arise out of a worker's employment consume on average only 21 percent in legal and other transaction costs. Private health insurance typically spends about 10 cents of each premium dollar on such costs, while the Social Security disability program spends less, around 8 cents per dollar.[5] Such systems beg to be used in place of a tort system spending more than 50 cents of each dollar on transaction costs.

Nevertheless, it is not always wise to judge by first impressions. Deeper examination of the transaction costs of the tort system suggests that they may not be so inexcusably excessive as they may seem at first blush. This is not to minimize the problem: under any measure, it costs far too much to operate the tort system. One of this book's authors has long been motivated by tort law's fortuity, excessive costs, and unpardonable delay to champion no-fault, neo-no-fault, and other systems for dealing with the compensation needs of injured persons in a variety of accident settings.[6] Yet it is important to understand that society asks tort law to perform functions that other compensation systems do not. Those functions to a considerable extent demand the use of expensive procedures that run up tort law's operating bill. To some extent at least, those additional functions merit additional costs of the system. Before consigning the tort system to the waste bin, it would be prudent to examine further those relationships between tort law's functions and its costs.

That some of tort law's expenses make sense would be the reaction of Judge Small and lawyers familiar with tort cases in response to stinging attacks on the system's transaction costs. American society asks tort law to do hard work, they would point out. We are used to paying more for the performance of difficult tasks. Heads do not turn when those who collect, write, and edit the news cost us more than those who deliver the newspaper or when brain surgeons receive more than barbers for treating heads.

The tasks of the compensation systems identified above with low administrative costs are relatively easy. Before a life insurer pays benefits, it usually need only determine whether the policyholder is dead. The health insurer need only determine whether its policyholder actually was sick and received the treatment for which it is paying. The charity need only determine whether the recipient belongs to a clearly defined group that it has undertaken to help. Even the workers' compensation system initially need only decide whether the employee's injury is related to his employment.

By contrast, the tort system has to determine when it is appropriate to transfer considerable sums of money from one person or entity to another in situations where the proposed payor never made a promise to the injured claimant to help him out under any circumstances. For the most part, tort law has to decide whether a defendant (or its product) was at fault in a specific setting. It also has to decide whether defendant's faulty conduct or product caused the claimant's injuries. In addition, it has to take account of the claimant's own fault, if any, in causing the injury. The fault decisions that tort law must make are tough ones. Tort law must evaluate arguably wrongful behavior about which society has been so equivocal that it has not usually been barred by statute or regulation. In the kinds of tort cases with the highest transaction costs—medical malpractice, products liability, and toxic torts—lengthy investigation and technical expertise are almost always needed to uncover and evaluate the facts underlying both the fault and the causation decisions.

Moreover, tort law is asked to make its crucial determinations on a highly individualized basis. While other compensation systems focus solely on the claimant and the source of the injury (a claimant with whom the insurance company has and has had a continuing relationship), tort law must focus on the particular behaviors of the defendant and the claimant in the particular circumstances of the accident; and the claimant is not only a stranger to the insurer but an adversary. The rules of tort law are not a series of neat prohibitions, like motor vehicle codes. Normally, they do not simply require drivers to stop at particular places or proceed in particular ways: they vaguely require people to act as "reasonable drivers under all the circumstances." On those rare occasions when courts have attempted to set down concrete behavioral rules, easily applied to a host of common accident-prone situations (including one promulgated by no less a judge than Oliver Wendell Holmes), they have often been overruled and widely excoriated as trying to achieve "cookie cutter" justice.[7] Cases such as Howard Young's are typical of tort law's complexity. Considerable evidence will need to be developed and presented concerning, at least: (1) the perceptions of the train driver; (2) his actions preceding the accident; (3) the Transit Authority's rules about driver behavior, customary subway driver behavior, and the rationales behind those rules and behavior; (4) how quickly the train would have stopped had the train been driven and braked appropriately; (5) what injuries to Howard, if any, would have resulted from a proper stop; (6) what did the bystanders on the platform who failed to assist Howard perceive, what could they have done to aid him, at what risk to themselves, and how effective would that help probably have been; (7) the culpability of Howard's conduct, including the extent to which he knew or should have known about the dangers of taking the subway and standing near the tracks; and (8) the hiring, training, and supervision practices of the Transit Authority with respect to its subway drivers. All this information must be exhaustively explored if tort law is to diligently examine the totality of Howard's accident circumstances in order to make accurate judgments about fault and causation.

On top of such tough decisions, present in most cases where there is disagreement about a defendant's liability, society asks the tort system to make a fully individualized determination of the plaintiff's harm. The system isn't asked, as is workers' compensation, to come up with a category of injury that roughly fits the claimant's case and that will lead to scheduled predetermined payments—a maximum of, say, $400 a week for wage loss and a preordained medical fee of, say, $250 for setting a broken arm. It is asked to determine the particular physical and emotional harm done to this particular plaintiff, to determine not only the financial but the psychic repercussions of that harm, and then to put a precise dollar value on that harm and its repercussions. To do this, of course, the tort system investigates in great detail the realities of the claimant's postaccident life and then makes extensive use of experts to identify the postlitigation course of his life as an injury victim versus the course his life would have taken if he had not been injured.

All these difficult tasks—and more—must be accomplished in a contentious, adversarial litigation setting where there is much at stake. It is no surprise that transaction costs as a percentage of total compensation are often highest in those cases in which injuries are most severe. Where there is a lot to win or to lose, the parties quite naturally research and investigate more and present more evidence than they would if little were at risk. For many defendants in these kinds of high transaction cost cases, more is at stake than the even large dollars claimed by plaintiffs. In the medical injury cases, doctors feel their pride and reputations are on the line. Similar feelings may move defendant manufacturers in products liability cases, and such a defendant may also fear that a finding for the plaintiff will subject it to ruinous multiple litigation from other people similarly injured by the identically designed or marketed item from its product line. In toxic tort cases, defendants may see masses of people in the same lawsuit or may simply envision legions of similarly exposed and injured persons standing in line behind one plaintiff, waiting only for a verdict in his favor before they too sue.

To do the complicated, high-stakes job of processing the Youngs' claim through the tort system competently will take huge amounts of time from P. J. Cowcroft, Judge Small and her aides, and defense attorneys. If the tort system is to carry out this job, it must, of course, guarantee the Youngs the ability to participate fully. It should assure them legal services, which they—like most seriously injured people—cannot afford in the accident's immediate aftermath. In Britain, such access has often been assured by having the government pay for the plaintiff's lawyer pursuant to the Legal Aid program or by having the losing or settling party pay the winner's legal expenses. The contingency fee system in the United States is used to assure access to a lawyer for injured persons with plausible claims. (Even Britain recently went to a form of contingent fees.) This system grants the plaintiff less compensation relative to transaction costs. Thus, not only does society assign tort law its most difficult accident-related job, but it uses a technique for doing so that militates against full plaintiff compensation.

As to comparison of tort law's costs to those of other compensation systems, we should not be any quicker, it is argued, to compare the transaction costs of the health insurance system and the tort system than we would be to compare the costs of meals at a local restaurant and a local dinner theater. It would be laughable social policy to try to influence people to eat at Aunt Josie's diner rather than at the Showboat because the former delivers its good lasagna dinners for $5 while a similar dinner at the latter costs $25. To denigrate the Showboat for the costs of its lasagna dinner ignores what else it provides its customers for the money: a play.

So, too, the tort system purports to provide the American public more than only compensation for persons injured in accidents. When tort law compensates plaintiffs, it takes money away from defendants, whom it judges adversely. That sanction, and the availability of that sanction to anyone injured by another's faulty conduct or product, is meant, as we have seen, to serve as a deterrent to unsafe behavior. Unlike the more routinized compensation systems—health insurance and governmental disability programs—the tort system purports to provide a safer world. The country has vividly demonstrated its willingness to pay considerable sums for what it hopes will be protection from illness or injury, most notably through expensive federal and state regulatory agencies like the Environmental Protection Agency, the Occupational Safety and Health Administration, the Consumer Product Safety Commission, and a host of others. Insofar as tort law provides some of this safety, it would seem to be worth paying more for its operation than for the operation of a system, like health insurance, that provides only compensation.

The tort system, moreover, is supposed to supply more than just dinner and a play. In addition to compensation and safety, it purports to deliver justice. Tort law redresses grievances. It sanctions the guilty. It makes judgments and defines right and wrong in the world of accidental injuries. Tort law also aims at providing many accident victims and potential victims assistance that is important to regaining, maintaining, or attaining psychological health.

If the tort system provides all these advantages (and, admittedly, to tort law's critics, that is a big *if*), one cannot possibly conclude that it costs too much to run the system merely on the basis of its much higher costs per dollar of compensation compared with alternate compensation systems. We must also ask how valuable are the benefits that tort law provides over and above its defects, and how does this compare to the benefits-defects ratio of alternate compensation systems. We began our efforts to evaluate the tort system in

Chapters 3 and 4. That evaluation will continue in the next chapters. At this stage, it suffices to reemphasize that the extent of social dismay at tort's transaction costs along with its delays and uncertainties should be influenced heavily by judgments about what social goods that system produces.

Dismay at transaction costs is also fueled by concerns about which transaction costs produce inadequate concomitant benefits and whether those costs can be controlled or mitigated.

There have been two principal responses to recent studies of how expensive tort lawsuits are. One—the public policy response—has sought to drastically curtail tort law, while sometimes calling for the use of other systems to deal with accidental injuries.[8] The other—the insiders' response—has been to tinker with the tort system in ways designed to streamline it. The former response operates from a sense that tort law does too little of social value.[9] The latter rejects any such assessment. Rather, it accepts tort law's domination in the law's response to accidental injuries and seeks to make it work in a less costly fashion in particular contexts.[10] Resolving accident disputes more cheaply in a middle way is at the heart of a third kind of response to tort law's high transaction costs, delays, and uncertainties. That response—which we shall offer later in this book—identifies and reduces the factors that make the tort system so expensive while identifying and retaining essential features that make tort law valuable.

Some of what makes the tort system so expensive is obvious. To what extent can some of that be reduced, while holding intact the strengths of modern tort law? This chapter provides an opportune place to examine *what* factors add large costs to tort claims processing and *why* those factors exist. Examination of the *why* will help us to figure out how such factors might be reduced. In Chapter 9, then, after closer evaluation of tort law's other values, those more radical measures to reduce transaction costs while preserving positive aspects of tort law will be examined.

As indicated in the paragraphs above on tort law's "hard job," a significant factor in keeping transaction costs high is the legal and

factual complexity of many tort cases. It seems unlikely that anything can be done to change the complex way accidents happen.
Legal changes could, however, render many of the factual complexities irrelevant to a liability decision. Tort law could conceivably
move to a regime of imposing liability without reference to any fault
or product defect. It could award damages according to carefully
drawn schedules or only for out-of-pocket loss (not for an indeter-
minate item like pain and suffering), as has long been done under
workers' compensation. Elimination of consideration of plaintiffs'
or defendants' fault and the more amorphous items of an accident
victim's loss would dramatically reduce the amount of factual investigation in most tort cases. It also would eliminate a good portion
of the wrangling over the legal import of those facts and would
remove a significant part of the uncertainty that so often impedes
settlement of cases.

Apart from enactment of no-fault auto insurance laws, few courts
or legislatures in the United States have shown the slightest interest
in these dramatic steps that might bring tort transaction costs much
closer to those of the workers' compensation system. The fact that
the law has moved so little in these directions may provide evidence
that society values highly the central place of fault as a justification
for loss-shifting, as well as full, individualized compensation for
persons injured through another's fault.

The other main source of transaction costs is the adversary system itself. Here, too, eliminating the two principal issues argued
over—fault and the uncertain value of intangible losses—could
greatly curtail adversarial costs. But even lacking that, in various
geographical areas and substantive realms, courts have tried a variety of reforms to reduce the preparation and presentation demanded
of lawyers under the tort system. Among them are such devices as
court-annexed arbitration and summary jury trials. In the former,
courts divert certain kinds of cases to relatively informal hearings
before one or more experienced lawyers, who render a decision on
liability and damages; the parties are free to reject the decision in
favor of a full court trial. In the latter, the attorneys describe and

defend their respective clients' positions for a strictly limited period of time—often an hour each—to a six-person jury. The judge or magistrate presides and gives the jury a brief statement of the applicable law. The jury deliberates and then provides either a verdict or a special report of the views of each juror. The jury's determination is not binding but is followed up by a meeting with the judge to set a schedule for settlement negotiations, which ideally will be facilitated by the mock-jury verdict.

Although some commentators have been enthusiastic about the potential cost reductions of these methods—primarily through facilitating early settlement—there is little clear evidence of the methods' effectiveness. Indeed, a recent detailed study of court-annexed arbitration in New Jersey in auto accident cases found no reduction in attorney fees or in time devoted to the cases.[11] Perhaps this should not surprise us, for as long as such intractable issues of "who or what was at fault" and "the economic value of noneconomic loss" are present, the forum deciding those issues makes little difference.

Systemic efforts have been applied to reduce the obviously massive transaction costs associated with resolution of mass toxic tort cases. Class actions, aggregation and sampling, consolidation, and computerized case analysis have been used in order to facilitate the processing of cases in situations in which the limits of courts threatened to delay such processing until the twenty-first century. In some measure, those resolutions occurred much the way they would have within the tort system—without, however, the individualized attention to particular plaintiffs that would have been characteristic of the typical tort case.

With respect to the second transaction-cost booster inherent in the adversary system, human behavior, even less obvious prospects for cost reduction exist as long as tort law remains largely intact. Although it is widely believed that attorney behavior stretches injury litigation out beyond what any disinterested observer would regard as necessary, it is unclear how that behavior can be corralled. Settlement too often awaits the long-delayed eve of trial. Defense attorneys often proceed slowly, to stretch out litigation, in the knowledge that delays in the receipt of compensation put pressure on plaintiffs to accept lower settlements in order to get needed cash. (And also— whisper it—to increase their own defense legal fees.) Often plaintiffs' attorneys with a large portfolio of cases do not seem to push very hard for quick settlements, nor can their usually subservient clients (with only one case in *their* portfolio) push them to hurry the pace.

There are some judicial measures that might reduce these costs by encouraging attorneys to be less dilatory. Judges can cajole, inform, and twist arms to get settlements—particularly in situations in which it seems to the judge that delay is coming from defendants' strategic behavior. Plaintiffs can be spoken to by judges early in the litigation and encouraged to keep pressure on their attorneys for speedy resolution.[12] Early trial dates can be set and adhered to, thereby defusing the delay inherent in common attorney tendencies to let careful case analysis and preparation slide to the eve of trial. Legislators can require the assessment of prejudgment or even pre-settlement interest in tort cases from the time of claim, in order to discourage deliberate defense delay. Overall, judges could, in theory, actively discourage the sort of unnecessarily adversarial behavior that foments cost- and time-increasing methods of disputation.

But all these measures have long been tried: none of them changes significantly the nature of tort litigation.

Before turning to other more viable means of preserving vital elements of tort law, we need insight into which of its features make tort law valuable despite its shortcomings. For the most part, that value has been defined in terms of the monetary effects of tort. Tort verdicts give money to plaintiffs, so we focus on its value as a compensation device. Tort law strips money from culpable defendants and thereby threatens others with punishment for risky behavior, so we also focus on its value as a deterrent device. But the preceding chapters should have made us aware of the serious questions raised about the compensatory and deterrent value of tort law. With those questions in mind, as well as this chapter's itemization of the serious costs of the system, we need to look harder to see whether other values of tort law could justify retention of much of its basic forms.

CHAPTER SIX

Just Proceedings?

If you asked Howard and Nicole Young what their tort lawsuit would give them besides monetary help in reestablishing their former lives, they might respond: "Justice." So might their children, Elissa and Laura, although they might be more likely to describe their lawsuits as making things fair. Interestingly, the officials of the Transit Authority involved with the case, the train driver, and the sued bystanders all might echo that response in describing the value of *their* participation in the defense of the suit. Certainly we outsiders, happily not involved in the lawsuit, expect the law to be serving justice when it decides the Youngs' or anyone else's disputes. If people perceive tort lawsuits as being principally about justice, it makes sense to examine the accuracy and significance of that perception.

Unfortunately, though the Youngs and the defendants are likely to agree that they are seeking justice from the tort system, they are likely to disagree about whether the system provides justice. When the result comes from a verdict, one side of a tort lawsuit—the side whose expectations are dashed—will feel justice was denied them. In the case of settlement (which happens more than 90 percent of the time) *both* sides may feel ill used. In such a world, where overwhelmingly more than half of the main participants will feel that the tort system has treated them unjustly, perhaps very unjustly, it is hard to understand how any conclusions can be reached confidently about the justice or fairness that the system provides.

Nevertheless, tort law's proponents argue that there are good reasons to believe that we do get a considerable amount of justice from the system. In fact, the justice it provides may be the principal advantage tort law has over other ways of dealing with accidental injuries, ways that may well be as effective or more so at providing compensation and deterrence, yet seem significantly less costly than tort.

There are also good reasons to believe that finding a great deal of justice in the tort system (if true) is an important discovery, perhaps important enough to make society tolerate the tort system's relatively high costs. While they may also have other goals in mind, people who take part in tort litigation clearly understand their participation as implicating justice. If people are seeking just resolutions of their disputes in tort law, it seems important that such justice be there. After all, a restaurant serving good fajitas will be highly valued vis-à-vis other eateries in a community where diners go out to eat with fajitas prominently on their minds. So, too, when people turn to legal institutions with justice on their minds, an institution that provides such justice should be prized.

Of course, it is not just the tort system's "customers" who have considered justice an important aspect of tort law. Ordinary people, mostly uninvolved in tort lawsuits, see disputes that involve a victim's claim for compensation from someone who injured him as calling for resolutions based at least partially on justice. Many of the deepest thinkers about law generally and about tort law in particular have emphasized justice's prominent role. John Rawls has described justice as the "first virtue of social institutions." The father of modern efficiency theory in tort, the former Yale Law School dean Guido Calabresi, now a federal appellate judge, regarded tort rules that efficiently reduced accident costs as palatable only so long as society regarded them as just. Various other tort scholars describe tort law primarily in terms of its role as a system of corrective justice—justice concerned with repairing the situation created when someone wrongs someone else.[1] The most recent large-scale examination of the tort system—the American Law Institute's Reporters' Study on Enterprise Liability—described justice as the "simplest and most venerable" rationale underlying tort law.

But make no mistake: the notion that tort law provides a considerable amount of justice is a tough one to sell in today's marketplace of ideas. Charges of injustice abound in current commentary on tort law. Some critics fault tort law for its failure to provide corrective justice. In spite of its veneration for justice, the American Law Institute study quickly dismissed it as a justification for tort law. How can there be corrective justice, asked the study authors, when tort law so rarely extracts payment from the actual wrongdoer?[2] Rather, payment more often comes from the employer or insurer of the actual wrongdoer, or gets passed on to the purchasers of the wrongdoer's goods or services. Similarly, one of this book's authors has been in the front ranks of those who speak out about tort's lottery-like characteristics: it may compensate the Youngs while offering no such compensation to people similarly injured in an identical subway station by a sudden stroke, a collision like Howard Young's that the driver or other passengers could not have avoided, or a mugging by unidentified assailants.[3]

Other critics bemoan not just tort's failure to supply justice but also its provision of injustice. Highlighted among these criticisms is the alleged inconsistency in tort decisions. Like cases are not treated alike. Courts in some states find a product to be defective, courts in other states find it is not. Some juries find that mothers' ingestion of Bendectin during pregnancy caused their children's birth defects, most juries find it did not. People with what appear to be similarly serious injuries are awarded a few hundred thousand dollars in damages in some cases and several million dollars in others.

Others assail tort for assessing damages that are disproportionate to the defendant's wrong. The train driver or the Transit Authority in the Youngs' case, for example, would complain if forced to pay damages for all the resultant injuries in that they were thereby being heavily punished for actions that were only slightly blameworthy. After all, the driver would say, I was only going a little over the speed limit. Many drivers do that to make up time. Anyone can be distracted for a moment. To make me or my company pay some huge judgment for such an insignificant lapse is punishing us more than we deserve (especially, he might add, when the victim was very drunk).

These criticisms, often valid, highlight flaws in tort as a system of corrective justice. That is the context for most discussions of justice in tort. Tort law does not traditionally aspire to change the allocation of wealth or property in this country. Rather, it has usually concerned itself with repairing wrongful disturbances in the existing distribution of wealth, property, health, and other forms of good fortune.

Nevertheless, criticism has expanded recently to include tort law's effects on distributive justice—the fair distribution of the world's benefits and burdens. Some challenge tort law simply because it helps maintain an unjust allocation of goods. Others say that it actively contributes to distributive injustice by favoring the wealthy over the less wealthy. That favoring does not occur directly. In theory, poor people's injuries are compensated just as fully as those of the wealthy. As we have seen, however, an injured poor person generally requires less money to put her back in the same position she occupied before the accident than does a similarly disabled wealthy person. A major portion of tort damages goes to replace lost earnings. Lawyers like Howard Young have a lot more lost earnings when they are disabled than do street sweepers, domestic workers, or Burger King cashiers. However, when Howard Young and these other workers pay for their subway tokens, which include in their price the seller's costs of paying tort compensation, they all pay the same amount. If the Transit Authority were liable only for the level of damages of poorer people, its token prices would be lower. Thus, the poor pay more for the goods and services they buy so that wealthier workers like Howard Young can be fully compensated if they are wrongfully injured. Compounding this injustice is the fact that a higher proportion of such wrongfully injured wealthy people will be inclined and able to interest a plaintiffs' lawyer in representing them in a tort lawsuit. Because their settlement or award is apt to be larger than those of similarly disabled poor people, their lawsuit is likely to generate higher fees. Both the probability of hiring a lawyer and the percentage of losses recovered can vary directly with a victim's wealth.

Skepticism about the meaning of justice in tort law is another obstacle to confidence in the system. Many would say that there is simply too little agreement about what justice is in the tort context for us to be able to reach any confident conclusions about whether we get much justice from tort law. These skeptics would point to differing concepts of justice, elegantly constructed by current and classical philosophers, and observe that neither American society nor American law has clearly chosen one of those visions of justice as the true one.[4] Moreover, the skeptics would claim, even where there is some agreement about what constitutes justice—for example, that rules are just if people would have agreed to them *ex ante* while ignorant of the nature of their own lives in society—that agreement takes place at such a level of abstraction that it tells us very little about whether actual tort rules or decisions in particular tort cases are or are not just.[5]

Perhaps this skepticism explains the paucity of attention given to tort law's justice role before the 1980s. In the most influential tort book of the past thirty years—*The Cost of Accidents* by Guido Calabresi—justice is only an ultimate check on the adoption of tort rules that otherwise would be adopted based primarily on the author's accident-cost-reduction theories. With a few notable exceptions, other major tort scholars and casebook authors have paid little attention to the justice component of the tort system. There has been much serious scholarly attention to justice in tort law in the past decade, but the recent American Law Institute Reporters' Study still gave it only a few pages of discussion in a lengthy two-volume work.

Many of the critics' and skeptics' challenges to the existence of justice within the tort system have considerable force. But adherents of tort law point to the inadequacies of other ways society does or might deal with accidental injuries. Moreover, the way the tort system operates encourages its adherents to argue that it will produce considerably more substantive justice and fairness across the board than will those other ways (such as, say, workers' compensation or automobile no-fault).

Finding substantive justice in tort law, or in any other system handling personal injury claims, means finding just resolutions of the disputes that people bring to the system. There are two usual ways to evaluate the justice of such outcomes: the first seeks to identify whether tort law's rules are just by comparing them to abstract principles of corrective justice. This technique assumes that rules which match up with general principles of corrective justice will lead to just outcomes in particular cases. Another evaluative method requires that we identify the collection of adjudicatory practices that make up tort law and then examine the ability of such practices to reach just outcomes in individual tort cases.

The first method has been widely tried but has run into serious obstacles. It requires an analyst—most often a tort scholar or judge—to take a particular rule or case decision and carefully examine how it matches up against some standard of justice. This is a common reaction to issues of right and wrong: determine what is right and what is wrong, and then measure the action in question against each definition to see which category fits it.

Each of us commonly does this, in a somewhat casual way, with respect to many, many situations in our lives, and learned philosophers have attempted to establish such standards in a rigorous way in their writings about justice and law—even about justice and tort law in particular. But the results of their efforts tells us much about the fallacy of this match-up approach. These great minds simply don't agree about the basic standards of justice. Some say general social utility must be the yardstick against which all rules are measured. Others contend that principles of individual autonomy must govern. Still others argue that communitarian values be the measure.[6] These sorts of differences put Judge Small in a tough position if she wants to do justice in deciding whether Howard Young has a claim against the fellow passengers who failed to help him off the tracks. Theorists focusing on individual autonomy say it is unjust to impose a legal duty on people to help a stranger in distress. Communitarian and feminist theorists disagree.[7]

This sort of disagreement should be no surprise: these arguments about justice have their roots in centuries-old philosophical debates. Nevertheless, the persistence of such disagreement among these learned people—people far more similar to one another in background and attitudes than are most of us in this society of substantially different cultures, education, incomes, and ages—should serve as a warning that we will not have enough consensus about appropriate standards of justice to make this analytical approach work all that well. It is hard, in other words, to get *unum* out of *pluribus* on precise standards of justice.

That warning seems even more clear when we think about trying to reach some consensus about how standards of justice in fact match up with particular rules of tort law. Even when philosophers agree which basic principles of justice should apply to tort law, they seem unable to agree on what those principles require in the way of even the most basic decisions about tort rules. For example, in a very careful, thoughtful article, one of the country's leading products liability scholars praised another scholar for his thorough attention to the key principles of justice. Yet he concluded that his insightful colleague had simply gotten the application of those principles wrong: justice did *not* require that manufacturers be held strictly liable for product injuries—liable, that is, even when, say, a flawed product inexplicably emits from a scrupulously supervised assembly line. Rather, wrote the dissenting scholar, justice required that manufacturers be held liable only for faulty behavior.[8] A greater difference on a more basic element of tort law could not occur. Yet it came from two thoughtful philosophers who agreed on what principles of justice were basic.

We turn to the second, more pragmatic, method for evaluating the justice of tort outcomes in light of these difficulties in the match-up method. Unlike the match-up method, this approach recognizes and accepts society's full variety of informed viewpoints about what is just in particular situations. The pragmatic method focuses on the legal practices that lead to decisions in tort cases. It would mark tort law as achieving justice to the extent that these practices are likely to lead to outcomes consistent with contemporary community standards of what is fair and just.

It is in these practices of tort law—the way in which its rules are formed and its decisions made—that some find its substantial justice. They see essential practices of tort law as simple. As in the Youngs' case, the plaintiffs and the defendants hire lawyers, who guide their clients through a judicial process that consists most often of judge and jury sharing decision making at the trial level, followed by several opportunities for judicial review of what has happened. Decisions in the trial process are typically made in the context of extensive information about the particular accident that gave rise to the plaintiff's injuries and about the extent of the harm the plaintiff suffered. While at most only about 5 to 10 percent of tort lawsuits go all the way through the trial process, settlement decisions are heavily influenced by the outcomes expected from that process— outcomes that in turn are influenced by the precedent set in those few cases that are litigated and the even fewer that are in fact appealed to final appellate court adjudication.

These practices contrast sharply with those of most alternative ways proposed or adopted to deal with accidental injuries. Workers' compensation and automobile no-fault systems represent the most widely used such alternatives. Neither of those systems looks very fully at the accident that caused the claimant's injury or at the extent of one's injuries. They don't care whether the injury-causing conduct by either party was wrongful. Nor do these systems deal with the full ramifications of the injury for the claimant: they pay her medical bills and a fixed percentage of weekly wages at the time of injury until she can resume work. Nor do juries share in the decision making. Judicial review of decisions is likely to be less comprehensive. Some or all of these differences exist in all alternatives to tort.

Tort law's practices purport to promise justice—at least much more justice than will be found in alternative institutional arrangements—through the roles played by lawyers, judges, and juries in resolving disputes about responsibility for and the extent of injuries from accidents. Lawyers, particularly plaintiffs' lawyers like P. J. Cowcroft, function in the tort system to provide injured persons with something that aggrieved citizens dealing with other areas of law often lack: access to the courts and equality of representation. Because most tort plaintiffs hire their lawyers on a contingency fee basis, even the injured poor have access to the tort system. That access is admittedly far from complete: the poor, for example, are less inclined to hire a lawyer. Nevertheless, many injured people— including those least likely to be compensated adequately through public and private insurance systems—do have access to the tort system. And, it is argued, thanks to plaintiff lawyers' potential for lucrative contingency fees, injured persons with valid tort claims are more likely than most victimized individuals to learn that the legal system's doors are open. Plaintiffs' personal injury lawyers are the most aggressive marketers of legal services for the general public— particularly in their use of radio and TV advertising. While often so aggressive as to be offensive, these client-alerting efforts, believers in the system argue, at least help maximize the percentage of persons who will investigate the possibility of a lawsuit after being injured by tortious behavior.

What's more, that same contingency fee arrangement that opens the courtroom doors even to the poor also increases markedly the chances that plaintiffs and defendants will receive equally good legal representation. Because of their ability to earn a substantial percentage of awards large and small, good plaintiffs' personal injury lawyers can earn substantial sums of money. Very good ones can get *very* rich—earning $5–10 million or more *annually,* with many others earning high in the six-figure range. That opportunity attracts good lawyers to the plaintiffs' side of personal injury litigation and keeps them there. In addition, the large fees available to plaintiffs' lawyers often enable them to develop and present the plaintiff's case as fully and as expertly as her opposite number can do for the defendants. Increased use of networks by plaintiffs' lawyers for sharing

information about similar kinds of cases likewise has improved the
chances that the antagonists' litigation resources will be in rough
balance. In short, although the insurance companies and other corporations that most often show up as the defense in tort cases have
considerable resource advantages over typical individual plaintiffs
like the Youngs, those plaintiffs are much less likely to be over-
matched than in almost any other kind of David-and-Goliath litigation that takes place in our legal system.

This rough equality of advocacy in the tort system takes on
particular importance for the existence of justice in the system's
decision-making practices. It means that there will often be an acceptable balance in the kinds of information presented to tort decision
makers—in contrast to the imbalances that permeate most kinds
of individual-versus-institution disputes. Just outcomes in tort cases
depend heavily on such information. The legal rules in tort cases demand presentation of full stories about how an accident happened
and what harms resulted. Tort law's general rules invite decision
makers to consider all of the large number of factors relevant to
the cost-benefit ratio of injury-causing behavior. So too do rules
about damages, which require a decision maker to award a victorious plaintiff an amount of money calculated to go as far as possible
to put him back in the position he would have been in had the
defendant not acted wrongfully. Such determinations, of course,
require judges and juries to examine a wealth of detail about the
plaintiff's past, present, and expected future life. Lawyers are under
a duty to develop, organize, and present these kinds of information
to the judge and jury in ways designed to help the decision makers
understand, from the perspective of their clients, what really happened in the way of accident, injury, and aftermath. Without a rough
equality of lawyering ability and resources between plaintiffs and
defendant, important pieces of this complex puzzle of information
often would not reach decision makers. To the extent that the tort
system minimizes that inequality, the chances of just outcomes
increase.

For tort law's adherents, all this means that judge and jury decision making takes place in a rich context of full, concrete understanding about the people and the circumstances connected with the injurious accident. When judges, even appellate judges, make decisions about what tort law should be, this context for their decisions makes it more likely that they understand and appreciate at least some of the realities of the accident world. That understanding is enhanced by the articulate presentations of capable lawyers whose job is to clarify judges' and juries' understanding of what happened and how such happenings should be related to legal rules.

Tort "law" is the product of hundreds of these sorts of fully contextualized decisions. Trial judges make rulings that, even if controversial, at least can be examined by intermediate appellate judges (albeit with a heavy presumption in favor of a trial court ruling) and perhaps in turn by judges on the Supreme Court of the state. Adherents of tort law take comfort in the self-correcting nature of the judicial process: all these decisions, made in concrete settings, become more clearly law that will apply to many other situations. Decisions also draw more fully on what previous generations have said was the law, on what other courts have said more recently about this area of law in related contexts, and on scholarly commentaries about the law in this kind of case. In other words, into each formulation of tort law goes the thinking of many other judges, prodded by practicing and academic lawyers, who have tried to grapple with the question of what is just in circumstances like those facing the court.

Thus tort law remains, its proponents argue, always dynamic, always attempting to respond to the shifting realities of the world and the shifting understandings and evaluations of those realities through which individuals and communities evolve. People are being hurt in accidents all the time. With lawyers' help, they make claims for just treatment through the tort system, claims that are resisted by those against whom they are made. This goes on in at least fifty different tort systems all the time. State courts which respond to those claims and defenses are sufficiently independent that a decision handed down by one may represent a "new" outcome. Yet, these fifty-plus jurisdictions are sufficiently interdependent that when one does something new, others will pay attention to that novel view and must make a conscious choice, in the face of ardent support for—or opposition to—that novel position, either to accept, reject, or modify that new law.

The sheer numbers of decisions that thus go into determining what tort law is and what it means suggest that the legal rules may well reflect, over time, a consensus about what is just. That consensus—formed as it is by hundreds of past and present judges' decisions, in concrete contexts—will be, for those who value tort law, an educated, thoughtful (if perhaps controversial) verification of what is just.

The more particularized results that we look for in the outcomes of particular tort cases come in part from the application of these general rules. They come equally, if not more, in the view of tort law's adherents, from the powerful role of the jury in tort law. That role is powerful in large part because of the open-endedness inherent in tort law's most commonly applied basic legal rules, outlined above: (1) there will normally be no liability unless the defendant (or its product) performed unreasonably (and the plaintiff behaved reasonably—or comparatively so); and (2) plaintiffs proving such should receive compensation in an amount that will restore them to the life they would have had if the accident had not happened. The jury, it is argued, exercises its power in ways that are likely to reflect the community's sense of what is fair and just because (1) jury decisions are collective decisions, arrived at by consensus; (2) juries are made up of persons who represent the diverse perspectives of our society; and (3) each jury exists only to decide one case.

Thus, according to tort law's adherents, the practice of collective decision making is likely to lead to just outcomes for several reasons. First, a group of six to twelve persons will probably remember more about the extensive information presented to them about a case than will any one individual. The group's members will thus understand better the realities of the situation facing them. Second, in order to make their decisions about liability—about a just outcome—the members of the jury have to talk and listen to each other. The jury must come back from its secret deliberations with at least overwhelming agreement about both liability and damages. They cannot simply walk into a jury room, vote 7–5 or 8–4 in favor of one party, and then return to court with a verdict. Such talking and listening, tort proponents argue, maximizes the chances that the differing attitudes, understandings, and perceptions inherent in each person's individuality are explored and dealt with insofar as those differences pertain to the outcome. This group process, according to the system's adherents, enhances the chances that a jury will "get it right." A sophisticated social scientist recently concluded that the jury—the most studied part of the legal process—is "one of our society's most reliable decision-making institutions."[9] Equally related to our concerns about justice, this group process assures that strong, differing notions of what is a just and fair outcome for a *particular* injury will be fused in the decision about disputes over responsibility for that injury and its extent.

The inclusion of many different kinds of people on juries likewise purports to assure that this amalgamation of varying senses of justice will embody, over time, the varying senses of justice within our society. Ordinary people, drawn from all walks of life, sit on juries. This means that while any one jury decision may not encompass the community's full sense of justice, those decisions taken as a whole—which make up tort law—probably do. That *general* validity may admittedly give little comfort to a litigant whose case has been decided "unjustly." But it is this "whole" that influences most tort resolutions. Although the vast majority of tort lawsuits are settled before they ever reach a jury, those settlements are guided by what juries "as a whole" do, because settlements are based on the lawyers' predictions of what probably would be the outcome of jury deliberations.

Finally, jury decision making, the proponents of tort law maintain, is likely to embody community notions of what is fair and just because each jury is a one-shot entity. One jury is selected to hear one tort case. It does not decide any others. Accordingly, when the jury decides the case, it will focus solely on the people before it and on what in fact happened in the accident. Its understanding of those realities will not be contaminated by having looked closely at many other injurious accidents. The jury will see Howard Young's drunkenness, not his mixed with the drunkenness of some intoxicated driver who ran down a child in last month's case. It will look only at Elissa Young's suffering, not at hers mixed with the suffering of a child in last week's case, who had a broken leg and uncaring parents. In being able to see the realities of this particular accident and injuries more clearly than repeat decision makers—the sort that dominate some alternatives to tort law, such as a workers' compensation board—the jury should enhance the extent to which outcomes in the aggregate reflect sensitivity to the real accident world. In addition, the one-shot nature of jury decision making means it is extremely difficult for any group or institution interested in the shape of tort law across the years to influence decisions in a particular direction. While specially interested entities may be able to "capture" administrative agencies or even the judiciary—witness what some see as the Roosevelt-Truman or the Reagan-Bush administrations' ideological manipulation of the federal judiciary—they cannot do so with a jury, the composition of which is unknown before a trial and irrelevant thereafter. The import of the jury's nebulousness for justice lies in the inability of any *one* view of what is just to gain ascendance in its decision making. The way to influence juries' sense of what is just and fair is to influence society's sense.

In addition, it is argued, the operation of the tort system allows for correction of whatever injustices may arise from jury verdicts. The trial judge reviews the verdict; so does at least one appellate court, and sometimes two or three, if asked. Many judges do not hesitate to step in where they feel confident a jury has decided unrealistically. Monthly the law reports are full of cases in which appellate courts reverse or reduce verdicts for plaintiffs. Unlike possible alternatives to the tort system, those decisions about proper levels of compensation or about proper liability outcomes are made in the context of particular cases. Each judge has a very concrete sense of what she is deciding, and, for the most part, each makes her decision after hearing careful articulation by capable advocates of appropriate perspectives on the concrete situation before her.

Tort law's adherents argue that another perspective supports an expectation that judge and jury decision making will lead to just outcomes. The tort system, it is argued, invites justice into its workings. It works on disputes involving accidental injuries in a context infused with justice. Lawsuits are brought to the civil "system of justice." In many places, the courts are referred to, literally and figuratively, as halls of justice. More substantively, lawyers and judges are said to understand themselves as having an obligation to observe and respect principles of justice in the processing of disputes. Justice and fairness are the language of courtrooms and are urged on judges and juries by advocates as the basis for decisions in their favor. Compared with other institutions that respond to the needs of accident victims—the relatively impersonal and automatic payment under workers' compensation and no-fault automobile insurance, to name again the most prominent—tort law, it is said, is more likely to listen and feel obliged to respond to arguments that its rules or its decisions in particular cases are unjust, or would be more just another way.

Tort law's very public nature likewise, its supporters contend, invites justice into its workings. The claims and defenses in a lawsuit, and much of the evidence relevant to it, are matters of public record. Verdicts, and even many settlements, attract considerable public attention, attention that seems unlikely to subside in an era in which million-dollar verdicts and major group-brought lawsuits proliferate. Regardless of whether the public spotlight—and, thus, public commentary—glares at a particular tort decision, it can be appealed if one of the parties believes substantial injustice has been done. And appeals most often trigger written opinions by a panel of judges, who spell out the reasons for or against their decision. Any injustice will often catch the attention of other legal professionals and scholars, eager to shoot their darts into anything that resembles a balloon filled more with hot air than with justice. Justice thus will be discussed beyond the confines of the parties to a lawsuit.

Moreover, as suggested earlier, proponents argue that the tort system works to cultivate justice in its prime decision makers. Tort lawsuits force the realities of the individual people and situations involved in accidents into the forefront of these decision makers' consciousness. Should the Youngs' cases proceed to trial, the members of the jury will come to know more about Howard Young and how he was hurt than they do about anyone else, outside of their own families, who has been accidentally injured. Judge Small and the jury will learn the good and the bad about Howard's conduct relevant to his injury, and they will learn much about the other people involved with the accident. Learning all this, confronting the full meaning of the accident for the people involved, the judge and jury will find it difficult not to care about the people involved. Even if they were not inclined at the outset to care about both the plaintiff and defendant, the parties' lawyers will seek to make them care. Trials awaken strong feelings about people outside our normal circles of family and close friends. Those feelings in turn, tort partisans contend, awaken in the jury concerns about justice, concerns that lie dormant in most other areas of their lives where they, like most of us, are allowed to distance themselves from the realities of other people's lives.[10] It follows, in this view, that such an awakening makes concerns about justice much more palpable in tort decisions than in less fully contextualized settings for decision making.

Answers to the criticism that tort law is itself unjust also arise from this individualized context, when the tort system makes decisions about facts and the application of legal rules to those facts. Among the assertions that tort law is itself unjust, perhaps the most persistent is that its judgments and damage awards are wildly inconsistent. Tort law's adherents answer that this criticism derives from a worldview that demands one true standard of justice. Judgments and damage awards *are* inconsistent if there is one true answer to the questions before judges and juries in the thousands of tort trials every year. But the divergent responses of juries and judges may simply reflect the reality that there are many valid answers to these questions, even when the system is adhering to agreed-on principles and the answer givers are acting dutifully and rationally. In this diverse society, in which people bring many different viewpoints to questions like "To what extent has Elissa Young been harmed by her father's accident?" a wide variety of answers can be expected.

Professor Michael Saks, a social scientist specializing in law, highlights this element in pointing out that damage awards in each tort case represents only one sample of what the appropriate damages should be.[11] If the case were tried ten times, there would be ten different awards, probably clustered around a midpoint. We might then be more confident what the "real" value of the injury done to the plaintiff was and more willing to brand as unfair an award that deviated greatly from all the others, but we still could not conclude that any one award was right and the others wrong. Where there are so many possible "right" answers to a question like "What is the dollar equivalent of the plaintiff's injuries?" criticism of the "inconsistency" of those answers, he argues, is misplaced. Within an acceptable range, in this view, such a variety of "right" answers probably more fairly reflects the uncertainty inherent in the real world than would an alternative system's uniform awards.

(Unconvinced, critics of the tort system point to the deep disenchantment with tort law among some of those caught by its vicissitudes—including that very uncertainty in any given case, as well as its concomitant delays and transaction costs. It was Learned Hand, the greatest American judge not to make it to the U.S. Supreme Court, who once wrote, "After now some dozen years of experience [as a judge], I must say that as a litigant I should dread a lawsuit beyond almost anything else short of sickness and death." How much more dread is involved, ask critics of the tort system, for a badly injured litigant waiting for years while in need of funds to replace lost wages and secure medical care?)

Two other major criticisms of the effectiveness of tort law's corrective justice efforts seem misplaced to the system's adherents. The first says tort law dilutes justice because awards are usually paid not by the wrongdoer but by his insurance company or by his employer. But a tort judgment is directed against a wrongdoer, not his insurance company, tort adherents respond. Society requires the insurance company to pay for and defend the wrongdoer because the insurer and wrongdoer made a contract requiring just such payment and defense. If society thought such contracts wrong, they could be ruled invalid as against public policy—which is what some courts have ruled with respect to insurance against punitive damage awards.

Moreover, insurance and the legal doctrine of employer liability for employees' torts actually expand the number of wrongdoers whom tort law can sanction, while facilitating the "correction" of the injustice to the injured plaintiff. Tort law tries to do justice by making wrongdoers pay. Not only *can't* the tort system make a person of modest means pay more than his means—which certainly won't cover even a "small" $20,000 judgment—the system won't even try to do so. The wronged plaintiff and her lawyer can't afford to bring a lawsuit that would earn them the kind of payment people of modest means could afford. Accordingly, an effective tort judgment (or more likely a settlement) against a wrongdoer can be gained in many more situations because defendants or employers have insurance. In many of those situations, if not most, even the insured or employed wrongdoer can face unpleasant consequences: insurance premiums can go up or coverage be canceled; employers may severely reprimand the wrongdoer, put him on some sort of probation, fire him, or even (theoretically, at least) sue him for what they had to pay for his wrong. (Actually, more than 95 percent of all tort settlements and judgments are borne not by individuals but by insurance companies or large corporations that self-insure.)

Likewise, wrongdoers who pass their tort payments on to customers are not thereby immune from sanction. Entities may find themselves at a competitive disadvantage if they try to add the costs of tort judgments or settlements to the costs of the goods and services they provide. Increases in their prices will cause loss of many customers unless demand for their goods or service is somehow highly inelastic. (On the other hand, tort's critics argue, most institutional insureds pay insurance premiums based on the kind and location of their business rather than on their individual safety records.)

A related criticism of tort law based on insurance—that the injustice of injury is not corrected by tort payments because most injured people have other sources of compensation, such as health insurance—seems to tort law's adherents even less fairly placed at tort law's door. Those who are least adequately compensated elsewhere for their injuries are most likely to make use of the tort system, according to a Harvard study of medical malpractice claims. (On the other hand, workers' compensation data show that almost half [42 percent] of all products liability payments go to those who have already collected substantially for medical expense and wage loss.)

Tort law's adherents argue that those who do receive substantial compensation from other sources often had agreed beforehand to refund that compensation from their tort suit proceeds. This common arrangement likely allows potential tort victims to buy health insurance at lower rates. From that perspective, then, the tort system helps all injured people "correct" ahead of time the effects of injuries done to them. (Critics of tort law respond, though, that those nontort sources of compensation often don't bother to collect their share of tort recovery in so-called subrogation claims because of the expense and delay involved, thus resulting in wasteful—and even corrupting—double payment to injury victims.)

The second major criticism of tort law's supposed failure in its corrective justice function alleges that the system doesn't compensate people in many situations in which corrective justice would seem to demand it. But the fact that some wrongdoers have inadequate or no insurance coverage or other sources of recompense reflects society's problems, not those of tort law, its adherents argue: if society demanded it, the government could pass and enforce "financial responsibility" laws requiring all citizens to carry adequate coverage.

Adherents of tort law go on to argue that the system's inability to compensate innocent victims of disease or accident where there was no wrongdoer does not make tort law unjust but only incomplete. Incompleteness need not imply injustice in the compensation of American injuries any more than hunger relief efforts in one part of Africa are impliedly unjust because they do not encompass other needy areas. Incompleteness equals injustice only where there are no principles or other good reasons guiding the choice of which segment gets helped. Tort law, with its focus on wrongdoing causally connected to the injury, certainly purports to make its choices based on principle—indeed on a principle that seems widely accepted within our society.

Tort law then, in the eyes of its adherents, enjoys substantial advantages in the provision of justice over other more routine ways of dealing with accidental injuries, such as workers' compensation or no-fault auto insurance. Such justice—dependent as it is on full, individualized decision making—does not come cheaply. There may be ways, which will be explored in the concluding chapter of this book, to retain some of the ingredients of tort law essential to the existence of such justice while still reducing some of tort law's costs. Even then, however, tort law will remain an expensive dispute resolution machinery compared with alternatives that promise quicker, less disputable (if admittedly less individualized) compensation to needy victims of accident or illness. Indeed, tort law may be intolerably expensive for the advantages it provides.[12] And for many of its advantages touted in this chapter, competing disadvantages can be cited.

As to tort cases being decided in a rich context of detailed litigation, it can be argued that personal injury cases are *too* contextual—dominated by the individual considerations of the individual case, thereby overlooking a broader and perhaps better view. Take, for example, the apparently easy case of deciding that GM was grossly negligent in placing gas tanks on the side of its trucks. The death of seventeen-year-old Shannon Mosely in such a truck after a fire following a collision with a drunk driver led to an angry $105 million verdict by a jury determined to punish GM for its supposedly irresponsible actions in causing *this* horribly burned motorist in *this* case. But not in front of the jury were the many people who may have been *protected* by GM's design. Without getting lost in the technicalities of automobile engineering, nor indeed purporting to decide the merits of the case, logic suggests that any possible placement of the gas tank can cause some accidents and prevent others. Impeccably credentialed engineers have tried various locations for gas tanks—in the rear, in the front, inside the passenger compartment, or underneath it. What is the tradeoff of enhancing a fire in a side-impact collision (which GM's actions did) versus avoiding dangers in a front-end collision (far more common in fatality cases than side crashes)? The point is, as we saw earlier, that it is very hard for a defendant to be persuasive about avoiding hypothetical dangers in *other* instances in the context of an actual single case concerning horrible injuries to the individual plaintiff before the court.

As the auto design case discussed above suggests, it is not at all clear that courts constitute the ideal forum for risk management. Judges and juries may fail to account for the trade-offs or inherent imperfections in a needed product. As indicated earlier, Peter Huber, in a controversial survey of courts' performances in overseeing risks to the public, determines that whereas some public control of public risks is necessary, courts provide an undesirable, sometimes disastrous forum for exercising such control. He sees courts are often "institutionally predisposed" to favor the wrong risk choices, due largely to their preference for old sources of risk over newer, even safer sources—old, outdated oral contraceptives versus new IUDs or sponges, for example. Judicial review of technology thus becomes "review of technological *change*." Such a skeptical, even hostile attitude toward technology is founded all too often "on the Panglossian belief that we already reside in the safest of all possible worlds and the Malthusian conviction that the future has nothing to offer but a snake." Huber concludes that "'natural' selection of tort litigation—controlled largely by the . . . plaintiff's bar—fails to operate as a rational ordering device for selecting among good and bad public risks."[13]

As to the jury's reflection of the community's sense of justice, there is considerable resistance to this notion. That resistance stems in part primarily from concerns that juries are often overcome with sympathy when faced with someone who has been hurt—especially when injured individuals sue a large corporation such as a manufacturer, a hospital, or an insurance company. Others question the competence of inexpert jurors to decide complex matters. Even so conservative an authority as the late Dean Erwin Griswold of the Harvard Law School raised this doubt: "The jury at best is the apotheosis of the amateur. Why should anyone think that 12 persons brought in from the street selected in various ways for their lack of general ability should have any capacity for deciding controversies between persons?"[14] (Believers in the jury rebut with studies indicating that these so-called inexpert juries generally decide cases the way presumably expert judges would. They point out that defendants in tort trials are exonerated at least as often by juries as by judges, disproving the notion of jurors' soft-hearted sentimentality.)

Even assuming that tort law adherents are correct that trials are objective and fair, critics argue that trials take far too long—delays of two to three years or even longer are commonplace. Critics also point out problems inherent in the complexity of judicial procedures, including application of the rules of evidence and instructions to the jury on the applicable law, leading to much strategic maneuvering on both sides. Defense lawyers, for example, often adopt a strategy of "getting error into the record" in order to earn a basis of appeal (with all *its* delays and uncertainties) and thus extract concessions in the way of much reduced awards even to plaintiffs victorious at trial.

Finally, whereas supporters insist that tort law itself is not to blame for the fact that many potential wrongdoers, especially motorists, have no insurance to cover their liability, critics point out that the huge cost of tort liability insurance—not only its expense but the waste that attends it—is the reason for all that uninsurance. Paying insurance against automotive tort claims, including pain and suffering, often exceeds $1,000 a year for the minimum coverage in many urban areas, thus pricing out huge numbers of the poor and near poor. According to some estimates, 80 percent or more of the motorists in the inner cities of Detroit, New York, Chicago, and Los Angeles may be driving without insurance. Thus, it is argued, tort law, with all its expense, cannot disclaim responsibility for many motorists' lack of adequate insurance.

With all these pros and cons, then, we are obliged to look further to see what people involved in accidents, as well as society as a whole, get for the large amounts paid for tort law.

CHAPTER SEVEN

Human Transactions

Somehow in the early 1990s, prime-time network television became littered with shows about lawsuits. The cowboys-and-Indians and cops-and-robbers of our youth had given considerable way to lawyers-and-clients. It seems unlikely that this reflects a maturing of American television viewers' thinking, to a point where they yearn for programming about accident compensation and deterrence. Rather, the popularity of lawyer-and-client programs should remind us that lawsuits contain many of the basic elements of human drama that have long fascinated everyone. If *L.A. Law* and its progeny featured lawsuits by injured persons, it's because legal contests about injury claims are full of the tensions and passions that involve and intrigue people.

In light of the explosion of dramatic presentations of tort cases in the mass media, the idea that tort lawsuits have tremendous personal meaning for the people involved should surprise no one. Likewise, given the vicarious role drama has always played in societies' consciousness, no one should be surprised that the dramas played out in tort lawsuits can have substantial meaning for the mass of uninjured citizens as well. Certainly, Howard Young and his friends would not be surprised. His tort lawsuit is one of the defining activities of his life. Those who know him cannot help but recognize, in the drama of his claims for compensation from those who he charges wronged him, some meaning for their lives in a dangerous world.

What *is* surprising, in light of this obvious dramatic significance of tort lawsuits, is how little attention professional analysts pay to all that those lawsuits mean for those involved and for others who become aware of them. The professionals concerned with the tort system would gauge the value, or lack thereof, of the Youngs' tort lawsuits by looking only at the amounts of money that the Youngs take away. Those amounts will be compared to the economic losses the family suffered as a result of Howard's accident. Sophisticated observers might also compare the settlements and awards with the amounts spent on the resolution of the case. They may try to examine whether defendants like the Transit Authority behave more safely as the result of this sort of lawsuit.

What the professional analysts rarely do, however, is listen. The data that are collected and fed into the analysis mill after Howard and Nicole Young's suits are finished will not include any reports of interviews with them nor any observations about what their experiences were like in the course of their lawsuit. That could be a shame. The professionals could be missing something. For Howard Young, in particular, his tort lawsuit might not only be about pursuing money. It could also be about pointing the finger at those who he believes helped ruin his life and about getting an explanation for what happened to him. It could also be about coming to grips with his own contributory role in the accident, about having *his* story heard, and about reestablishing a way of living in the world.

Of course, what Howard Young's tort lawsuit means for him is not the same as what his wife's lawsuit means for her or what his children's lawsuits mean for them. Nicole simply wants, *needs,* money to salvage her home, to ward off the creditors, and to reestablish some modicum of security for her family. She needs that money *now*. Neither she nor her kids may be much interested in blame.

Others will find different meanings in tort law. Different people, from different circumstances, injured in different ways, will react differently to the prospects or actualities of a tort lawsuit. Obviously, a suit's significance is drastically different for the persons who are accused of wrongdoing. For example, the driver of the subway train that injured Howard might find the lawsuit a profoundly distressing experience, as the finger of blame is pointed publicly and relentlessly in his direction. Even so, he might find the experience cathartic. For him, as for Howard, the suit could be a source of understanding and a forum for coming to terms with a horrible accident. Even so, with the city's Corporation Counsel fully in charge of the litigation, and the city the ultimate source of any money damages, the driver might find himself involved in the litigation only peripherally, in ways that hardly touch his life. In that sense, he would resemble many other individual tort defendants, insulated and isolated from responsibility for the whole affair.

Even though these tort lawsuits mean different things to different people, their significance for the people involved should not be ignored in efforts to understand or evaluate the tort system in the United States. The preceding chapters have highlighted the importance of the tort system's quantifiable outcomes: compensation, deterrence, and expense (especially transaction costs). To a significant degree, analysts can measure those outcomes in definite terms: the dollars recovered by plaintiffs or the dollars spent by the participants and society in the litigation. Being relatively easy to analyze, these outcomes constitute the dominant features of most analysis of tort law. Even those who are most active in that analysis acknowledge, however, that such analyses are incomplete—that attention must be paid to justice and injustice. After all, we are dealing with what purports to be a system of justice. And justice is hard to quantify.

We are also dealing with a system that is chockablock with people. Real people—many (but not all, let it be admitted) with real injuries—are the source of all the outcomes that analysts measure. These people go into the tort system—initiate it, in fact—for many reasons, and then have many different experiences with it. Those of us who watch and listen have a variety of experiences as well. Our experiences provide information about the significance of tort law that may deserve as much attention as does information that is more easily quantified. In thinking about what happens in a tort suit to the Howard and Nicole Youngs and the train drivers and Transit Authorities of the world, we may better understand what it is about tort law that grips us and others enough to merit prime-time television attention.

Individual plaintiffs like Howard and Nicole Young are the people for whom a tort lawsuit most obviously has significance beyond the dollar outcome. Tort law's adherents argue that the lawsuit can help them cope with the serious injuries that have befallen them. Howard Young's life has been shattered; money can help to rebuild it, but dollars alone will do only so much to repair Howard's self-esteem, ease his bewilderment, or soothe what may be his sense of violation and outrage. His entire experience in his tort lawsuit, on the other hand, it is argued, may help to rehabilitate Howard in those ways at the same time it rehabilitates his pocketbook; the tort system may allow him to tell his story of the accident and be heard, perhaps restore some of his sense of control over his world, help him acquire important understanding of what has happened to him, vindicate him while permitting him retribution, and assist him to develop important social relationships that provide him power and a fuller sense of community. Each of these rehabilitative pieces needs exploration in order to understand the potential significance of a tort lawsuit for Howard Young and other victims of accidents.

Tort law's adherents argue that it offers victims of accidents at least the hope of an opportunity to tell their stories in a setting where they are closely listened to. Many plaintiffs who believe they have been wronged emphasize that it is important to them to tell their stories, to "have my day in court." One of the main themes of the many veterans who sued chemical companies for exposing them to Agent Orange during their duty in Vietnam—themes expressed in testimony by them and their wives in opposition to the proposed settlement of the massive class-action suit—was that they were being denied their opportunity to tell their stories. Plaintiffs in sex abuse cases have reported their beliefs that telling about their abuse, in a formal legal setting, will allow them to stop reliving its trauma.[1] Tort victims tell their story in a special way, in the context of an official claim for redress of their injuries. Skilled, powerful professionals like P. J. Cowcroft listen ever-so-carefully to victims' stories, and then help to present those stories to others with a force and lucidity beyond the capacity of the victims themselves.

For tort law adherents, then, not only can the system facilitate a particularly strong "telling" of one's story, it also can provide a forum in which the teller is particularly likely to be heard. With their lawyer at their side, Nicole and Howard Young are listened to much more respectfully by insurance claims adjusters, by the defendants allegedly responsible for their injuries, and by judges, juries, and other legal officials. The party accused of wronging them has to sit and listen to what they have to say. Being listened to may give Howard and Nicole the same feelings of dignity and respect that all of us feel when persons of substance listen to what we say about matters of importance to us. Moreover, in the formality of the litigation process, that listening has a different, more profound, quality than it does in ordinary social and work interactions, as important as it is for people to be listened to in these settings as well.

Equally significant to many litigants, tort proponents argue, may be the measure of control over their lives that they begin to assert—or reassert—in a tort lawsuit. Before his injury, for all his insecurities, Howard Young felt that he had a significant amount of control over his life's course, and over his family's lives as well. Whether Howard was right or wrong to have those feelings may be a conundrum in American society, where the Horatio Alger myth competes vigorously and constantly with the fatalism of "shit happens" bumper stickers. But many observers regard an emphasis on personal control over one's general environment as one of the defining characteristics of American culture.[2] Certainly, there is little doubt that many if not most of us strive mightily to assert control over what happens in our lives. We work hard to achieve and maintain a firm base on which to stand in life. That base is an understanding of ourselves as the ones in charge.

A serious accident like Howard's seriously erodes that base. The outside world has intruded into the very essence of his individual autonomy: control over his own body. He no longer can earn a living. His network of social relationships, from his family to his workplace, has been seriously diminished. After a serious injury, no matter how much "in charge" an individual had been, he is likely to feel and be in charge of very little, at least temporarily.

A tort lawsuit, the system's proponents contend, can assist victims like Howard to regain some of that important sense of being in charge. In the first place, the lawsuit tries to examine the events that led to the plaintiff's injury and organize them into a rational framework. Regardless of the verdict, the suit itself purports to assign responsibility for the injury based on a legally structured calculation of who was in control of the events and how their failings brought about the accident. While the lawsuit is in the planning and action stages, the plaintiff is actually *doing something* about his or her injury—perhaps for the first time. His actions—with the aid of his lawyer—make powerful forces react, pay attention, and respond with explanations of their own for what happened.

Adding to the plaintiff's sense of control, tort partisans argue, is the lawsuit's role in helping an injured person acquire an understanding of precisely what has happened to him and why. When bad things happen to them, people want an explanation. At a recent funeral in New York City, for a mother accidentally shot as motorists quarreled, a priest articulated a common response: "Our first instinct is to ask, 'Why?' . . . Our minds are logical. Our minds want to know reasons. . . . I'm not sure there is even a reason why to know. But if we could know the cause, then we could control it."[3] Interviews with plaintiffs in lawsuits claiming discriminatory treatment reveal that their suits largely reflect the victim's efforts to learn "Why is this happening to me?"[4]

Tort lawsuits, then, can help to provide explanations and valuable understandings. Like other persons injured badly enough to be able to interest a lawyer in their case, the Youngs can count on an investigation into the circumstances of their injuries that arguably will be far superior to any that they or any governmental agency could conduct. P. J. Cowcroft is expert in the assignment of responsibility for accidents. Whether acting for a professional like Howard Young or for a farmer or factory worker, Ms. Cowcroft as a matter of course provides the tough questioning of others involved with an accident that can help to uncover the full story of what happened. Absent such lawyer involvement, injured persons usually find that their own frailties and the social distance that often exists between them and the people or institutions who injured them keep them from asking even moderately challenging questions, much less the probing questions that are the stock in trade of experienced plaintiffs' lawyers. Moreover, the tort plaintiff may undergo extensive medical and psychological evaluations necessary to support his damage claims. His lawyer will use her skills as a professional storyteller to help the plaintiff weave the extensive information gathered into a comprehensible story of his accidental injury and subsequent existence. To withstand challenge, that story should be solidly anchored in reality (although, of course, it will be constructed in the light most favorable to the plaintiff). In preparing to tell that story in a public setting and in the face of professional skepticism, the plaintiff may acquire a different and fuller understanding of what has befallen him.

What this acquisition of understanding and enhanced feeling of control mean to Howard Young and others like him is uncertain and unquantifiable. Tort law's adherents argue that it is important, particularly for those whom tragedy has touched, to have such perceptions. Some believe that understanding what has happened and developing a renewed sense of control are necessary parts of the healing process for those who have been seriously injured. For Elissa and Laura Young, for example, it is argued, the tort lawsuit may be an important stage in the grieving process, as they tell about the loss of their father-who-was and thus reconcile themselves in a fashion to their present lives. Before Howard Young can begin to deal productively with the world again, tort proponents maintain, he needs to trust that world somewhat: it must become sufficiently controllable so that he need not be terrified of further injury. It may even be valuable in encouraging his reengagement with the world for Howard to hear officially the extent to which he is responsible for his own predicament. But at the same time he may come to grips with the fact that he was not totally, perhaps not even primarily, to blame; others may be shown to be blameworthy as well, as his lawyer and expert witnesses try to put his lapses in the context of a day of professional trauma.

Of course, feelings of confusion and loss of control may not be all that injured persons bring to a tort lawsuit. They can also bring anger—huge, sometimes unmanageable anger at what has been done to them. They can carry with them a sense of having been violated and feelings of outrage at that violation. One victim of a man-made disaster told a researcher that he felt the "way someone who has been sentenced to prison for a crime he did not commit" must have felt. Unlike persons injured by random accidents, illness, or natural forces, those injured by another's wrongdoing often feel diminished—well beyond the reduction in their physical capacities. In the eyes of such a victim, the injurer has demeaned him by treating him less respectfully than he deserved. Insult has been added to injury. (Admittedly, though, tort law's critics might point out that, as Howard Young's own conduct indicates, casting blame can be a complex process psychologically, with its burdens as well as benefits.)

The tort lawsuit, then, can contain the hope of vengeance and vindication for tort victims. The plaintiff calls the alleged wrongdoer into a very formal public setting to account for the wrongs arguably done him. At the worst, the alleged wrongdoer has to respond. At best, the plaintiff earns a favorable settlement, or even a victory at trial, either of which can carry strong connotations—if not explicit statements—of wrongdoing on the defendant's part. Regardless of victory in the lawsuit, the plaintiff, proponents of the system argue, has fought back against those he believes victimized him; victory, of course, allows him to exult in the defeat of the enemy and his own vindication.

Tort law's adherents contend that the availability of vengeance and vindication can contribute significantly to the value of lawsuits for the injured: tort litigation allows these accident victims and their families to express anger in a socially acceptable manner—to "sue the bastards." They don't have to silence their anger. They can attack—and hurt—the wrongdoer without having to give physical vent to the violent aspects of their impulses. They can gain revenge on the injurer without having to perform acts of punishment that they and others might well find immoral.

Insofar as they can act in this socially accepted way to avenge the wrongs they believe done them, accident victims and their families avoid having to bottle their anger inside them. Such repressed anger can fester. Unexpressed, it may emerge in troublesome ways: in private acts of vengeance, in the further disruption of the victim's important ongoing relationships, in retreats into isolation. Instead, victims of wrongdoing can gain deep satisfaction from defeating the wrongdoer in court; that public, formal defeat—against the wrongdoer's will—signifies in a very concrete manner, easily understood by plaintiffs, that the victim is the equal or superior of the wrongdoer. Giving someone who hurt you his just desserts can be importantly satisfying to persons for whom anger has been a strong, chronic emotion.

Side by side with vengeance in tort lawsuits, argue the system's adherents, goes vindication, and with it the opportunity for injured persons to regain some of the self-respect they have lost in the process of being wronged. The psychiatrist Bruno Bettelheim emphasized that recovery from victimization requires a process of reintegration, whereby the victim takes an active role in reestablishing a nonvictim relationship with the injurer. Comments by tort claimants often emphasize the desire for public vindication as a motivating factor in their decisions to sue. By having the reality of their injuries and the wrong done them acknowledged in official ways, tort claimants are, it is argued, validated in ways that can contribute significantly to the restoration of their damaged self-esteem.[5]

Finally, tort law adherents argue that the lawsuit may provide injured persons empowering access to social relations which their injuries have substantially curtailed. Serious injury tends to isolate people. They can't go to work. They often cannot leave hospital or home for a long time. Their preinjury social networks dwindle, from the victim's neglect or the discomfort of the nonvictims or both. The major event in the victim's life—his accident and injury—is at most a peripheral part of his friends' lives. A tort lawsuit may help the plaintiff to get past his timidity, confusion, and anger to get on productively with his life. In some instances, moreover—particularly in mass tort cases where many persons have been similarly injured—an injured person gains access through tort law to a community of similar victims. Families of the passengers who died when Pan Am Flight 103 exploded, for example, banded together around the identification of themselves as victims, with a commitment to doing something about that victimization. In many such instances a tort lawsuit can serve as a major vehicle for introducing these people to each other and for organizing ameliorative efforts. In the context of large numbers of similar tort lawsuits, injured people may find a social community of persons who share victimization as a central defining issue in their lives, yet who come together in a powerful setting, in which they are acting strongly to remedy the harm done them. It allows them to establish a camaraderie not *just* of victimhood, but also of power and action.

Tort law adherents also contend that these suits are not for the plaintiffs alone. Those who have escaped injury may likewise benefit from the lawsuits of people like Howard and Nicole Young in less obvious ways. Beyond the arguable deterrence to unsafe behavior discussed in Chapter 4, tort lawsuits provide a number of intangible benefits for the great majority of Americans who do not sue: those lawsuits purport to educate all of us—and particularly lawmakers and those who create danger—about life's hazards and about responsibility for them. These tort lawsuits can boost our morale by affirming our own value; they can, tort's proponents contend, increase the sense of many of us that we have a shared ownership of law in America.

Just as Howard Young's lawsuit may help him acquire a fuller understanding of his world of injury, tort law's adherents argue that his and others' lawsuits can help the rest of us understand the world of dangers—those myriad parts of our world that can become accidents: at the most basic level, tort law purports to help us understand what we have to watch out for—what is dangerous. Women in the United States now think differently about intrauterine devices, based on newsworthy tort litigation. Unions, schools, and individual citizens have become more alert to the presence of carcinogenic dangers in certain environments, in part because cancer victims have claimed in tort lawsuits that these exposures caused their diseases.

More generally, tort law's adherents argue as follows: tort lawsuits can help us all understand differently the meaning of everyday events and injuries. The claims made in lawsuits, and the law's treatment of them, can change how we think about accidents. Holding the Transit Authority liable for the actions of its train operator—the tort law doctrine of vicarious liability—can goad us to understand certain kinds of accidents as characteristic of subway transport, rather than to think of them as isolated, unrelated events. Injuries that occur to assembly line workers when safety guards have been removed from industrial machinery can be understood as cases of individual stupidity by workers who prefer to take chances; on the other hand, after tort claims urged by such injured workers, they may be understood as characteristic of workplaces in which safety becomes optional and in which workers may have little realistic choice about self-protection. Similarly, poisonings resulting from the leakage of hazardous substances from toxic waste dumps could be understood as inevitable concomitants of essentially safe activities. Or, with the help of tort claimants, those injuries could be understood as the products of activities that are abnormally dangerous—so dangerous, in fact, that some courts go so far as to hold dump operators strictly liable for any injuries their sites cause regardless of how carefully the operators may have behaved. So, too, tort lawsuits that hold entities which design and build roads liable for some automobile accidents may help us understand more fully the forces that underlie what appear on the surface to be accidents resulting only from driver error. In each of these situations, tort lawsuits by injured individuals, proponents of the system argue, force the law to deal with the often complex realities of particular injuries and to incorporate those realities into legal doctrines that in turn help shape people's wider perceptions of events.

For tort law's adherents, then, these lawsuits are valuable sources of fresh, more systemic perspectives on accidents. Under this view, even the most seriously injured accident victim will succeed in tort only if he can find a responsible party with enough money to pay his damages. As a result, plaintiffs' lawyers constantly face pressure to discover and understand the roles that affluent institutional actors played in the accidents that arguably injured their clients. Plaintiffs' lawyers are trained to look past the obvious causes of accidents into the network of forces that can cause injury. For example, many persons injured seriously in car accidents caused by intoxicated other drivers contacted lawyers. Often, the lawyer found out quickly that the drunk's automobile liability insurance would provide only a small fraction of the money needed to compensate his client for her injury. Accordingly, he explored other avenues of possible responsibility and brought tort claims against the business or individuals who, knowing the drunk had to drive, had supplied him with liquor, and, sometimes, against the carmakers whose inattention to safety in the design of his client's car had contributed to the injuries she suffered when a collision occurred. Such claims, even where unsuccessful in a particular case, contributed to a new way of thinking about drunk driving accidents: we began to look more deeply at how the obviously guilty individual became drunk and then became a drunk driver. We all—including ultimately even the automobile industry—began to think about car crash injuries in terms of the quality of the car as well as the quality of the driving involved. As we began to understand this kind of accident and injury as not just the product of an individual human weakness for intoxicants, society began to understand better that the injury problem might be reduced substantially through public policies about the serving of liquor and cars better equipped to withstand crashes. As plaintiffs and their lawyers regularly seek these more subtle explanations of accidents in lawsuits, tort proponents argue, all of us more regularly obtain such explanations.

Moreover, according to tort law's adherents, as a result of these lawsuits we expand our sense of responsibility for accidents, not just our understanding of how accidents happen. Tort lawsuits are one of the very few forums in our society where people talk meaningfully—seriously and concretely—about responsibility for harm. After all, in this world in which we see ourselves as the masters of our destiny—all the way from "we will conquer space" to "we will eradicate hunger" and "we will stop drugs"—accidents that cause injuries demand explanations. We seek those explanations first by looking for who is responsible, because that explanation is consistent with the common worldview that humans are in control of their lives. So tort lawsuits examine the question: "Who is responsible for this accident?" This examination takes place in the context of particular individual accidents. This means that concepts of responsibility are not merely invented at the top of the legal pyramid. These concepts work in ways that can transform and often challenge the ideas of the legal establishment. For example, the tort law of thirty years ago would have completely prevented Howard Young from getting any compensation from a negligent Transit Authority, because his own faulty behavior contributed to his accident. This was the legal doctrine of contributory negligence. Faced with individual lawsuits in which seriously injured people had been injured by glaringly negligent defendants as well as by their own foolishness, judges and (perhaps especially) juries gradually and surreptitiously altered that legal doctrine in practice. Many juries let plaintiffs win but gave them less than the full value of their injuries, to reflect their own contribution to the accident—their contributory fault. Some judges tended to create exceptions to the rule of contributory negligence in situations where they saw close up how it would otherwise work to let clearly culpable injurers completely escape responsibility for injuries they caused in part. Eventually legislators followed suit in enacting "comparative negligence" statutes, legitimizing the informal rule whereby a negligent accident victim would have his compensation lessened by the degree of his negligence compared with that of his injurer.

For tort law's adherents it is also important that the public reex-
amination of responsibility takes place in the context of individual
lawsuits because that allows the power of narratives to work on
social understanding of responsibility. In a tort lawsuit, the parties
tell their stories—often powerfully, for the parties are aided by professional storytellers: their lawyers. Everyone in the process—
judges, jurors, parties to the suit, and even those watching on *Court
TV* or encountering other reports—must deal with those stories as
they are told. Observers have long recognized the power of such
narratives in breaking down preconceptions about how the world
works. Narratives can create bridges across gaps in experience to
unite those involved in accidents with those who have not been,
bridges that can elicit empathic understanding. Such stories, it is
argued, assist tort law's decision makers and all of us in recognizing
realities in thinking about responsibility for accidents.[6]

Tort law's adherents further argue that these changed understandings that tort lawsuits foster may be critically important. First,
the attitudes of lawmakers—judges, legislators, and regulators—
and of those who create dangers (to themselves or others) toward
the problem of accidental injuries may change in productive ways.
Lawmakers and those who create danger may learn a great deal
about how accidents happen and who bears responsibility. Institutions in particular may learn from a tort lawsuit in which they *have*
to listen to the victim's story of what happened and how, and in
which they have to submit their own behavior to judgments about
its blameworthiness. Only tort law may assert with such directness
and power to a Transit Authority or some other defendant: you
committed a *wrong*. And the defendant must seriously weigh the
possibility of such a damning assessment in deciding whether to settle. Such statements can be a particularly powerful impetus to
change for an entity or person who believes in avoiding wrong.

Furthermore, tort law's adherents maintain that tort lawsuits
may, by changing understanding, encourage different reactions to
accidents among those lawmakers not directly exposed to lawsuits.
Changed social understandings of how accidents happen and where

responsibility for them lies will necessarily filter into the legal process. And more direct impact often comes from tort lawsuits' contributions to people's tendency to organize around particular issues. For example, the suit by the veterans exposed to Agent Orange in Vietnam can be seen simultaneously as a vehicle to bring veterans together around a single issue, to raise public consciousness of a serious problem, and to encourage greater legislative and administrative receptivity to the plight of suffering Vietnam veterans. Even individual lawsuits can achieve that end. Workers who bring tort lawsuits against abusive supervisors—for intentional infliction of emotional distress, for sexual harassment, or the like— can create awareness and inspire optimism among fellow workers that harmful supervisory behavior can be resisted and successfully challenged.[7]

Aside from this educational role, the argument continues, the threat of tort claims may be valuable for the noninjured in several ways. First, the existence of tort law gives us some power in relation to those whose conduct creates danger. A parent who walks to her daughter's school and notices that no one has removed ice from regularly traveled stairs there can mention that at the principal's office. Finding the same problem days later, she need not experience the typical feelings of powerlessness that so many feel when trying to deal with school or other bureaucracies. She can subtly mention to the principal how the family of some child who fell on those steps could sue the school district for a lot of money. Or she can forgo subtlety and threaten to sue the principal, the janitors, and the school if anything happens to her kids. Either way, the availability of tort law can alter our sense—and perhaps the actuality—of power in situations that pose danger to us or others. Furthermore, successes by tort plaintiffs can help other victims better understand that it may not have been only fate or their own failings that led to their injuries. Some observers have noted that for all the litigation in our society, individuals still tend to make claims for compensation at a far lower rate than that at which people are injured. They have explained that low claiming rate as due, at least in part, to people's tendency to see themselves at fault when they get hurt. Insofar as tort lawsuits remind them of the responsibility of others, they may be more likely to take action to remedy wrongs done them. The more action that is taken, the more victims and potential victims will tend not to see themselves as helpless.

Second, the argument goes, tort lawsuits may boost society's morale. Like criminal law, tort law purports to make formal statements about wrongful conduct when it renders judgments. Philosophers have long argued that this official condemnation of wrongdoing can contribute to social cohesion. It also can give satisfaction, the way ceremonies such as funerals do, by honoring a concept of fair treatment that we hold dear.[8] Like other ceremonies, tort lawsuits may make important statements to us that society values "us," the ordinary people. The crescendo of successful lawsuits by asbestos workers may have unmanageably clogged the courts, but to tort law adherents it also spoke loudly that big corporations were not going to get away with poisoning "us" workers. According to the tort law's adherents, the lawsuits by women whose bodies were allegedly invaded by producers of DES and Dalkon Shields may remind us that women can be systematically abused in this country, but they also powerfully remind us that those producers needn't get away with violating "us" women. So, too, argue tort law adherents, "us" veterans and "us" ordinary consumers can get a lift when giant multinational corporations are disciplined by tort law for exposing troops to Agent Orange or for exposing motorists to cars and trucks that are insufficiently safe.

Third, the argument goes, the noninjured benefit because tort lawsuits increase our sense of shared ownership of the law. People see law as a tremendously powerful force in America. Witness our statements to children that they have to buckle seatbelts because it is the law. Lawsuits and trials can remind us about the law and the ability of normal people like ourselves to use it. Tort lawsuits can give us a sense that this law is *our* law. Like the mother who complains about icy stairs to a school principal, we realize that we may gain redress from someone who can hurt us. We carry that little piece of power with us wherever we go. If we notice danger, and can have our fears soothed by the knowledge that those who create dangers will be less careless, lest we litigate, then we may well feel some affinity with the judges and lawyers who produce tort law. That affinity can enhance our sense of belonging in a powerful way in our community. (Not long ago a sophisticated Scandinavian declared how much he resented the relative immunity enjoyed by health care providers from being held liable under his country's sluggish tort law for even egregious acts of malpractice. "There may be problems with your medical malpractice law," he lamented, "but I envy you for it.") Conservatives and others in the United States who advocate more "empowerment" of people ought, under this view, embrace tort law.

But let it be quickly acknowledged that there is plenty of controversy about whether tort lawsuits in fact do all that the law's proponents claim they do for the injured plaintiffs themselves and for the rest of us. The rosy picture that tort law's partisans paint of its potential for enriching lives and understandings may obscure the law's darker sides, both for injured persons and for society. Tort law's critics point out that there are substantial indications that some tort litigation actually increases the hurt of the victims of accidents; likewise, tort litigation increases the hurt of even victorious accused wrongdoers. The book *Automobile Accident Costs and Payments* by Alfred Conard and James Morgan quotes claimants caught up in personal injury automobile accident litigation.

> "They were trying to humiliate me for a quick settlement."
> "If I had been financially able, I would have held out longer."
> "It was too long to wait for a settlement. It seems like insurance companies prolong cases too long."
> "It was pretty miserable—justice isn't for the little man. I've had enough of courts. If you have [a] sharp lawyer, you're all set."
> "It just dragged and dragged. It threw me from being a self-supporting woman, so that I'm dependent on others."

"The settlement was unfair, but the lawyer said take it or you
  might get nothing."
"[My lawyer] wanted me to say something that wasn't true. I
  wouldn't tell a lie for money."

Of primary significance in thinking about the meaning of tort
lawsuits for the people involved is a simple fact: in every trial, some-
body loses. In many cases, the *injured person* loses. Either he loses
completely at trial or, much more often, he is told by his own lawyer
either to give up or to accept a settlement payment that he may find
inadequate. For plaintiffs, losing either way can obviously under-
mine the feelings of vengeance and vindication described above as
potential values of a tort suit. Likewise, given the vicissitudes of litigation, results that provide deserving victims of accidents with little or no compensation or (at least relatively) undeserving victims
with generous awards may demoralize the rest of us, just as, on the
one hand, the initial Rodney King beating verdict was understood
by many as a message that people of color are fair game for police
brutality and, on the other, the beating verdict in the Reginald
Denny case was understood as indicating a compensatory bias in
favor of lawless conduct by blacks against whites.

Even when a deserving plaintiff is successful in a tort lawsuit,
however, critics of tort law contend that the suit's nonmonetary
costs may outweigh any intangible benefits a plaintiff is likely to
experience. The lawsuit may actually increase the injured person's
pain. This can occur from the very outset of a tort lawsuit because
there may be considerable stigma associated with the bringing of a
tort claim. When the Youngs file their lawsuit, the headlines may
read: "Subway Drunk Sues CTA for $3M." Regardless of whether
their case ever makes the newspapers, some of their neighbors may
understand the lawsuit in those terms. Some in the Youngs' community may see the lawsuit as violating strong American norms of
self-sufficiency and personal responsibility. Howard and his family
may be seen as people who "rock the boat," who try to escape
responsibility for their own actions, and as money grubbers who

seek to get rich not by dint of honest labor but by displaying their pathetic lives to overly sympathetic juries and judges. Even injured persons whose accidents were not caused by any misbehavior of their own may experience such reactions. American culture continues to possess a strong, probably dominant strain of individual responsibility, which frequently causes negative reactions when people turn to the courts to blame others for their misfortunes. Those negative reactions tend to be exaggerated when, as with tort lawsuits, the person trying to shift blame also seems to be trying to "get something for nothing."[9] All of this is exacerbated by many documented instances, insist critics of tort law, of padded and even fraudulent assertion of tort claims.

Once past the initial filing hurdle, the plaintiff can run into many other painful obstacles, including some created by his own lawyer. Tort lawsuits, in the eyes of lawyers, demand strategic presentation of a party's case. One common strategy for a plaintiff's lawyer is to depict his client as a victim. Howard Young may be portrayed as extraordinarily helpless. In the course of his lawsuit, he may be helped and encouraged to emphasize how terribly disabled and powerless he has become. He may be constantly on display, all but wearing a sandwich declaring, "My life is ruined." Should Howard Young countenance such a strategy, the lawsuit seems unlikely to produce in him the sense of being back in charge of his life, even if he wins. Research by Lester Keiser, chief of neuropsychiatry at Hollywood Florida's Memorial Hospital, found that the "ensuing wrangles with claims adjusters and lawyers" of the tort system intensifies the nervous strain expressed by accident victims. People can get so absorbed in nursing their symptoms as they pursue their claims that their lives are adversely altered further.[10]

Such a disempowering strategy relates as well to the importance stressed above that tort plaintiffs be able to tell their own story. What are told in a tort lawsuit are several different—adversarial— stories. The defense also tells a story about the plaintiff and his accident, one that the plaintiff will scarcely find lyrical. In Howard

Young's case, the defense story will be about Howard the drunk, who threw away his family's future just to indulge his soiled vanity with too much to drink. Should the trial focus on each of the Youngs' damages, the story told by the defense and its witnesses may get unpleasant—even nasty. It may tell of a Howard who might not have amounted to much as a lawyer anyway—for that story will reduce the amount of money Howard would get to compensate him for lost earnings. The story may even tell of Howard's failures as a husband and father, or of possible strained relationships in the Young family before the accident—for that story could reduce the amounts Nicole and the children receive for the loss of Howard's love and companionship. When he tries to tell his story, Howard's credibility and competence—at both remembering and telling—can be challenged at every turn. Even when not challenged by the defense, Howard's story may be manipulated by his own side's needs. Howard may not be allowed to explain his own anguished feelings of responsibility for what happened. He may have to suppress whatever responsibility he may bear for his misfortune and wear the mask of an innocent man, whose momentary slip could not have been foreseen. In the service of his case, Howard's understanding of reality may be radically truncated and edited so that the story he finally tells bears little resemblance to "his" true story.

A trial—even a deposition, a formal question-and-answer session of witnesses before trial by opposing lawyers with no judge present—is usually a bruising experience for injured persons. Not only do they have to continually parade their inability to take care of themselves before strangers who are not necessarily sympathetic, but, as suggested, they may also have to endure their adversary's efforts to mitigate—even perhaps belittle—their suffering and, where possible, to portray them as unsympathetic individuals. Some idea of the maelstrom that litigation can stir up for parties or witnesses caught in its vortex is conveyed in the following transcript from a deposition of an exchange between the country's most successful plaintiffs' lawyer, Joseph Jamail, and defense lawyer Edward

Carstarphen. The dispute between counsel concerned, among other things, Carstarphen's objections to Jamail's questions of the defense witness.

> *Jamail:* You don't run this deposition, you understand?
> *Carstarphen:* Neither do you, Joe.
> *Jamail:* You watch and see. You watch and see who does, Big Boy. . . . And don't be telling other lawyers to shut up. That isn't your goddamned job, Fat Boy.
> *Carstarphen:* Well that's not your job, Mr. Hairpiece.
> *The Witness:* As I said before, you have an incipient—
> *Jamail:* What do you want to do about it, asshole?
> *Witness:* I'd like to knock you on your ass.
> *Jamail:* Come over here and try it, you dumb son of a bitch. Come over here. . . .
> *Carstarphen:* You're not going to bully this guy.
> *Jamail:* Oh, you big fat tub of shit, sit down.
> *Carstarphen:* I don't care how many of you come up against me.
> *Jamail:* Oh, you big fat tub of shit, sit down. Sit down, you fat tub of shit.[11]

Even if a sensitive and competent plaintiff's lawyer like P. J. Cowcroft manages to sustain Howard and his family through the slings and arrows of litigation, through delays that may seem interminable, and helps Howard to tell "his" story rather than one constructed by other forces, the Youngs may well find the process more destructive than constructive. Tort litigation may be a way for plaintiffs to come to grips with what has happened to them, but it may instead be a way to prevent them from letting go of what happened to them. The litigation, which will insist that they revisit Howard's accident again and again, may well tend to keep their injuries alive more intensely than if they had not sued. Just as there are reasons to believe that the tort lawsuit is an injured person's healthy response of "doing something about it," there are reasons to believe that the lawsuit can represent an unhealthy response of "wallowing in it."[12]

Of course, however poorly plaintiffs do in their tort lawsuits, they at least have the ability to opt out. Defendants do not. If an injured person perceives that his tort lawsuit will be particularly unpleasant, he need not bring it or he can discontinue it. Those accused of wrongdoing have no such luxury. Once hailed into the lawsuit, they must take their lumps until they win, lose, settle, or are allowed out. There is no question that being sued for having negligently or intentionally injured someone is a most unpleasant and bruising experience. Most of the fury that health care professionals exhibit whenever a discussion turns to lawyers undoubtedly emanates from the pain they feel or think they will feel if sued.[13] Admittedly, a high percentage of tort lawsuits involve actions either against corporations or governments, and an even higher percentage are borne ultimately by insurance companies. Even so, individual motorists, corporate employees, and especially health care providers feel the sting of being the objects of a public accusatory process. Victory may help vindicate such defendants, but it can't wipe out the prolonged agony of having to defend oneself. And defense victories rarely if ever grab the attention that huge plaintiffs' claims or victories do.

Doubts, then, about tort law's advantages include the suspicion both that some of these benefits may not exist for many accident victims and that even where they exist they may be inadequate.

Among the tort lawsuit's nonmonetary benefits about which we have speculated is the possibility that it can help the injured person regain some of his sense of being in charge of his life. But tort law's critics contend that a suit may often reemphasize the plaintiff's lack of control. In the massive number of cases brought by workers injured by exposure to asbestos, for example, many litigants felt that they had little or no say over how their cases were handled.[14] This need not mean, of course, that the plaintiff will not experience some enhancement of his sense of being in charge from the power of the lawsuit alone and its characteristics of organizing, investigating, and assigning responsibility. Nevertheless, tort law critics insist, we need to acknowledge that the system's potential contribution to feelings of empowerment can often be diluted, or even undone, by contrary feelings.

Similarly, tort law critics point to the possibility that a tort suit will provide the injured person with neither vengeance nor vindication. Obviously, a plaintiff will find no revenge or vindication from a lost lawsuit. And plaintiffs lose a substantial number of their lawsuits, in the range of half—or more—of those that go to trial. Although they may receive some payment in settlement of their claims in a significantly higher percentage of claims, tort plaintiffs may clearly find those settlements far less satisfying or vindicating. Settlements are private in nature and usually include continued formal denial of wrongdoing by the defendant ("solely in the interest of avoiding further legal expense . . . "). Further, settlement amounts, always long delayed, may seem insignificant compared with the magnitude of the damage done to claimants' lives. And litigants in the Agent Orange, asbestos, and other mass torts have bitterly criticized the amounts paid to lawyers compared with what the claimants themselves received.

Benefits that tort partisans have suggested exist for the rest of us—the society of uninjured persons—may also be exaggerated. Tort law's critics admit that lawsuits can undoubtedly be powerful educators about accidents and responsibility, but they point out that whenever something educates there is the risk that it miseducates. Greater understanding that electromagnetic fields may hold dangers for those regularly exposed may be valuable knowledge. Yet greater "understanding" can also convince us that using cellular telephones causes brain cancer. That recent scare was inspired by the filing of one tort lawsuit. It sent the stock prices of at least one cellular telephone manufacturer into a tailspin, apparently with no concrete basis for the link between cellular telephoning and the clusters of cancers that have arisen. Likewise, the Audi car manufacturer claimed that it was forced to stop production of one of its models because of a wave of lawsuits about its gearshift mechanism that turned out to be groundless. Similarly, tort law's critics argue that the dangers of breast implants trumpeted by litigation have been grossly exaggerated, as have, they assert, those associated with GM pickup trucks—exaggerations, it is asserted, orchestrated by plaintiffs' lawyers and expert witnesses in their hire.

And although tort lawsuits may boost our morale when we see those who injure "us" get their just desserts, they may demoralize others when they see people getting rich from injury claims. If little Elissa and Laura Young receive large sums for the loss of their father's love and companionship, they may become quite wealthy. To other families, their wealth may appear to denigrate values of self-reliance and hard work that they have struggled for years to develop. Certainly it is not unheard of for many people in a community to react with resentment when relatives of disaster victims take to the courts to "cash in" on their losses.[15]

Furthermore, even if the eagerness of many people to pursue tort claims and the resultant changes in social attitudes about responsibility for accidents are regarded as impressive evidence that tort lawsuits do in fact contribute to the betterment of the lives of both individual plaintiffs and society in general, questions remain about such "betterment." As outlined earlier, tort law is a very expensive, acrimonious, dilatory, haphazard, and expensive way to deal with injury victims' claims for compensation. As was the case in our earlier considerations of other possibly positive effects of tort law—compensation, deterrence, and justice—the psychological and educational benefits that tort law might provide must be very significant before they can justify the heavy costs of an accusatory fault-based system for determining injury-related controversies. Moreover, those significant benefits must outweigh the psychological and educational costs that the tort system itself imposes on both those who sue and are sued.

Unfortunately, we know too little about these "human" dimensions of tort law to draw any confident conclusions about the value of lawsuits for the people involved or for the rest of us. Perhaps, in the end, the only conclusion we can reach with confidence is that society must struggle even harder to appraise the human benefits and burdens of tort law—and the various forms it can take—if its overall value in society is to be accurately assessed and dealt with.

One further note here: the psychological impact of tort lawsuits may become more obvious if we examine the different roles of an alleged victim in a tort case and in criminal litigation arising out of the same incident. Because sexual abuse cases have sometimes involved both tort and criminal proceedings, they may usefully illustrate common differences. In the criminal trial, the state—acting through a prosecutor employed by the government—will have its lawyer, as will the defendant accused of a crime. The allegedly abused person will be interviewed by the prosecutor but will have virtually no control over the way in which the litigation is carried out. Frequently, the criminal case is settled by an agreement, a plea bargain, solely between the prosecutor on the one hand and the accused and his lawyer on the other. Furthermore, the victim of even a convicted abuser has no say in the punishment eventually meted out to the abuser—unless she resides in one of the small number of jurisdictions in which victims are invited to make statements at the time of sentencing. In contrast, the accused abuser stands at the center of the proceeding. Before anything happens to him, a jury must find *beyond a reasonable doubt* that he unlawfully abused the victim. His—and society's—interests in avoiding convicting an innocent man generally trump the alleged victim's interests. And even in deciding to sentence a convicted abuser, the court is likely to center its attention on the defendant and his characteristics as much as on the events for which he is punished.

In contrast to the peripheral participation of the alleged victim in the criminal proceeding, the tort system highlights the alleged victim at least as much as the alleged abuser. The plaintiff need only prove that the defendant *probably* abused her unlawfully. In cases such as sexual abuse, where the evidence is often the plaintiff's word against the defendant's, this easier requirement of proof makes it much less likely that an actual abuser will win the litigation. Of course, given the vicissitudes of litigation, it also makes it more likely that an innocent defendant will lose the case.[16] Moreover, in a tort case the alleged victim can control her own case. She has her own lawyer and can press the case or not. But this "control," without the filter of a prosecutor's discretion, can also mean that frivolous or even fraudulent claims can be pressed in the hopes of exacting a settlement from a defendant anxious to avoid the unpleasantness of answering a foul but false accusation. So the claimant's control is a double-edged sword.

Indeed, the current tort system, according to its critics, is riddled with corruption. It provides both adversaries, claimant and defendant, with incentives to exaggerate and even cheat—and they do so. As a result, it is argued, society loses in spades. RAND's Institute for Civil Justice estimates—as does the FBI—that pain and suffering claims, often based on a multiple of medical bills incurred (and usually paid by one's fringe benefit health insurance), produce huge and unnecessary health care expenditures.[17]

There are four distinct types of cheating committed by claimants: phony claims, staged accidents, jump-ins, and exaggerated claims.

In phony claims, neither the accident nor the injury actually occurs. An individual procures a damaged vehicle, for example, plus a tractor-trailer's license number, and sends the trucking company a phony accident report claiming that the tractor-trailer forced the vehicle off of the road. Photographs of the vehicle are enclosed to verify the report. In cases of staged accidents, an accident occurs, but little or no actual injury results. One common method of staging accidents is to cruise a wealthy neighborhood in a car full of occupants, searching for (preferably) a woman who is backing her car out of a driveway while distracted by small children. The "stage" car will cross behind her in order to be hit. The "victims" blame the woman, and their common story not only helps to "prove" that it is the woman's fault but also allows multiple (and inflated) claims to be filed against her insurer. Perhaps the most popular staged accident is the "swoop and squat" maneuver, which involves a minimum of three vehicles. The target vehicle—once again perhaps a young mother with her offspring in the car, or a truck (to take advantage of its slow maneuverability and high liability insurance limits)—is spotted driving along a multilane highway. The "swoop" vehicle makes a lane change in front of the cooperating "squat" car. The squat car then stops suddenly in front of the following target vehicle. Often a fourth vehicle, also part of the team, rides alongside the target vehicle to prevent a lane change. The resulting accident is the "fault" of the driver of the target vehicle, and the multiple occupants of the squat car (carefully belted) once again file phony and inflated claims.[18]

In a jump-in—which involves a real accident, but no injury— "ghost riders," who were never in the colliding vehicles, quickly board one of the vehicles, preferably a bus, to file false insurance claims, aided by unscrupulous lawyers, doctors, and chiropractors.[19]

Finally, some real accidents and real injuries produce exaggerated claims. Because "pain and suffering" damages are generally calculated as a multiple of medical bills, there is the incentive on the part of an injured claimant to pad those bills. Insurance fraud is lucrative not only for claimants, who receive several times their economic loss, but for doctors (especially chiropractors), who receive inflated payments, and for lawyers who receive their percentage contingent fee from a larger settlement. The RAND study distinguishes between hard injuries that are objectively verifiable—for example, the loss of a limb or a fracture detected by an X ray—and soft injuries like sprains and strains that are not usually objectively verifiable and thus present an opportunity to exaggerate their existence or seriousness. Under no-fault auto insurance laws in effect in New York and Michigan, the profit has been largely drained from unnecessary medical bills. RAND found that in those two states there are seven soft injury claims for every ten hard injury claims. In Hawaii, whose no-fault law provides a greater incentive for exaggerating claims, there are nine soft injury claims for every ten hard injury claims. But in California, a state without any no-fault law, where the tort system is therefore unimpeded by any barrier to tort claims, there are twenty-five soft injury claims for every ten hard ones.

In Massachusetts, after its automobile no-fault law was amended in 1988 to require a higher threshold of economic damages before tort claims would be allowed, the median number of treatment visits per claim for automobile injuries rose radically the next year from thirteen to thirty per claim, a 131 percent increase. Similarly, a study in Hawaii of 1990 auto tort claims revealed that the median number of treatment visits by claimants to chiropractors is a remarkable fifty-eight, with one-quarter of such claimants having more than eighty-four visits. The RAND study found that with a barrier of $1,000 in medical bills necessary before a tort claim could be brought, Hawaii claims peaked just above the $1,000 threshold, strongly suggesting widespread "build-ups" to exceed the statutory threshold.

But not all the cheating is done by claimants: insurers also have incentives under tort law to cheat. Motorists are often unaware that they can expect payment of roughly three times their medical bills for their pain and suffering. This being the case, ambulance-chasing insurance adjusters rival ambulance-chasing lawyers to reach the accident victim first. If the former win the race, they can cheat the victim in several ways. An adjuster can misrepresent the law and settle the claim for a fraction of its worth—refusing, for example, to pay for treatment already covered by health insurance (contrary to the law in many states) or to pay anything for pain and suffering. An insurance adjuster can even assure a potential but unsophisticated claimant that the insurer will eventually settle the case and then stall until the statute of limitations has expired. The terminology of insurance claims tells the story of chicanery on both sides all too graphically. Insurers characterize cases as "under control" or "out of control," depending upon whether the claimant has yet consulted a lawyer. An "out of control" claimant represents an exponentially increased risk of exaggerated medical expense and wage loss. But if a claim is "under control," an insurer is freer to stall, hoping that unfavorable witnesses to the accident will die, move away, or suffer fading memory—or, in the case of serious accident victims, that the victim's desperate need for medical treatment and wage replacement will drive him to settle for relatively little.

The RAND study addressed not only excess claims for pain and suffering but also the excess size of claims due to padding on valid soft injury claims. RAND estimates that such illicit claiming costs insurers $9–13 billion annually in compensation for noneconomic loss and other costs, which in turn adds $100 to $130 annually to every auto insurance policy.

But not all the padding is due to claimants' marginal behavior. A reputable claimant's lawyer may find that unless he keeps his client incurring medical bills, whether marginally necessary or not, an insurer, knowing its ultimate exposure through the stabilized condition of the claimant—and knowing also that a claimant must wait years to get to court for the sum certain involved—will often offer relatively meager amounts in settlement. Similarly, an insurer may harass a claimant's lawyer with unnecessary motions and depositions to cut into the profit from the lawyer's contingent fee. To put it bluntly, institutional tort defendants wail long and loud about "frivolous claims" while ignoring the often equally pernicious problem of "frivolous defenses."

A tort law specialist tells the following tale, illustrating how improper insurance intransigence can itself cause false claims:

> One early evening I was in my backyard cooking on the grill when my neighbor—a doctor as well as a friend—came over and apologetically said to me, "Hank, I hate to bother you with this, but my wife's car was hit from behind when she was stopped at a red light many weeks ago. I promptly submitted the car repair bill to the other driver's insurer as I was told to do. I have called the company representative about the matter many times, but can't get *any* response. They won't even return my calls. What should I do?"
>
> "What you should do, Jerry, is call one more time and leave this message with the adjuster's secretary—don't record it on an

answering machine: 'Are you going to pay for my wife's car, or do I tell you about her bad back?'"

"Oh my God, Hank, there's nothing wrong with my wife's back, and I don't want to get involved in *that* game!"

"No, Jerry, you don't understand. The words I'm asking you to utter are not meant to be literally true. They are really a sort of incantation—a war dance, if you like. You utter these words—almost like rattling a spear—and that will cause a responding little dance from the adjuster."

The doctor did as he was told and, sure enough, within days a check for the car damage arrived.

A related tale: For years some insurance companies kept a limitation clause in their uninsured motorist coverage, under which an insurer agrees to pay damages to its own policyholder whose car is hit by a negligent uninsured motorist. The clause provided that the coverage would be exhausted by any payments from the policyholder's health insurance, even if the losses exceeded the amount of that coverage. In one case, for example, the uninsured motorist coverage limit was $10,000 and the insured suffered about $20,000 in losses. Because the insured received $10,000 from health insurance, the auto policy paid nothing, despite the additional $10,000 of losses beyond the uninsured motorist coverage limits. In jurisdiction after jurisdiction courts ruled such a clause invalid as unconscionable. But insurers nonetheless long kept the clause in their contracts, and adjusters would routinely deny claims to claimants based on the (now illegal) clause. Eventually, some knowledgeable claimants caught on, went to lawyers, and insurers often found themselves paying huge settlements to avoid angry verdicts from juries. During a deposition in the case cited above, the insurance company lawyer asked the claimant's expert witness, "Isn't it likely that an insurer, given the complexity of an automobile policy, might have just inadvertently kept the clause in the policy?" The witness replied that he would be much more inclined to believe that explanation if the insurer could point to clauses inadvertently kept in insurance policies when insurers were *losing* money on them. The insurance company's lawyer promptly ended the deposition and the matter was quickly settled for a six-figure sum, dwarfing the claimant's $10,000 damages, so fearful was the insurance company of a jury's ire.

There are also incentives on both sides to cheat at the trial itself. Some lawyers have paid witnesses to change their stories or to testify falsely that they were at the scene of an accident. One lawyer pressing lawsuits against New York City for accidents caused by improper street maintenance was prosecuted for using a shrunken ruler in an official evidence photograph in order to make a pothole appear larger.[20]

Tort law's critics contend that the system's intractable variables in proving who or what was at fault and the value of pain and suffering uniquely encourage marginal—even outright corrupt—behavior. When so much is at stake through such inherently unstable factors, bitter exploitation of the unknowns on both sides shouldn't surprise us, argue tort law's critics. The potential widespread misery—even in an open-and-shut case of tort liability—is captured by the following excerpt from a review of the best seller, *A Civil Action*, by Jonathan Harr:

> The book has the texture and narrative drive of a true-crime saga, even though it's really about the (theoretically) stodgier world of litigation. As viewers of Court TV and CNN flock to infotainment spectaculars like the O. J. Simpson murder trial, Harr's book offers troubling evidence that the most luridly dramatic stories our courts have to tell may be found not in criminal trials, but in civil ones. Maybe it will spawn a new genre: the true-lawsuit book.
>
> But Harr's book is more than just a page-turner. It's a subtle and edifying tale about how even the "best" lawsuits—those where the plaintiffs are battling a clear injustice—can create misery. And not just for the defendants, but for the plaintiffs and even—now here's the real surprise—for the plaintiffs' attorney.

At the center of the book is Jan Schlichtmann, an ambulance-chasing attorney whose obsession with the . . . case [against the deep-pocket corporate defendants Beatrice Foods and W. R. Grace for contaminating city water supplies] seems to mix equal parts of greed and idealism.

. . . Schlichtmann is a great lawyer, but he also has his meter running, and as the book progresses the reader becomes increasingly aware that the costs of proving corporate harm are consuming more and more of victory's likely spoils. This is true of all big lawsuits, but it seems especially true of [this] case, both because Schlichtmann is a maniacal perfectionist willing to spend untold sums on top experts, and because he has a taste for extravagance. Throughout the book Schlichtmann is seen renting expensive rooms in hotels like New York's Helmsley Palace and Boston's Ritz-Carlton to conduct settlement discussions. . . .

I won't spoil the book's ending . . . and reveal exactly how much of the families' booty [from a huge settlement] was gone by the time Schlichtmann's lawsuit was done. Nor will I describe precisely how ghastly is the picture that emerges of ruthless corporate [defense] lawyers and rather slow-witted and (in one instance, at least) clearly biased judges. Suffice it to say that the reader leaves *A Civil Action* convinced that a courtroom is almost never a logical place to go if you want to solve society's problems, even when justice is on your side.[21]

CHAPTER EIGHT

Context

<hr>

While scholars, policymakers, and maybe even some judges mull over the grand questions about the costs and benefits of the tort system, P. J. Cowcroft has a law practice to maintain. She has bills to pay, clients to care for, and, perhaps soon, a case to try. Last week, slightly more than two years after the Youngs first approached her, P.J. finally succeeded in convincing Judge Constance Small to set a date for the trial of the Youngs' case against the Transit Authority and the train driver. The other defendants— the bystanders who had not helped Howard as he lay on the tracks—had long ago been discharged from the lawsuit by Judge Small, who had seen no reason to deviate from the state courts' traditional rules, which rarely require other individuals to help someone in distress.

As so often happens in tort suits, settlement negotiations got serious only as trial neared. Yesterday, the lawyer for the Transit Authority presented P.J. with a new monetary offer for the Youngs if they would agree to drop their lawsuit. This settlement offer was significantly higher than any the Transit Authority had offered previously. P.J. had immediately called the Youngs and set up a meeting to discuss the pros and cons of accepting the settlement offer. Now P.J. was agonizing about what to recommend to her clients. She knew they would ask her what she thought they should do.

Often P.J. had little trouble deciding on a recommendation. Rightly or wrongly, her years as a trial specialist had left her quite comfortable estimating her clients' chances of success at trial and the level of damages a jury was likely to award if the client did win. But in the Youngs' case, politics, among other factors, was rearing its ugly head. One house of the state legislature had already passed a bill limiting the total amount of tort damages a person could collect in a lawsuit against an agency of local government. P.J. worried that if the other chamber passed—and the probusiness governor signed—such legislation in the two months before the Youngs' trial, her clients might wind up with less than a third of what they would get if they won the case under present law. No political pundit, P.J. felt uncomfortably uncertain.

Frustrated that her predictive advice to the Youngs might not be very sound, P.J. was kicking herself for not having paid more attention to the information that her state trial lawyers association had been putting out for the last five years about "tort reform." As P.J. sat doodling out the pros and cons of the Transit Authority offer, she was equally disturbed to realize that her professional future and the future of the people who came to her for help might increasingly be decided in the political arena.

P.J. felt confident about her ability to get many judges or a jury to listen and respond to her clients' tales of distress. A trial lawyer by training and disposition, P.J. felt not at all confident that she or her clients would be listened to when the legislature—the politicians—decided matters about tort law. She remembered well the dire warnings of her law partner, Nat Martin, that the glory days of plaintiffs' personal injury lawyering would soon be over. Martin had considered all the talk about the merits and demerits of the tort system to be so much hot air—those ivory-tower types were still trying to figure out how many angels can dance on the head of a pin. "Hot air doesn't do much to stop a juggernaut," Martin had said, "and so-called 'tort reform' is just that: a juggernaut that's going to crush plaintiffs just as surely as that subway train crushed that client of yours." This had never seemed truer than after the emphatically conservative, probusiness results nationwide in the 1994 elections.

Nat Martin was probably right. Widespread serious reform of tort law—by legislatures, rather than the courts—seems more and more likely in the last years of the century. In fact, some state legislatures have already been churning out significant changes in some

pieces of tort law for a decade or more. How widespread and sweeping the trend is likely to be is subject to dispute, but reform is driven
by sufficiently strong social forces that its movement through and
across at least several of the major features of current tort law seems
to many unstoppable. Accordingly, a discussion of the important
features of the law of torts would be remiss without attention to the
social and political forces at work outside the courtroom. As Nat
Martin's comments suggest, those forces provide the context in
which the debates about tort's strengths and weaknesses will be
heard, understood, considered, and acted on.

The tort system's political problems are viewed by some as quite
simple at their core. Tort lawsuits, settlements, and judgments hurt
governments, businesses, and insurance companies—and thereby at
least arguably all those who pay for goods or services. Lately, tort
lawsuits seem to be hurting those entities all the more. Because they
do not like to be hurt, they try to make tort lawsuits go away, or,
at least, hurt less. Finding the courts insufficiently helpful in eliminating or reducing their pain (though courts have been pulling in
their tort horns of late), businesses and professionals have turned
to the legislative branch and public opinion to alleviate their tort
headaches.

Some people, most notably consumer groups and plaintiffs'
lawyers, have concluded that these businesses and professionals
should have a tort headache, perhaps an even more painful one than
they now suffer. These proplaintiffs groups strongly oppose efforts
by business and professional groups to escape the pain of tort lawsuits by changing tort law. They argue that business and professional groups should instead avoid hurting people in order to reduce
their own hurt. Plaintiffs' lawyers—who primarily fuel the political
opposition to the business groups' tort reform efforts—find substantial motivation from the fact that those groups' pain is their
gain. A third or more of the money paid by businesses and professionals in tort judgments and settlements goes into the pockets of
the injured persons' lawyers, not to speak of what must be paid to

defense lawyers. Curtailment of claimants' tort rights means huge financial losses for lawyers.

When these two groups are pitted against each other in efforts to elect or influence certain legislators, to advance or retard legislation, and to influence the public's attitudes toward tort law, the law loses much claim to being a creature of careful analysis and neutral decision making. Instead, it becomes a creature of public persuasion and influence—in short, of politics. One can, of course, overstate just how magisterially neutral court-mandated tort law can be. Tort law's critics can argue that, at the state level, judges are usually elected—and the rest are selected by elected officials. Increasingly battles over judicial elections or selections are waged with partisan—indeed often bitter—participation by proplaintiff and prodefense interests. Also common is "forum shopping," whereby lawyers use flexible jurisdictorial rules to have a case heard before courts sympathetic to one side or the other. Jury selection, too, is often notoriously subject to similar jockeying to ensure bias toward one side or the other. But granting all that, the nature of pure electoral politics is probably much more nakedly partisan than court-driven law.

Once a relatively sleepy backwater—and not so long ago—tort law now seems destined to occupy the legal spotlight for quite a while. All the ingredients are there for continued political struggle over what will be the essential components of tort law. Business and professional groups are feeling and will continue to feel pain from tort lawsuits for quite some time. As their pain from tort law has increased, these groups often find legislatures and the public more susceptible than courts to their ideas about how tort lawsuits should be limited. As a result, the business groups are using their financial and political power directly to push specific legislative changes. Plaintiffs' groups shove back. The political nature of this pushing and shoving about tort law is reinforced and probably aggravated by the ways it tracks partisan Democrat-Republican politics. Business groups are also using their power indirectly, in advertising and other methods for promoting ideas among the public that tort law needs serious, probusiness reform.

Tort lawsuits are painful for businesses and professional groups in several ways. First, they feel pain because tort lawsuits cost them money. Even those whose activities are unlikely to injure anyone have to pay for or set aside funds as liability insurance—insurance that will cover them if, through a judgment or settlement of a tort claim, the law says they are liable to pay someone for her injuries. An individual motorist's expensive liability insurance may be a drop in the bucket compared with the liability insurance premiums of most professionals and businesses—though perhaps not as a percentage of income. Many businesses and professionals—even quite careful ones—inevitably cause injury in the course of their myriad activities. So if an injured person makes a claim to recover damages from them, they may have to pay considerable sums. If found liable, they may pay damage awards in six, seven, even eight or nine, figures to persons whom their activities have seriously injured.

Even if judged not liable, defendants pay. They pay the costs of the lawyers, experts, and other functionaries whose expensive services are necessary to defend against a tort claim, win or lose. In litigated proceedings, those costs, too, can quickly run into six figures or more.

Moreover, these direct costs are not the only raid on business and professional pocketbooks. As their costs of doing business rise because of these payments to avoid or respond to tort liability, the affected groups argue that they find themselves having to raise prices; as their prices go up, generally their income goes down, particularly if they have competitors who are not paying similarly high costs of tort liability. This concern supposedly underlay the deep involvement in tort reform issues by former President George Bush's Council on Competitiveness, energetically headed by then–Vice President Dan Quayle. More recently, tort reform was a major clause in the Republican Contract with America for the 1994 congressional campaign. Bush's council forcefully articulated the view of many businesses that tort lawsuits hampered American companies' ability to compete with foreign businesses who did not face such threats and assaults. Even within the United States, businesses increasingly claim that their too-liberal state tort and workers' compensation laws hamper their ability to compete with businesses based in other less liberal states.

Not only do tort lawsuits cost money, they also have serious emotional and temporal costs for those sued. The most obvious psychological costs of tort lawsuits can be seen in the medical profession. Perhaps because their mistakes can cause much worse injuries than the mistakes that most of us make, many doctors have been sued. Even if they haven't, they know colleagues who have been. Arguably, doctors don't feel much of a financial pinch from tort law: malpractice insurance pays for any suit, and the premiums can be "passed through" to patients and deducted from taxable income as a business expense. Doctors also suffer little if any competitive disadvantage because colleagues in a given specialty and area pay virtually identical insurance rates. Yet doctors have been the leaders in the assault on legislatures in the name of tort reform. They passionately resent being sued—being publicly accused, not to say branded as guilty, of malpractice (how they hate that word). They view lawyers as vultures hovering over their medical practices, ready to pounce on them as soon as a patient fails to get some ideal expected medical outcome. Their most vexing day-to-day problem is voluminous record keeping, often designed just to cover their behinds in case they get sued. Patients can become potential adversaries, and important doctor-patient relationships, dependent on trust, can be seriously undermined.[1]

Though perhaps not so often personally assaulted by the tort system, business executives have similar strong distastes. Not only do tort lawsuits attack their individual and corporate reputations, but executives resent the disruption of their work that the suits entail. As with doctors, business people involved in decisions and activities that some "know-nothing" lawyer links to an accident find themselves trapped in time-consuming litigation that has no productive value. Once an accident happens, a doctor or business executive must spend many, many hours—often in emotional turmoil—pulling together and reviewing records, meeting with others within the organization about the events, and telling one's story in contentious pretrial proceedings and in court. Time, lots of time, is lost by people who never have enough of it in the first place.

Finally, for businesses, tort law undermines their ability to plan. In economic hard times like U.S. businesses have experienced recently, executives need to make hard choices in order to streamline their operations and to keep their companies afloat and competitive. However, executives cannot take the axe to tort law's costs the way they often can to the company's other costs. They can't decide: "OK, let's spend 10 percent less on tort suits next fiscal year." Tort costs exist relatively independently of their actions year-to-year, even if investments in safety might conceivably cut the costs in the more distant future.

Tort defendants embrace legislatures and, to a lesser extent, the public, as cures for their tort-induced pain in the hope that those bodies of opinion will be more sympathetic to their concerns than the courts. Not that the courts are hopelessly prejudiced in favor of injured people—though many institutional tort defendants think so. Actually, empirical evidence indicates that juries—the supposed source of proplaintiff bias—generally make reasonable and rational decisions in tort cases.[2] But businesses and professionals are inclined to think that legislatures and the public hear and respond to their points of view more fully, perhaps because competing proplaintiffs' voices may be weaker in those forums than in courtrooms.

Certainly it's true that when tort law is made by judicial decisions, plaintiffs generally have a strong voice in the lawmaking process. Howard Young and his family come to court with P. J. Cowcroft at their side, well equipped to contest the Transit Authority on all the issues regarding its liability to them. The Youngs have a lot at stake and they know it. They are willing to pay a talented lawyer a lot of money in order to win their case. The contingency fee system gives them the wherewithal to hire such talent. Accordingly, when a decision about a rule of tort law is made by trial or appellate judges, the view of injured persons as to the merits of those decisions usually will have been fully presented and argued to the court. The court's decision will be limited and reality-tested, argue tort law's adherents: it will be limited to the few and precise legal issues that must be resolved in the particular case before the court. For example, when faced with the formal claims for legal protection the bystanders whom Howard Young originally sued for failing to help him off the tracks, the court would not decide whether people generally should be held liable for failing to help persons in distress. Rather, Judge Small would decide only whether bystanders on a subway platform can be held liable when they did not help an intoxicated person up from the tracks in these particular circumstances of danger, confusion, and distance from Howard. (In this case, as we have seen, it was ruled early on that the bystanders could not be held liable.) Whatever decision Judge Small or an appeals court makes about the law will be reality-tested: the actual circumstances of the accident, the defendants' knowledge and behavior, and the plaintiffs' needs will be presented in detail to the court. Consequently, it is argued, the law will be anchored in a carefully garnered understanding of the reality of a specific situation.

Tort law's adherents argue as a corollary that neither the accumulation of legislators' votes nor the formation of public opinion includes such significant participation of injury victims or such reality anchoring. Plaintiffs, they assert, are relatively unheard in the legislative process, compared with business and professional groups. Those who have recovered whatever compensatory damages tort law is going to give them know that their already adjudicated rights will not be affected by pending legislation. So they don't lobby. Conversely, the people who may be affected as future accident victims by any legislature-made tort law do not show up to present their perspectives to the legislature because they do not know ahead of time that they will be hurt. Nor do former plaintiffs or plaintiffs-to-be generally try to influence the public's understanding of the world of accident victims: plaintiffs are one-shot players on the tort stage. People like the Youngs may care what people in their community think about *their* lawsuit, but they don't much care what the public thinks about tort lawsuits generally. Moreover, even if a significant number of accident victims was concerned about particular legislation or public attitudes, the group would need substantial money and organization to compete with the business groups' messages about those issues.

Business and professional groups, on the other hand, it is argued, know they have a considerable stake in legislative changes in tort law. They are repeat players—parties involved again and again in tort litigation. Even if individual businesses and professionals don't foresee getting sued in the future, they recognize that their liability insurance charges are likely to go up as others in their industry or profession are sued. Changes in tort law that make it harder for plaintiffs to win lawsuits, or that reduce collectible damages, will reduce the amounts that defendants have to pay out in future lawsuits. This knowledge makes it worthwhile for business and professional groups to put substantial time, effort, and money into efforts to influence legislative decisions.

Of course, even if plaintiffs are by and large missing from legislative considerations of tort reform, their lawyers are not. Plaintiffs' lawyers recognize that legislative reforms which make it more difficult for victims to recover full damages in tort lawsuits take money out of *their* pockets. Therefore, the Association of Trial Lawyers of America (ATLA), or one of its state affiliates, will show up in the legislatures to oppose the business groups' efforts. In the past decade, these plaintiffs' lawyers' organizations have focused most of their efforts on blocking or rescinding legislative initiatives that change judge-made tort rules rather than on offering proplaintiff legislative initiatives of their own. Added to ATLA's efforts are those of consumer advocates like Ralph Nader and his cohorts.

Before we look more closely at the respective troop strengths in the political wars that are waged between the business and professional groups on one hand and plaintiffs' lawyers and consumer groups on the other, we should recall that legislators make decisions based on factors quite different from what judges must consider.

When judges make tort law, they do so anchored in the detailed specifics of particular accidents. The focus of the legislative process is much more general. Legislators are much more likely than judges to hear about the societal effects of the tort rules that they are being asked to change. Actual data about those effects are arguably in short supply.[3] Therefore, legislators commonly may hear widely different versions of reality, no one of which is necessarily subject to rigorous cross-examination by a knowledgeable adversary. Insofar as they hear about a particular incident of carelessness that harmed a particular individual, legislators will probably hear a caricature of the accident, which fits it into the debate as an example of the foolishness or wisdom of the tort rules at issue, rather than the sort of concrete, detailed evidence that is introduced in courts. When the spotlight is on the general societal well-being rather than on the horrors of individual accident and injury, the social benefits of a tort rule change may well be more apparent that its effect on some injury victims of that change. Thus, tort proponents argue, the business and professional groups' interests may well receive more attention from the legislature than in court. (On the other hand, juries may be *too* immersed in the particulars of a given case and unaware of the general effects of their decision: its impact on insurance rates, for example.)

In addition, when judges decide tort rules, they are relatively well protected from the wrath of the disappointed party: the judge often has solid job security. Many are appointed. Even elected judges, unlike their counterparts in the legislature, usually serve long terms, and often face reelection in nonpartisan balloting, running not against an opponent but on their own records. Granting the increasing partisan participation of proplaintiff and prodefense groups in the election and selection of judges, in legislative debates about tort law legislators generally pay much closer attention to how their votes will play with the groups who might provide substantial support or opposition in an upcoming election.

Not only may the business and professional groups find themselves heard better in the legislature, they may also find their expressions of concern about tort law more powerful on the streets than in the courts. As indicated earlier, American society has long been some-what hostile to persons who bring lawsuits to get money for acci-dental injuries. For some, it offends basic notions of personal responsibility—that individuals should take care of themselves and should get money only when they have earned it.[4] So business groups can sow hostility to lawsuits on fertile ground when they communicate in their myriad ways with the public on tort issues. That ground has proven so fertile that the head of the American Tort Reform Association (ATRA), a major umbrella organization advancing business interests in tort law, claims that reform has become a "grassroots movement."[5]

Bringing tort law into the political arena has entailed a tremen-dous surge in political organization and spending around issues that as recently as fifteen years ago were regarded as pretty much the business of the courts. Although the business and professional groups have by no means given up on changing tort law in the courts (and have achieved some success there), they have multiplied enormously their efforts to achieve reform directly through influencing legis-lation and indirectly through influencing public opinion. Proplain-tiff groups, particularly ATLA and its affiliates, are meeting these efforts head on.

The tort-reform groups have been tremendously active in the leg-islatures on both the state and national levels. Local, state, and national medical societies, for example, have often made use of both their financial clout and their high status in the community to obtain reforms. More than three hundred tort-reform statutes dealing with medical malpractice alone were enacted by state legislatures in the 1980s. Some notion of the power of the medical lobby is suggested by the enactment of legislation in more than forty states—entitled "Good Samaritan" legislation—that relieved physicians of liability for negligent care in the course of treating injured or sick persons whom they encountered fortuitously and stopped to render care to. This wave of legislation took place because of doctors' fears of being sued in such instances. (Actually, we have been unable to find a single reported case in the country in which a physician had been held liable for stopping to render such emergency assistance; on the other hand, reported cases don't reflect all the cases where litigation was instituted, settled, or even tried without being appealed.)

The business lobby is also powerful, if far more fragmented. ATRA claims about four hundred nonprofit organizations, public agencies, professional and trade associations, and businesses as members. Its well-financed Washington office coordinates legislative reform efforts around the nation through weekly "legislative watch" mailings. ATRA helps business groups throughout the nation to set up state and local affiliates. Its Texas affiliate alone spent more than $1 million on lobbying in 1992, while another Texas progeny, the Citizens Against Lawsuit Abuse, reportedly enlisted sixteen thousand members within a year after it began a campaign of ads against "lawsuit abuse"—ads produced and supplied by ATRA.[6]

Nor does ATRA work alone. When reform of products liability law—along with medical malpractice the most significant area of tort litigation—is at issue, it is joined by the Product Liability Coordinating Committee, a coalition of more than seven hundred thousand businesses, and by the Product Liability Alliance, which claims some three hundred trade associations and corporations. Of course, businesses and their trade groups involve themselves very directly in lobbying for particular reforms. When a products liability reform bill reached the U.S. Senate floor in 1992, for example, the National Association of Manufacturers organized fly-ins by many corporate chief executives to lobby their senators the day before the vote. (In spite of their effort, the bill was defeated.) A host of insurance industry organizations, moreover, have been described by an industry publication as "heavily involved in the crusade to modify tort laws." The Insurance Information Institute, for example, spent $6.5 million on tort reform television advertising in 1985–86, and the American Insurance Association, the Alliance of American Insurers, the National Association of Mutual Insurance Companies, and the National Association of Independent Insurers have also been active in the campaign.[7]

The task of defending the existing tort system, meanwhile, has fallen to ATLA, the plaintiffs' lawyers' organization, allied with such consumer organizations as Consumers' Union, Ralph Nader's Public Citizen, and the National Insurance Consumer Organization, founded by Nader and now merged with the Consumer Federation of America. And ATLA, like Nader, is no slouch. It consists of a class of persons perhaps unique to the United States. As a group, plaintiffs' lawyers are well-to-do. Some, indeed, are fabulously wealthy, probably the best-paid group of lawyers in the nation. Why? Because, unlike most lawyers, they get a piece of the action through their contingent fees. Corporate lawyers—even on Wall Street at $1,000 an hour—are, after all, limited by how many hours there are in a day (granting imaginative computations by some lawyers). But a third (or more) of $1 million or $10 million or higher, can easily dwarf any hourly fee. In 1988 the *Washington Post* estimated that Jack Olender, Washington's leading plaintiffs' medical malpractice lawyer but by no means nationally renowned, netted $2–5 million a year. In 1989, *Forbes* magazine listed sixty-three plaintiffs' lawyers who made more than $2 million each in both 1987 and 1988, with at least fifteen others likely in that category, plus another fifty in the $1–2-million range. *Forbes*'s 1995 list of the top earners in the trial bar included annual earnings of $90 million for Joseph Jamail, $40 million for John O'Quinn, and $26 million for Wayne Reaud.[8] Such earnings are almost totally dependent on the continuation of the tort system. Plaintiffs' lawyers also tend to be among the elite in quickness, wit, articulateness, and self-confidence—all of which help them as witnesses in legislative chambers.

These characteristics have enabled ATLA to stage effective campaigns against tort reform. Many regard the plaintiffs' lawyers—along with some dissident insurers—as the major factor in the sudden arrest of no-fault auto accident legislation in the 1970s. Others credit ATLA with having slowed the tort reform juggernaut in the 1990s. Even if ATLA and its state and local affiliates cannot marshal the financial muscle and numbers of concerned persons that business and professional groups can, it can compensate for those deficits by its single-minded intensity on tort reform issues. More than most of the business groups, ATLA has a single legislative focus. Plaintiffs' lawyers and their money will stay with a legislator who votes with them on tort reform issues. And that money is substantial: According to a study by the American Tort Reform Association, based on a conservative estimate, between January 1989 and December 1994 contributions from individual plaintiffs' lawyers to all congressional candidates totaled $18,066,433. Combined with ATLA-PAC contributions of $12,872,886 over the same period, a total of more than $30 million came from plaintiffs' lawyers for federal elections. Further combining these figures with an additional $26 million in trial lawyer contributions in seven states, ATRA documents plaintiffs' lawyer state and federal contributions of $56 million. To put that $30 million in three federal election cycles in perspective, ATRA reports that the five largest labor union contributors since 1989 contributed a total of $29,727,165; the "big three" automakers (GM, Ford, and Chrysler) contributed $2,195,233 over the same three election cycles, with ten of the largest oil and gas companies in the United States giving a total of $6,975,764.[9]

One result of this politicization is to open up bountiful stores of funding for politicians. In Illinois, where stringent legislative reforms of tort law have been enacted, the State Medical Society's political action group likewise was deeply committed to sympathetic political candidates, to the tune of $600,000 in the 1992 elections. With moneyed groups sufficiently anxious about the success or failure of tort reform legislation, legislators have tapped into a mother lode of campaign financing. Keep in mind that lobbyists on both sides share in the largesse as long as the stalemate lasts. The director of Illinois' Common Cause claimed that the ready availability of money from both probusiness and proplaintiff groups gave legislators an incentive not to resolve tort reform issues, so as to keep campaign contributions flowing their way.[10] That, incidentally, may help explain why for fifteen straight years attempts in Congress to pass legislation marginally reforming products liability law have been frustrated. What this means is that any public interest in weighty tort reform can be stalled as legislators and lobbyists on both sides revel in stalemate.

With legislators' and lobbyists' more unsavory interests contributing to political battles over tort reform, Republicans tend to latch onto tort reform as a campaign issue, while Democrats seem to be increasingly reliant on plaintiffs' lawyers for campaign financing. Thus, tort reform battles increasingly mirror, and are aggravated by, traditional party politics. If this was not obvious before 1992, it became so during that presidential campaign. Then-President George Bush, accepting his party's nomination, told the Republican convention: "I'm fighting to reform our legal system, to put an end to crazy lawsuits. If that means climbing into the ring with the plaintiffs' lawyers, well, let me just say, round one starts tonight." By September, when Bush's pollsters were telling him that his assault on plaintiffs' lawyers was the only helpful tack he and the party had taken at the convention, the Bush-Quayle campaign was running anti-Clinton ads titled "Stop the Trial Lawyer Takeover of the White House." Similarly, Bob Dole made tort reform part of his presidential campaign in 1996.[11]

The 1992 Clinton campaign was aware that close association with the much-maligned tort system or with "tassel-loafered" plaintiffs' lawyers was no way to win the election. In the vice presidential debates, candidate Al Gore was quick to point to Arkansas' low liability insurance rates as evidence that then-Governor Clinton was second to none in his ability to handle the tort problem. Nevertheless, ATLA members in both 1992 and 1996 organized important fund-raising efforts for Clinton. As the 1992 campaign ended, Alabama Senator Howell Heflin was caught by the *Wall Street Journal* reminding the Democratic Caucus in the Senate to vote against products liability reform because, he said, plaintiffs' lawyers, along with "Jews and the labor unions," were the most important contributors to the Democratic Party.[12]

Plaintiffs' lawyers have long had particular importance to Democrats at the state level as well as the national. Disproportionately

Democrats, they tend also to be, like Democrats, generally disproportionately ethnic—Irish, Italian, Jewish, black, and Hispanic. And they have a lot of money—a relatively rare condition for Democrats. They have long recognized the need to obtain legislative support and have thus contributed lavishly to legislative campaigns. Best of all for their donees, the antiestablishment, provictim nature of plaintiffs' lawyers puts them in the mainstream of Democratic positions. By the nature of their work—and perhaps by their personalities—plaintiffs' lawyers tend to be fiercely independent of and instinctively averse to the establishment. They are, after all, in the business of suing the establishment. They are solidly, and profitably, in the Democratic camp on social and economic issues, especially those dealing with redistribution of income. In return for their support, plaintiffs' lawyers ask for legislators' help only on tort reform issues—in contrast to insurers, manufacturers, and health care providers, who have myriad issues affecting them before legislatures. Regardless of their personal inclinations on tort law, Democratic politicians find this occasional vote a small price to pay for the significant, regular help they get from plaintiffs' lawyers. With labor unions in long decline nationally, and with tort law issues so important to plaintiffs' lawyers, Democrats increasingly are compelled to attend to their voices.

As we have seen, plaintiffs' lawyers have long been skillful in enlisting the efforts of consumer groups in fronting anti–tort reform lobbying. Many sources have reported the extent of funding of Ralph Nader's organizations by the plaintiffs' personal injury bar. Nader himself has perhaps fueled such stories by his refusal to open up his books on the grounds that many of his contributors wish to remain confidential. At any rate, there is no question that Nader and his colleagues have rallied effectively to the cause of curbing tort reform. In this connection Nader's detractors—legion, of course, in the business community—have often accused him of cynically living off what they deem a corrupt tort system. But here they underestimate him. Like everyone, Nader has his faults, but cynicism is not one of them. Indeed one of his great strengths is his manifest sincerity. One can fault him sometimes for his zealotry but not for disingenuousness. If pressed in private, Nader might well concede some of the inadequacies of tort law, but his basic thesis is that our society—especially large-scale providers of goods and services—often pays insufficient attention to the interests of safety. (Recall that Nader made his reputation by his attacks on GM's unsafe cars.) Although a believer in regulation, Nader recognizes the tendency of regulators to be captured, or at least overwhelmed, by the regulated. (He even quarreled furiously with his own protégée, Joan Claybrook, when she was charged with regulating the safety of automobiles in the Carter administration.) Thus Nader turns to the plaintiffs' personal injury bar as a unique resource in our society: sophisticated, affluent, expert individuals—by definition not part of the establishment—with enormous incentives under tort law to chastise the commercial and professional elites of this country, arguably in the interests of greater safety. Thus, in turn, Nader becomes a vigorous defender of that same tort law.

Note, too, that the plaintiffs' personal injury bar, although also often seen as cynically devoted to its own self-interest in defending the tort system, is largely composed of people who believe sincerely in what they do in representing the lonely, injured individual—often impecunious by nature of the accident, if for no other reason—against a large, impersonal, often vastly wealthy, and even on occasion overreaching corporation.

Conversely, Republicans, flush with 1994 electoral success, found their natural money-giving constituency among business and health care groups. At a time when a national survey reported that legal reform is the number one concern of small businesses and when business and professional groups are pouring millions of dollars into tort reform campaigns around the country, it was no shock to find Republican candidates engaging in trial-lawyer bashing and pushing tort reform as part of their campaign and legislative platforms. Republican attacks on tort law become even more acute as lawmakers realize that tort reform legislation helps to drain money from Democratic supporters while simultaneously pleasing the GOP's business and health care constituencies.

This politicization means that the issues which tort law traditionally must resolve may be increasingly decided on the basis of whose interests are served by a particular proposal. When the legislature makes tort law, the final shape of the law will be influenced— perhaps controlled—by its effects on those who are politically most powerful. But isn't that also the case when courts make tort law? There, tort proponents respond, the opposing parties are constrained, on the surface at least, to argue for their positions on the basis of common law traditions.

As we have seen, the neutrality of court-mandated law is debatable. And according to tort law's critics, biased jury selection, aimed at exploiting socioeconomic and political factors, can be all-important. A plaintiffs' lawyer, for example, will often reject retired people, many of whom live on fixed incomes and are assumed to be "too tight with a buck." One leading plaintiffs' lawyer favors African-Americans and Jews, on the other hand, on the principle that, having tasted discrimination, they will tend to identify with an underdog plaintiff. Blue-collar workers may also be favored by plaintiffs' lawyers, in that they can be expected to empathize more with accident victims, given that their own bodies are their livelihood. Conversely, a defense lawyer will prefer retired people, along with older blue-collar and middle-management workers, on the grounds that they are accustomed to shifting for themselves and are thereby inclined to be conservative with their awards. A defense lawyer may resist younger jurors because of what one calls their "tendency to have a social-worker, do-gooder mentality." And yet a defense lawyer may also seek to exploit racial and class differences in jury selection in order to encourage jury dissension, for a quarrelsome jury will rarely grant large awards. But even the most baldly packed jury is seldom as nakedly partisan a forum as the typical legislature, where tort reform is a "hot-button" issue and every "reform" a hostage to one or another party's political fortunes. In electoral politics, the merits of the arguments tend to give way to the service of team interests.

Thus public perceptions come into play ever more as the battle shifts to the legislatures. One way to loosen the ties of elected officials to plaintiffs' lawyers is to convince officials that such an alliance will be political suicide. That means convincing the public that tort reform is good and necessary, so that voters react negatively to those politicians who oppose it. Of course, convincing the public of the evils of the current tort system can work to business and professional groups' advantage in court as well: jurors in tort cases come from that same public. If jurors walk into a courtroom predisposed to believe that most tort claims are frivolous or that many people feign injuries in order to cash in on defendants' wealth, they will be more likely to find no liability or to award lower amounts in damages. If judges, too, with their ears to the ground of public opinion, become skeptical of the value of tort law for society or become more convinced that "runaway juries" tend to throw money at accident victims irrationally, then they may well tend to constrict the instances in which the law permits injured persons to recover damages and be more likely to reduce the damages determined by a jury.

Tort reform advocates have seized upon these potential points of influence. Business and professional groups have produced massive campaigns to impugn the tort system in the eyes of ordinary people—whether jurors or voters. A major piece of this campaign is straightforward advertising. ATRA has been particularly energetic in its efforts to convince the public of the evils of tort. With its ample financial base, ATRA has been able to produce sophisticated print and video advertising that plays on society's basic skepticism about tort claims. Approaching Americans whose individualist ethic makes them suspicious of persons who get money without earning it, ATRA has produced tens of thousands of posters, as well as television commercials, focused on the theme of "lawsuit abuse." One television spot, screened at ATRA's annual meeting as integral to the development of its "grassroots" campaign for tort reform, shows a

man falling as he tries to reach a light bulb from the top of a step
ladder, which he has balanced perilously on top of a stack of phone
books. As he tumbles three separate times, the voiceover intones,
"Some people misuse products and then look for someone to
blame." ATRA ads appeal to those skeptical of tort law wisdom
with pictures of cars sporting bumper stickers reading, "Hit me. I
need the money," and with stories of burglars who recover tort
damages when they injure themselves trying to get into buildings.
For those Americans feeling the effects of a beleaguered economy,
ATRA's ads tell viewers that frivolous lawsuits add $280 to the fam-
ily grocery bill each year and $300 to the cost of delivering a baby.
The man-tumbling-off-the-ladder commercial says that lawsuits
account for 20 percent of a ladder's costs. For those Americans who
may have missed the point—that they are personally being hurt by
tort law—ATRA ads show a pregnant woman in front of a closed
obstetrics office, unhappy children at a closed swimming pool, and
an informational video shows "The Day They Canceled the Fourth
of July." Insurance companies and businesses exploit similar themes
with print ads that emphasize the destructive impact of the tort liability system on American companies' ability to compete with those
in other nations and that show the tombstones of the companies
driven to bankruptcy by the "asbestos lawsuit lottery," with "tens
of thousands of jobs lost."

ATRA's Lawsuit Abuse ads have been placed—with the coopera-
tion of the Transit Authorities—in buses, subways, and stations in
the Philadelphia, Chicago, New York, Fort Lauderdale, and even
Long Beach, California, transit systems. ATRA mailed its Lawsuit
Abuse poster of the pregnant woman to eighteen thousand obstetricians in selected states. It placed its thirty-minute video against
the tort system on American Airlines flights. Insurers' advertisements appear across one or more full pages in national news magazines and newspapers.

At the same time, senior fellows at the Manhattan Institute—a
conservative think tank—have produced controversial books,
widely reviewed in the press, that rely (unfairly, in the eyes of tort

law's adherents) on material about the tort system's malfunctioning to convince the public of the system's foolish and socially destructive qualities.

Are these steps effective? Researchers have found jurors subject to such publicity more skeptical of tort claimants and have identified trends in judicial perceptions and actions that operate in favor of tort defendants.[13] Reports from those areas where ATRA ads ran in mass transit systems indicated that the number of lawsuits against transit authorities had dropped. ATRA's polls in those areas where its coalitions' ads have been heaviest show that as many as 80 percent of citizens believe frivolous lawsuits to be a serious problem and that similarly high percentages of the public favored particular prodefense tort reforms and opposed political candidates who accepted contributions from plaintiffs' lawyers. But if business and professional groups seem to some to be winning the battle for the hearts and souls of the American public on the issue of tort reform, one cannot help note the barrage of television ads, night and day, from plaintiffs' lawyers urging viewers with a possible claim to consult them. Presumably such persistent ads would not run to an unresponsive public.

Is serious tort reform inevitable? Even with all the efforts of business and professional groups to reach the public, even with their tremendous lobbying resources, reformers had actually achieved relatively little in the way of significant reforms in state legislatures through the mid-1990s. Nevertheless, by themselves, these political forces—in combination with important commercial, economic, political, and intellectual trends—will keep in the forefront the issue of whether the United States will effect major changes in the tort system by the end of the century.

A vivid example of the factors that will be in play in the push-and-shove of debate about the future of tort law is the impact of tort liability insurance on health insurance and vice versa. Even with the defeat of the Clinton health insurance plan, health insurance is expanding and is likely to remain high on the political agenda. But as is well acknowledged, even mere maintenance of current levels of health insurance and health care services—not to speak of expanding them—is bound to be very expensive. A major issue will be how to keep the costs of health insurance, whether publicly or privately funded, within bounds. That, in turn, means keeping the use of health care services to a minimum adequate level.

But data cited in Chapter 7 suggest that persons with tort claims make many more visits to health care providers than do those without such claims. A big reason for this, as we said, is to increase the size of one's tort claim—especially for pain and suffering, routinely measured as a multiple of one's losses, including medical bills. In response to this and other inflationary effects of health insurance, the country is increasingly turning to managed care organizations (MCOs). MCOs are designed to suppress the number and extent of health care services by "capitation" schemes, whereby, for example, an MCO is provided with a flat fee to care for a patient within a given period, thus providing the MCO with incentives to keep down health care services during that period.

These incentives under such "point of service plans" are in direct contrast to traditional "fee for service" health care plans, which have traditionally rewarded health care providers for providing more and more services. Under an MCO, then, patients with a tort claim are not allowed by their MCO to simply run up health care costs by more and more treatment. On the other hand, even "point of service" plans increasingly allow patients to go "out of network"— outside the plan's panel of approved health care providers—for further services, with the plan paying a large portion (but not all) of the outside medical bills. Thus a patient with a tort claim could still go "out of network" to a "fee for service" provider and so retain an incentive to pad medical bills. Furthermore, even to the extent that "point of service" plans succeed in depressing the number and extent of health care services, given the imaginative tactics likely to be employed by plaintiffs' lawyers in seeking the enormous profits in tort claims, lawyers will likely encourage their clients, in the alternative to further doctor visits, simply to stay away longer from work, thereby overutilizing sick leave and disability plans as a means of inflating economic loss, in turn causing inflated pain and suffering claims, with a consequent rise in employment absenteeism.

Moreover, regardless of incentives to pad claims, simply to the extent injured persons are able to obtain even uninflated medical care, their capacity to more aggressively hold out in pursuit of a tort lawsuit increases also.[14] In other words, if injured parties are insulated from need (by, say, increased health insurance) and can postpone paying a lawyer (via the contingent fee) until a settlement or a judgment is reached, they are in a position to resist early and relatively low offers from a defendant and thereby bargain for much larger sums. All this means that high levels of health care and disability insurance, though deemed socially desirable, are not only bound to be very expensive in themselves but to have a manifestly inflationary effect on tort liability insurance as well.

MCOs are likely to have even a further inflationary effect on tort litigation. A new wave of medical malpractice claims has already begun against them. Because health care providers associated with MCOs are under pressure to minimize levels and types of care administered, MCOs are an obvious target for malpractice litigation after a refusal to cover arguably necessary services in the interest of decreasing costs—and (whisper it) increasing profits. Although a highly ambiguous congressional law (the Employers' Retirement Income Security Act—ERISA) has so far been tortuously interpreted by the United States Supreme Court to throw some roadblocks in front of malpractice suits against MCOs, such suits are increasingly being brought and will probably grow in number, perhaps with explicit congressional approval, given the public outrage that cost-driven denial of health care services can engender.

Many health care providers employed or otherwise engaged by MCOs bitterly resent MCO control of medical procedures, and health care providers excluded from practicing under the auspices of an MCO (increasingly the principal medical practice game in town) are even more resentful. As a result, there will be an almost infinitely expanded bank of expert witnesses not only willing but eager to testify against MCOs for not only condoning but encouraging and even in effect mandating "medical malpractice."

Furthermore, malpractice litigation against MCOs can be expected to grow at an even faster rate than has typical malpractice litigation in the past because the basis of suit is greatly simplified. Before the recent and dramatic rise of MCOs, the incentive on health care providers was to overutilize health care in the interest of higher fees. (Indeed, it was that incentive and the consequent exponentially explosive growth in health care costs that has led to the Draconian solution of MCOs.) Thus malpractice litigation has traditionally focused on instances of, say, surgical error: more than 80 percent of the cases typically grew out of the operating room. Such cases are *relatively* rare and almost always hard to prove, given the complexity of surgery as it is actually conducted. But with MCOs the exponentially more common issue of *failure* to render care is at the fore. Consider a plaintiff's lawyer seeing a patient whose worsened condition arguably would have benefited from a form of treatment that was not performed. Such treatment may indeed have been reasonably contraindicated because of statistical unlikelihood of efficacy. But the plaintiffs' lawyer in this case need not bury herself in the arcane intricacies of surgery or some other affirmative form of treatment. Rather, she can with relative simplicity point only to (1) the lack of treatment for her impaired client, who is poignantly before the jury; (2) the (perhaps tenuous but still arguable) connection between the lack of treatment and her client's further impaired state; and (3) most explosive and easily understandable of all, the incentive to higher profits for the MCO in refusing to cover the treatment, which in the hands of a skillful lawyer becomes an elevation of profit over the patient's health. The refusal to cover the treatment will look particularly egregious because (a) a newly created pool of aggrieved and disenchanted expert witnesses is furious at what commercially preoccupied MCOs have done and are doing to their ancient and honorable profession of the healing arts, and (b) defendants are no longer individual doctors (with their possible jury appeal and relatively low limits of coverage) but faceless, cost-cutting, profit-maximizing, deep-pocket corporations.

It seems, then, that any rational plan for rationing health care—and such plans not only exist but are multiplying all the while—will just as inevitably become fodder for the personal injury bar.

Furthermore, quite apart from the effects of health insurance on tort law, more sweeping no-fault auto insurance reforms loom on the horizon. Such reforms will cause many plaintiffs' lawyers, deprived of the rich lode of car crash cases—relatively easy to prepare and try—to have to turn to more complex personal injury cases, especially medical malpractice and products liability suits. Indeed, it was no coincidence that mushrooming medical malpractice and products liability cases since the 1970s coincided with the enactment of relatively modest no-fault auto insurance laws. Many personal injury lawyers, in other words, seeing that the easy money of car crash cases was likely to dwindle if not dry up, turned, in order to gain portfolio diversification, to the admittedly much more taxing cases of medical malpractice and products liability, which they formerly would turn away as not worth all the trouble. With the possibility of even broader no-fault auto laws, limiting large as well as small car crash cases, the rush to other accident cases, including medical malpractice, can be expected to accelerate even further.

Now those who believe in the tort system as a deterrent will applaud this new round of malpractice litigation as a healthy and necessary corrective to the excesses of MCOs. But those who deplore the excesses of tort litigation itself will see huge incentives to even more of it as all the more reason to seek alternatives.

The forces operating in the tort and related worlds, then, strongly hint that substantial tort reform looms. Economic and intellectual trends seem likely to give momentum to such reforms. Economically, except for auto insurance, the country has for the past few years not experienced the kinds of sharp increases in tort liability insurance premiums that have sparked previous tort reform waves in the mid-1970s and 1980s. History suggests that a period of such increases may come in this decade. When it does, the pressure to do even more to the tort system than the piecemeal reforms of the past could be irresistible. Such pressure will come, furthermore, against a backdrop of possible major reforms that some tort law theorists have been developing for more than twenty years. The major features of such possible reforms will be outlined in the next chapter. Regardless of their merits, they have already been envisioned, and some actually tried. If then-Governor Mario Cuomo of New York— a lawyer, Democrat, and a leading liberal and voice for the disadvantaged—could propose taking completely out of the tort system the cases of newborns suffering disastrous neurological injury, could back products liability reform, and could seriously consider a sweeping no-fault system to replace all medical malpractice law, then major reform ideas could well become part of the intellectual mainstream, quite apart from right-left political partisanship.

One further factor that might also be considered as a likely influence on tort reform is increased international trade. It is uncertain, though, just how that influence will play out. Just as producers who face conflicting state tort law provisions push for greater standardization to the point where Congress is pressured to enact a federal products liability law, so too will many of them push for the United States to bring its expansive tort rules more in line with the much more limited laws of other countries. And yet, while one might expect that increased standardization among major trading nations to approach the lower level of tort protections afforded in Europe and Japan, one might also point to developments in the European Community and Japan for products liability law that is much closer to the current American model. Certainly medical malpractice claims have risen spectacularly in Britain in recent decades. As a result, the push of internationalization of tort law could conceivably thrust the rest of the world closer to American tort law rather than vice versa.

Politicization of tort law means that whatever changes occur over the next decade will not necessarily be the right ones. In preceding chapters, we have considered the major benefits and burdens of tort law as it operates today in the United States. In the concluding

chapter, we will examine major suggestions for tort reform that have
been advanced by those concerned with these real burdens and benefits. If our society is to maximize the net benefit we get from accident law, we need to evaluate possible changes in light of the real
problems that need fixing. Those problems, as we have seen, certainly begin with the massive transaction costs and delays involved
in resolving tort disputes. They also arguably include injustices and
inadequacies in both compensating the injured and making defendants pay—including both illicit prosecution and illicit defense of
claims. They thus arguably include mistreatment of both plaintiffs
and defendants by tort litigation.

The politicization of tort law means that decisions about the
changes in tort law are at least substantially made on the basis of
whose ox is being gored—or fed. Those groups whom the legislatures and the public hear best—perhaps because of their money,
their public relations skills, or their political affiliation—will aggressively seek to be protected from goring and allowed to be fed. How
this affects the whole society may well be subordinated to how it
affects the politically powerful.

Politicization also means that tort law—like many other issues—
is often reduced to sound bites. (Recall the simplistic salvos between
Democrats and Republicans over a balanced federal budget.) Tort
law is "lawsuit abuse"; tort law is a nation of crybabies, eager to
blame others for harms that are really their own responsibility; tort
law is runaway juries who throw money at undeserving claimants
for no sound reason. Or, on the other hand, tort law is bringing to
heel shady businesses and professionals who carelessly—even cal-
lously—maim the innocent, then use their vast resources to evade,
or unconscionably lessen or delay, any responsibility for their irre-
sponsible acts. Sound bites help arouse the public's skepticism about
those who seek, or seek to avoid, compensation for injury. Sound
bites do not, however, do much to enlighten public consideration of
the difficult dilemmas presented by tort law.

Many changes have been made in tort law during the past decade.
For the most part, those changes (while marginal) have been made

in an atmosphere of sensationalism. That should be no surprise: if reformers believe, for example, that lawsuit abuse and irrational decision making by jurors are the major problems in the tort system, then the kinds of reforms they enact to remedy those problems will be very different from the kinds of reforms that would take place if they thought high transaction costs, resort to illegitimate pursuit and defense of claims, over- and undercompensation, and over- and underdeterrence were the problems.

Therefore, it becomes important to conclude by considering which of the many proposals to reform tort law hold out hope of assuaging the system's real problems without abandoning its real strengths. Perhaps indeed the political balance remains sufficiently close to permit such worthy considerations to be a major force in the reforms to come.

CHAPTER NINE

Changes

Tort reform—most of it moderate—has been going on fairly seriously around the United States for about two decades. Such reforms—along with more significant reform proposals—are being urged on state and federal legislators daily. More reform seems inevitable. Even tort law's adherents want to change it here and there to make it better.

Howard and Nicole Young and their children have passed through the tort system. After a jury found the Transit Authority liable for the negligent driving of its subway train driver, it awarded Howard $2.5 million in damages, which took into account the 50 percent responsibility it assigned to Howard for his own injuries. Judge Small dismissed the claims of Elissa and Laura, following many cases in tort law that do not allow children to recover damages for the loss of a parent's love, companionship, or personal involvement in their lives. Following the verdict for Howard, the Transit Authority agreed to pay Nicole and Howard the $2.5 million right away, and not to appeal the verdict in his favor, in return for Nicole's agreement not to pursue her favorable verdict on her claim for her losses. After paying P. J. Cowcroft her $1 million fee and paying expenses of the suit, the Youngs took home $1.1 million.

Even with that sum, the costs of Howard's medical and rehabilitation services meant that the family had to move out of its home, to a more modest home farther from the city. Financially, the family will survive to live a moderately secure middle-class life. Howard will improve to a point where he becomes largely self-sufficient, but he will never be emotionally able to cope with the only kinds of jobs he can do: menial labor requiring little ability to concentrate. Emotionally, Elissa, Laura, Nicole, and Howard's lives will be forever darkened by the shadow that descended on the night he was crushed on the subway tracks.

The Youngs no longer care much about what happens to the tort system. There are a few others in urban areas, waiting on subway platforms as you read this, who will care, passionately, sooner than they know. People are injured in subway accidents every month. The Transit Authority still cares. So do P. J. Cowcroft and her law partners. They are wondering: what next?

Many people purport to have answers to that question, framed in statements that begin: "What should happen to the tort system in America is . . . " This concluding chapter presents brief sketches of the major kinds of such answers. It does not attempt here to advocate one right answer.[1] Granted that there are strengths and weaknesses in the tort system, each of the reform plans also has strengths and weaknesses. This chapter seeks to help the reader examine reform plans with an eye toward how well the social costs of the tort system are ameliorated and how well its social benefits are retained or amplified, keeping in mind the costs and benefits which have been described earlier.

The basic approaches to tort law reform are surprisingly few, given the number of academic and legislative proposals that have been floated during the past twenty years. Some reformers—prominent among the business and professional lobbies—propose to keep the tort system but change some of its parts. They are the "tinkers." Others—the "shakers"—want to throw out the tort system completely, or almost completely, in favor of an entirely different system for compensating accident victims. Finally, some reformers—the "movers"—seek their change through the establishment of alternative compensation systems while maintaining access to the tort system under some circumstances. Within each reform camp, the details of proposals vary widely. One kind of reform proposal—"choice" plans—seems to include both tinkerers and movers.

Within each basic type of reform are major debates about (1) what criteria should govern eligibility for compensation; (2) what sorts of compensation will be payable; (3) what will be the source of funding for the compensation payable; and (4) how will the systems be administered (publicly or privately, by court or administrative board)?

Many of the reforms that are proposed would apply to all the kinds of injuries currently treated under tort law. Others, recognizing basic differences among different kinds of accidents, would limit the reforms they propose to a particular kind of accident—such as auto accidents, or accidents at hospitals. These different approaches remind us that substantial differences arguably exist between the sorts of accidents that occur as an outgrowth of the provision of health care or manufactured products and the more run-of-the-mill types that occur in the street or in the home. Many reformers take pains to distinguish between the most common kinds of claim-inspiring street accidents—automobile accidents—and the medical malpractice and products liability accident categories. Mass tort and environmental accidents—which often overlap, as in the asbestos exposure cases—often are regarded as a separate category for reform.

This means that as we examine the basics of the three kinds of reform proposals, it is important to keep in mind the need of each kind to resolve important questions about criteria for payment, level and source of funding and compensation, and type of administration—and to keep in mind as well the possibility that a reform which suits one kind of accident may not suit another.

Starting with the more ambitious proposals, the nontort, or no-fault, reforms have already seized a substantial hold in dealing with certain categories of accidents. If the recent stream of no-fault proposals from prominent tort scholars is any indication, a new wave of no-fault reforms will soon be advanced in many legislatures.[2] Those reforms may be the sort of "focused no-fault" proposals—replacement of tort only in a limited injury area, such as vaccine-related injuries—that have often dominated the most serious discussion of nontort ways of dealing with accidental injuries. Some reformers, however, want to implement "general no-fault" plans, replacing the tort system completely and perhaps implementing other measures to make up for tort's lost functions.

The general no-fault plans most clearly exemplify the heart of nontort proposals. The focus is on compensation of injured persons. Compensation is achieved by having injured persons make claims for whatever assistance they need beyond the sources of help already present in their lives (such as health insurance, disability insurance, sick leave, and Social Security).

The best known of the general no-fault plans worldwide is in effect in New Zealand under its Accident Compensation Scheme, established in 1974, and amended somewhat since. Like most no-fault plans, New Zealand's still requires an injured person to make a claim, but to make it to a governmental administrative body rather than a court. The claimant need only prove he has suffered a "personal injury by accident," without regard to anyone's fault. (Victims of disease are not protected under the plan unless the disease results from employment.) Usually the injured person need prove no more. After waiting a short time, he will receive 80 percent of his lost earnings per week as long as he is unable to work. (Most no-fault plans pay 60–85 percent of lost wages, rather than 100 percent, in recognition of the lesser expenses that a nonworking person incurs and to provide incentive to return to work.) Like most no-fault plans, the New Zealand system has a cap on payment for lost earnings, so that the highest wage earners may have a lower percentage of their wages replaced. Medical expenses are covered. Until 1992, the Accident Compensation Scheme allowed limited recovery for intangible injuries: up to $17,000 NZ (about $11,334 U.S.) for loss of bodily part or function and up to $10,000 NZ (about $6,667 U.S.) for loss of enjoyment of life, disfigurement, and pain and suffering. The latter category was eliminated in 1992 as a means of reducing costs.[3]

The New Zealand system is funded in part by levies on employers and employees, by a gasoline tax, and by general revenues. The levies on employers vary with the assessed dangerousness of the occupation.

An even more ambitious general no-fault system has been proposed for the United States by Stephen Sugarman of the University of California Law School.[4] Sugarman's plan would displace tort liability and provide payment for all disabled persons, regardless of the source of the disability. For short-term needs (less than six months—a common cutoff under private and public disability coverages) medical expenses or income loss payment would come from expanded private employment-based insurance. For longer-term needs and the needs of those not employed, coverage would be provided by an expanded Social Security system. Other than for the short term, the plan would be funded by Social Security payroll taxes and by a gasoline tax. Given the radical nature and unknowable new costs of Sugarman's plan, its enactment seems most unlikely in the foreseeable future.

Focused no-fault plans usually differ from the general plans in a couple of critical ways. First, only a limited category of injuries—such as those suffered on the job or those suffered because of the administration of childhood vaccines or those suffered in automobile accidents—is covered by the plan. Focused no-fault plans have proliferated in Western nations, and more seem to be on the way. They have developed most commonly in the areas of workplace and automobile accidents but have been applied as well to birth-related neurological injuries, nuclear accidents, and black lung disease from coal mining, and have been proposed for other areas, particularly medical malpractice generally.[5]

These systems, like the general ones, dispense with tort law and its inquiry into the fault of involved parties. Instead, they pay out compensation based on the occurrence of an injury that is related in some way to the specific category of accidents. In the workers' compensation system, for example, the claimant must have received a personal injury as a result of an accident that "arose out of and in the course of" his employment. If that condition is satisfied, he will be paid his medical expenses and some money for lost earnings, most often two-thirds of his gross wages, again with ceilings commonly set based on the average weekly wage in the state. Payment for pain and suffering is not included.

The plans vary somewhat in administration and funding. In workers' compensation, the injured employee usually files an injury report with the state administrative agency overseeing the plan, which then turns the initial processing over to the employer's insurance carrier. In 70–90 percent of the cases, the insurer agrees on a compensation amount with the injured employee. The payments are funded by the employer, either through insurance or self-insurance. Most often, the employer's insurance rates depend on the general hazards of the work and the employer's particular claims experience.

The consumer writer Andrew Tobias sponsored an initiative measure on the California ballot in 1996 that would have totally replaced tort liability for auto accidents with a no-fault scheme, paying up to $1 million for medical expenses and wage loss. Nothing would be paid for losses already covered by other forms of insurance or for pain and suffering. The California ballot also included a controversial proposal—based on one from the second-named author of this book—dealing with plaintiffs' lawyers contingent fees. Both initiatives lost.

These no-fault plans of "shakers" certainly will shake things up by closing down the tort system, even if only in some limited areas of the accident world. There are some clear advantages to that shake-up, but clear disadvantages as well. Deciding no-fault claims simply costs less than the same sort of claim in tort. Recent studies differ on the amount of transaction cost savings no-fault realizes compared with tort, but all agree that the savings are substantial.[6] Because transaction costs—the bane of tort law—can be reduced substantially, and because payments for pain and suffering are eliminated in many if not most cases, more injured people can be given more money earmarked for compensation of economic losses. Freed from the need to prove that they were injured through someone's fault, a higher percentage of injured people will receive compensation for their economic loss from injuries.

Claims will be resolved more quickly as well: one recent study comparing victim compensation in Quebec's auto no-fault and tort systems found that only 35 percent of tort claimants received compensation within six months, while 96 percent of no-fault claimants had received payments within that period. Even if the compensation paid successful claimants is less than that paid successful tort claimants, the speed with which the compensation is paid and its adequacy at covering the claimants' "most important" losses arguably makes this difference acceptable in most cases. Besides, many more people will claim and many more will be successful. In that respect, no-fault moderates the more severe of tort law's fortuitous compensation ills, discussed in Chapter 3.

Particular no-fault proposals contain special wrinkles. For example, Stephen Sugarman has suggested a special auto insurance plan, funded by an addition to gasoline taxes, which includes damages for pain and suffering but puts them on a schedule and limits them to the most seriously injured. This feature addresses concerns that the tort system may grant excessive compensation for pain and suffering in small claims. This proposal, of course, could just as easily be part of the piecemeal changes in tort law, as our discussion of recovery for intangible damages such as pain and suffering will shortly reveal. The willingness of some proponents of no-fault coverage to allow tort claims for intentional or malicious injuries enables a no-fault system to accommodate victims' needs for vengeance in precisely the kinds of situations in which that need is paramount.

Lunch is not free at the no-fault table, however. Its benefits—and the reduction in transaction costs—come with their own costs. Transaction costs go down because no-fault systems don't do some of the hard jobs that society has always asked tort law to do. No-fault provides little individualized justice. It may fall short as a deterrent to unsafe behavior. And, perhaps most significantly, once tort has been retired, the critics of no-fault argue that it may be a fragile vessel indeed in which to face the storms of a body politic hostile to injury claims.

In no-fault systems, no blame is assessed. No one decides the value of the claimant's full injuries: what his actual earnings would have been; how much he has suffered; or what his life will be like in the future (other than whether he will be able to work and what his extra medical costs will be). If the no-fault system really wants to keep its transaction costs low, no one will ever decide in a general no-fault system (like New Zealand's) whether an injurer's faulty actions caused the claimant's injuries. No one goes to a no-fault system for individualized justice. It is more like going to the automated teller machine at the bank: punch in the right numbers and money will come out. Tort law's elegant, rich (some would say baroque) deliberative processes, by which community notions of fairness enter into and shape the system's "law," are notably absent.

In no-fault systems, injured people usually cannot call their injurer to account or make him face their accusations. Whatever story they get to tell will be very brief, truncated to only those parts necessary to satisfy no-fault's impersonal qualifying categories and its limited concerns about the extent of one's harm.

No-fault proposals arguably overlook the significance of abandoning these tasks. Perhaps they are not such important tasks. Yet the long history of tort liability in this country suggests that society considers them so. In spite of some strong feints toward "strict" (no-fault) liability, tort law has almost unanimously insisted that a defendant or its product must have performed in a faulty way before it will transfer money from him to someone he has injured.[7] The few instances in which courts have tried to impose real no-fault liability in the products liability area evoked extremely strong reactions from commentators and quick repudiation by other courts. Also, all states deny a claimant injured by another's faulty conduct or product some or all of the compensation he needs if the claimant, too, was at fault.

Many clearly believe it important that fault be proven before money is transferred from one party to a victim. If so, why should fault suddenly become unimportant when the transfer is called *no-fault* rather than *tort*? The same questions must be confronted if the transfer is done indirectly—for example, by levies against automobile manufacturers or gasoline purchasers to fund the no-fault automobile accident fund. Where the principle behind taking money from one entity is that the money is needed by people whom the payor is putting at risk, should society suddenly no longer care whether the payor was at fault?

No-fault is not without defense against charges that it fails to do justice. Its clear rules promise victims a consistency of treatment that tort law, with all its vicissitudes, including one-shot juries, fails to attain. In no-fault, if you are seriously injured, you get, say, two-thirds of what you have actually lost in earnings, up to a maximum based on social insurance principles—typically, two-thirds of an average weekly wage. So does the next claimant, and the next. In no-fault auto systems, mail clerks don't end up subsidizing lawyers. When a Howard Young buys no-fault insurance, his insurer knows that it is agreeing to pay the maximum allowable lost earnings if Howard is crippled. The cost of Howard's insurance reflects that expected payout. If his law firm's mail clerk, who earns less than the state's average wage, buys insurance from the same company, his premium will be lower than Howard's because the insurer is facing a lower lost-earnings payout if a serious accident occurs. Under tort law, though, the clerk must buy insurance to pay the lawyer's lost income.

Perhaps the most serious failing of no-fault plans, in the eyes of some of their critics, has been their failure to take much of a crack at tort law's deterrent task. If compensation is the main or only focus, its proponents can boast that no-fault plans shine. But when the accident-resolution system is asked to provide incentives to safety, no-fault plans are attacked as being empty at their core, paying alike as they do to people at fault and free from fault, and freeing those at fault from tort liability. In New Zealand's general no-fault schemes, payments are totally unrelated to anyone's faulty behavior. In the focused no-fault systems, the tendency is inevitable, critics argue, to focus more than under the tort system on one's membership in a group (drivers) or one's relationship to the injured (employer), and less on one's unsafe behavior in an individual case.

All no-fault systems grapple with this problem. Many make some efforts to provide safety incentives. New Zealand kept statistics on its no-fault payouts, expressly so that it could identify more dangerous industries and have those industries contribute more heavily to the funding of the Accident Compensation Scheme. But in fact,

New Zealand did little to reward or sanction those companies within an industry that were either more diligent or more cavalier than most about safety. To his credit, Professor Sugarman, the leading American proponent of a general no-fault scheme, recognizes this problem. He deals with it in his big California auto accident plan by having fairly cut-and-dried methods to identify the "bad" drivers and the "less safe" cars. Bad drivers and purchasers of less safe cars pay more for insurance under his scheme. Those easy handles for determining more or less dangerous activities or entities are not available outside the auto accident area, so Sugarman's general no-fault proposal relies on novel and ambitious methods for improving the quality of governmental safety regulation. Whatever merit those methods have in theory—which is debatable—the institution of such ambitious new regulatory reform in the foreseeable future seems fanciful. Moreover, regulatory reforms could just as easily come about in the context of a tort system that already provides some incentive to safety as in the context of a no-fault system that provides less deterrence.

Insofar as society continues to demand, in the face of numerous arguments to the contrary, that tort law do these other jobs—finding fault, determining cause, individualizing damages—it continues to suggest that these are important jobs. If they are important, then are they worth paying for? If so, are they worth as much as tort law now costs? If they are not really important jobs, then can tort law shed them—or at least some of them, such as paying as much as it does for noneconomic losses or in legal fees? And to that extent, could transaction costs be lowered enough to begin to approach those of its pure no-fault competitors?

One final concern needs to be raised with respect to all no-fault plans, even plans generous to accident victims and concerned with safety incentives. All of us potential accident victims have to ask what will happen if we sign on as a society to one of these plans and mothball tort law.

First, if tort law goes, can it ever come back? Notice, for example, that there has been no serious move to reinstate tort law for workplace injuries anywhere in the United States in the eighty or so years of workers' compensation. There was no such move even though benefit levels for workers' compensation claims had sunk so low in many states by the late 1960s—a decade in which radical consumerism was born—that a national commission expressed biting disapproval.[8] Admittedly inadequate workers' compensation may well have contributed to the rise of tort claims by injured workers against third parties (such as the punch press manufacturer providing equipment to the employer) that contributed to injuries and were not exempt from tort liability. But this only serves to emphasize the point that tort liability was alive to serve as a corrective to inadequate features of a nontort compensation system.

The reasons that tort may stay buried are precisely the reasons people should perhaps be very reluctant to bid it farewell in the first place. As the preceding chapter makes clear, there is a powerful array of forces in this society that find tort law painful. It is hard in any society to get rid of something—like the common law of torts—that has been around so long. If the antitort forces can ever overcome society's reluctance to abandon a longtime legal companion, they may well have the strength to forestall any efforts to force its return.

So what, one may ask, if we get a no-fault system, like, say, workers' compensation, that, whatever its difficulties, delivers vital compensation to more people, much faster and more evenhandedly than tort law ever did or will? Even assuming that these no-fault advantages were not, to some extent anyway, neutralized by tort's advantages in doing other jobs, the answer would be that in accepting no-fault, we may well have put ourselves more fully in the hands of the entities who will be paying for the compensation that potential accident victims get. What happens when the no-fault system becomes too painful to the providers of goods for services that are in turn responsible for much of the injury in society? Won't there be pressure to reduce benefits or tighten qualifying standards? Look at what has been happening lately to the most venerable no-fault system, workers' compensation. At a time when no-fault systems were being touted as the answers to the spiraling costs of the tort system, political battles erupted in several states as business groups tried to force cutbacks in workers' compensation benefits. In Maine and California, where troubled economies forced heated budget disputes in both legislative and executive branches, governors sought large reductions in benefits. In Maine, the political forces had reached agreement on a budget package, with the sole exception of the governor's demand for a 35 percent cut in workers' compensation. That single dispute was so important to his backers that the governor allowed the state government to shut down and ten thousand state workers to go idle rather than give in. The sides finally agreed to a 26 percent cutback, phased in over several years. California's battle also contributed to months of government without a budget or money to pay state workers. Granted, in both states critics pointed to claim abuses in the workers' compensation systems. But agitation for reductions in benefits often takes place in the context of workers' compensation systems whose benefits levels were already in the eyes of some so low as to be of questionable adequacy.[9]

These are not isolated incidents. New Zealand, in 1992, substantially cut back on the benefits obtainable through its exclusive no-fault accident scheme. According to one observer, the Trust Fund created in the United States by the Federal National Childhood Vaccine Injury Act of 1986, designed to route compensation claims for vaccine-related injuries out of the tort system into a no-fault scheme, has become "mired in case backlogs, underfunding and adversarial legal tactics."[10]

Tort law's adherents argue that it is more difficult, though not impossible, for the legislature to take away citizens' basic tort rights—witness the yearly futile battles in Congress to curb products liability claims. Even the waves of state tort reform of the past decade have left essential pieces of the tort system largely untouched. And if legislatures take significant common law tort rights away from the people, at least some state courts may insist, as a *constitutional* matter, that the people be given some significant benefit in return.[11] On the other hand, it may be much easier for the legislature to trim a no-fault program during an economic downturn by turning a 75 percent level of lost-wages compensation into a 65 percent level.

Within the systems themselves, the different kinds of decision makers can make a substantial difference in how reductions in benefits are implemented. In an administrative system like workers' compensation, if a program's chief administrator (perhaps with a word from higher political authority) sends out the word that standards have to tighten up and that awards must stop rising, the plan functionaries will in all likelihood see it as their duty to follow policy. In the tort system, there is no one to put out such a word. Even if there were, judges see their job, at least in part, as providing what they deem to be justice, not carrying out someone else's political or economic program. Juries are even less susceptible to a "get with the economy program" campaign. But here we reach an issue of real bite. It may well *not* be a good thing for one program of insurance—namely tort liability coverage—to be relatively immune from cost-cutting methods in tough economic times. Thus one finds cities and towns facing escalating tort liability costs while cutting back on vital services. (New York City pays more in tort settlements and awards annually than it pays for parks and libraries.) At any rate, defenders of the tort system urge that protections that exist thereunder for injured persons may be much sturdier when the political winds start blowing against them than those available in no-fault systems. Whether, given all the delays, corruption, and inefficiencies of the tort system, that is at bottom a plus or a minus is a topic of legitimate debate.

With regard to the "mover" group of reformers—those whose proposals include a place for *both* tort law and no-fault compensation plans, many of the same plaudits and criticisms are applicable. In this category of reforms fall many of the automobile no-fault plans that were adopted in the United States during the 1970s, as well as proposals to deal with exposures to toxic waste and a more general "neo-no-fault" plan that could deal with the whole universe of accidents. The desire of these proposals is to present sensible no-fault plans that often exist concurrently with tort regimes, in the expectation that a combination of the two would allow the strengths of each to prevail in appropriate circumstances.

The automobile accident no-fault plans originally presented the two sides of these "mover" plans. One type—threshold no-fault—bars access to the tort system unless the injured person is at least relatively seriously hurt. That level of severity was sometimes set by verbal descriptions (for example, "serious bodily impairment") and sometimes by a minimum dollar level of medical expenses (for example, $1,000). The other type—add-on no fault—allows any person to bring a negligence tort suit, with the hitch that he would have to subtract his no-fault benefits from any tort award. Both types of plans commonly had some provisions requiring a claimant to deduct from no-fault benefits some amounts received from another source, such as workers' compensation, to pay medical expenses or lost wages. The no-fault benefits resemble those described earlier for the general and focused no-fault plans.

But some observers consider allowing no-fault benefits plus access to tort suits unacceptably expensive, whether under add-on plans (which never abrogate right to claim for pain and suffering) or under threshold plans (which allow tort claims for pain and suffering for more serious injuries above the threshold).

The original hope was that no-fault laws would provide compensation to many more accident victims than are paid under traditional tort liability systems, and with faster payments and far lower lawyers' and adjusters' fees. Thus no-fault insurers could pay more people with less money. But some argue that the original no-fault concept has been "undermined" in the United States because the system is being used more and more frequently to accumulate enough health care costs to allow motorists both to collect no-fault benefits *and* to trigger a built-in right to sue, based on fault above the statutory threshold. (As suggested above, a "pure" no-fault proposal, ordaining only no-fault benefits and abolishing *all* tort claims, except against such defendants as drunken drivers, was soundly defeated as a California ballot initiative in March 1996.)

Another proposed change would give drivers the *choice* of purchasing no-fault for medical bills and wage loss, with such purchasers being both ineligible to sue and exempt from being sued for pain and suffering. (Drivers would still have to purchase fault-based property-damage insurance.) In states where no-fault plans are already in place, the waiver of pain and suffering claims would apply to tort claims above the threshold.

Purchasers of no-fault, then, would be allowed a tort claim against another motorist only for any economic loss in excess of their no-fault coverage. (If an injury were caused by alcohol or drug abuse, there would be no restriction on the right to sue.) In accidents between a driver covered by no-fault and one electing to stay under the tort system, the latter would make a claim based on fault against her own insurer, just as happens today under uninsured motorists (UM) coverage. Claims for economic loss in excess of that level of UM-like coverage would also be allowed against no-fault insureds.

Estimates by RAND indicate average minimum savings in total auto insurance premiums of more than 30 percent for motorists who choose no-fault. Savings for lower-income motorists would be close to 50 percent. Costs for motorists who elect to remain with fault-based coverage would be affected only minimally by the adoption of a choice plan. If 100 percent of insured drivers switched to the new coverage, annual premium savings across the country would have exceeded $40 billion in 1996, according to estimates of the Joint Economic Committee of the U.S. Congress, extrapolating from 1993 estimates by RAND.[12] (See Appendix for tables, including a state-by-state chart of projected savings.) The choice plan is incorporated in federal legislation proposed by then-Senator Bob Dole (R-Kan.) and incumbent Senators Mitch McConnell (R-Ky.), Daniel P. Moynihan (D-N.Y.), and Joseph Lieberman (D-Conn.).

Critics of such elective auto insurance plans protest against allowing consumers—often untutored in the niceties of tort law and insurance—to abandon their fundamental common law rights for auto insurance savings that may or may not materialize. They also object to requiring those who wish to remain under tort law to sue their own insurers rather than the wrongdoer when they collide with insureds who have switched to the new system.

A few "mover" reform proposals have evolved outside the world of auto accidents. But workable no-fault solutions for many other kinds of accidents are hard to come by. When a patient goes to a health care provider for treatment, can the law realistically decree that the provider must automatically pay for any adverse condition arising after treatment? Separating adverse conditions due to treatment from what made the patient ill in the first place is most vexing even on a no-fault basis. And even making every health care provider liable only for all conditions caused without fault by health care itself would force providers to face unknowable new claims and costs. Similarly as to products, assume you burn your hand badly on a stove. Does the stove manufacturer pay you? Why not, once anyone' s fault is not a factor? So abandoning fault for all kinds of products and services threatens society with huge new insurance claims and costs.[13]

A "neo-no-fault" proposal developed by one of the authors of this book, Jeffrey O'Connell, has potential applicability to *all* accident areas.[14] Unlike some other no-fault plans (like the hazardous waste–injury system just discussed), this proposal does not create any entity separate from tort law. Rather, it creates an "early offers/choice" plan, whereby any defendant of a personal injury claim is given the option of offering within 120 days to make periodic payment of the claimant's net economic loss—relatively prompt payment compared with the tort system. Such payment will cover any medical expenses, including rehabilitation, and wage loss, beyond any health or disability insurance already payable to the claimant, plus a reasonable hourly fee for the claimant's lawyer. A defendant in a tort suit promptly offering to pay these amounts to the claimant forecloses further pursuit of a tort claim; the claimant must accept. (Offers could be refused, however, and a normal tort claim pursued when the defendant's misconduct was intentional or wanton.) Note that under this proposal, no defendant is *forced* to offer such a settlement; this precludes the imposition of unmanageable new claims and costs to society.

When would a defendant be inclined to make such an "early offer"? If the defendant, after examining the claim, determines, for example, that the claimant never was in its hospital or never used its product, the defendant would obviously not offer to pay net economic loss. But apart from such cases, even if the defendant thinks it might be able to defeat a more threatening claim, it might also determine that it *is* after all a claim by its patient or a user of its product for an adverse condition that clearly resulted from a stay in the defendant's hospital or from use of the defendant's product. Although the defendant may believe the accident was not its fault, it would calculate what it would cost to pay the claimant periodically for his medical expense and wage loss. If that sum turns out to be less than what the defendant would pay to defense lawyers, plus its exposure to tort damages, including payment for pain and suffering, the defendant—and indeed the claimant—would arguably have found a good trade. Given the huge costs of defending tort cases and the gamble of having to pay large sums for noneconomic losses, many defendants would be prompted to pay for economic losses not just in cases they are sure to lose but even in many—perhaps most—cases in which the issue of liability is legitimately in doubt. One leading defense lawyer hypothesized that of the 250 cases his large office was then defending, all in various stages of litigation, he would advise making an offer to pay claimants' net economic losses in 200 if such a law were in effect.

It is argued this neo-no-fault proposal enables many injured persons to obtain relatively fast payment for their economic losses while being able to make use of the full tort apparatus if they are eligible. Incentives—but not requirements—are built in to encourage early resolution of tort disputes. They thereby attack, *within the tort system* itself, the grievously high costs of resolving tort disputes. The worst nightmares of delayed, inadequate compensation for seriously injured people are dramatically reduced, primarily for those plaintiffs for whom that is very important. Much of the tort system's deterrence is retained: the party paying the bill is the party responsible for the injury. In those instances in which the defendant's behavior is likely to be found clearly unreasonable, the full threat of tort damages remains as a disincentive to such behavior.

Furthermore, the guiding background for decisions about offering or accepting no-fault benefits is the tort system, with its full panoply of rules that reflect the community's notions of justice because they have been developed over time by a diverse multitude of justice-committed decision makers looking at concrete situations. In short, the parties' choices whether to engage in the neo-no-fault part of the process are shaped at least in part by considerations that society regards as just. Thus, choice plans seek to alleviate some of the weaknesses of tort law: its massive transaction costs and its long delays in the delivery of needed compensation. The plans also permit some of tort law's strengths to function—especially under the neo-no-fault plan—in forcing those arguably at fault to bear substantial burdens for injuries inflicted. No defendant under such a plan is relieved of full-scale tort liability unless he or she *earns* that relief through promptly reimbursing the injured victim's economic losses. Thus this plan purports to undercut any plaintiffs' lawyers attack on it as one-sided.

But choice plans are no panacea. Admittedly, the early-offer plan does not require defendants to make offers, though legislatures can supplement the neo-no-fault plans with incentives to encourage such offers from recalcitrant defendants. Defendants who do not make offers, for example, might by law be barred from asserting any legal defenses based on the claimant's own faulty conduct. At any rate, the opportunity to save on their substantial defense costs should arguably move most defendants to at least consider an early offer whenever a plaintiff seems to have a legitimate chance to win his case. Does the early-offer plan unfairly stack the deck against risk-averse people, who will give up a strong claim or a defense for fear of losing more in the tort trial? It is difficult, of course, to separate persons with very strong claims who are merely very risk averse from the larger group who simply are unsure—perhaps rightly so—about the merits of their claim or defense. That latter group especially includes many of the claimants whose cases should arguably be resolved quickly with "half a loaf" for each side. And, critics of tort law can argue, tort law itself doesn't treat the risk averse very well, given its delays and vicissitudes even in supposedly clear-cut cases. Nor can one blame just one side—either claimants or defendants—for this situation, given all the opportunity for disputation in the tort system.

Admittedly, choice plans do not go as far to eliminate the severe tort transaction costs as the nontort no-fault plans do, nor do they assure the same speedy delivery of compensation for as broad a group of injury victims. This concern with even broader compensation may argue for no-fault and tort mixes like the auto add-on and environmental two-tier plans; under those schemes, all truly injured people who will never be able to prove fault are assured of some financial help, while those with good tort claims can always pursue them. But that same factor might explain why such mixed proposals may not be politically acceptable, whereas the early-offer plan could be. The mixed proposals would seem to provide so much "adverse selection," whereby plaintiffs with weak claims go the no-fault route and plaintiffs with strong claims go the full compensation tort route, that they will be judged too likely to increase already high insurance costs.

Another "early offer" plan is somewhat narrower, concerning itself with plaintiffs' lawyers' contingent fees. The contingent fee, for all its virtues in helping to provide access to the courts for many injury victims, also provides rife opportunities for abuse. In September of 1989 in Alton, Texas, a soft-drink delivery truck struck a school bus, killing twenty-one children and injuring dozens of others. The bottling company's insurers quickly settled the case with the families of the victims for an estimated $122 million. Even though the case was settled early with no doubt about the issue of liability, the families' attorneys took a third of the settlement for themselves.[15] According to Lester Brickman of Benjamin Cardozo Law School, the $40 million-plus windfall amounted to at least $25,000 an hour for each plaintiff's lawyer. Less dramatic examples of abuse are prevalent. Suppose a judgment-proof driver with only the $20,000 state-mandated minimum of liability insurance crosses the center line, permanently and totally disabling a high wage earner in the opposite lane. There is no issue of liability, and it is obvious that the damages will greatly exceed the policy limits. A reputable insurer will very often promptly tender the full policy limits to the claimant. Notwithstanding that there is nothing to contest and, therefore, little work to be done, the claimant's lawyer will nonetheless typically pocket a third or more of the award.

A proposal by the second-named author of this book, along with Lester Brickman and Michael Horowitz, seeks to eliminate these types of abuse. The plan would allow a defendant in a civil suit sixty days after a claim is filed to make a settlement offer—in this case including damages for pain and suffering. If an offer is tendered and accepted, compensation for the plaintiff's lawyer would be limited to 10 percent of the first $100,000 and 5 percent of any amount in excess of $100,000. If a prompt offer is refused, the offer then would become the baseline for a contingency fee. For example, suppose a prompt offer of $90,000 is refused and the case is later settled for $120,000. The plaintiff's lawyer would receive $9,000 (10% of $90,000) plus a normal contingency fee of, say, one-third for the extra $30,000 ($10,000). If there is no prompt offer, then the lawyer's normal contingency fee applies to the entire award.

The plan is designed to pay lawyers only for results that they actually achieve. Plaintiffs' lawyers are to be paid 10 percent of any early settlement offer because admittedly their presence alone is often enough to force an insurer to take a claim more seriously. Lawyers are then compensated through the use of a normal contingency fee for any amount of money that the claimant receives beyond the original offer. In that case the lawyer is deemed to have earned any additional money through her own efforts at negotiation or litigation. By contrast, in a system in which lawyers receive a percentage of an entire judgment, lawyers are often receiving an extremely high percentage of money that would have been received without much reference to their services.

In addition, the plan's proponents argue that it will reduce defendants' incentives to stall. A prompt offer would pay 90–95 cents on the dollar to the claimant, whereas a later offer would deliver only 60–65 cents for every dollar. Therefore, a claimant will need—and bargain for—more from a later offer because he will receive less of it. Furthermore, it is contended, with a prompt offer insurers can reduce the transaction costs of their own legal defense costs by paying their lawyers for fewer hours (indeed, early offers could often be formulated "in house" by insurance company claims personnel without sending the case to much more expensive outside defense counsel). The Insurance Services Office estimated that insurers' legal defense costs accounted for 14 percent of total costs in 1992. As we have seen, a version of this contingency fee reform was on the California ballot as an initiative in March 1996, narrowly losing, 51–49 percent.

Opponents criticize the plan on the grounds that it will decrease access to the courtroom. They argue that personal injury lawyers earn their sizable fees: they risk nonpayment and underpayment; they pay more for advertising and malpractice insurance; and they enjoy little prestige with other lawyers and the public at large. In view of these disadvantages in practicing personal injury law, it is argued, a decreased profit margin would tend to drive lawyers away from personal injury work and create a shortage. In the opinion of the plan's critics, the contingency fee allows personal injury lawyers to diversify risks and stabilize their practice, which benefits both lawyers and clients.

Many of the plan's opponents prefer the current system of allowing judges to review fees and strike them down if they are "unconscionable." But, the plan's proponents reply, courts already see themselves as overwhelmed with crowded dockets. Also, as former lawyers, judges are often reluctant to discipline their erstwhile colleagues. Furthermore, it is argued, the biggest problem with "judicial review" is that about 95 percent of personal injury cases are settled out of court, so a judge will rarely have cause to review attorneys' fees.

The goal of both early-offer approaches is to drive down the waste of personal injury litigation by deterring litigants from resorting to prolonged and expensive legal strategies and providing lawyers and their clients with incentives to settle. The aim, according to Senator McConnell, is to keep cases from dragging on when the parties "just want to get it over with." Both parties, he thinks, would benefit—defendants by lessening risks of much larger losses and injured claimants by avoiding years of waiting and possibly receiving little or nothing. Personal injury lawyers on both claimant and defendant side counter, though, that there is more to law than just "getting it over with." Justice, they argue, often requires appropriate incentives to go to court.

In support of lawyers' objections to "quick and dirty" no-fault or neo-no-fault early-offer solutions is the considerable body of sophisticated research we presented earlier indicating that people—including those involved in an accident—feel the need to "tell their story." Indeed, their satisfaction with the legal process sometimes turns less on whether they win or lose than on their perception of the proceeding, including their opportunity to be heard.[16] Of course, with the settlement rate for personal injury tort cases well over 95 percent and with the courts already swamped with the few cases that do not settle, it may be wildly unrealistic to try to satisfy a widespread desire for full-scale hearings of whatever type.

Note, though, that the scheme allowing motorists to choose to insure themselves under either no-fault *or* tort criteria better serves the need in this connection of both those who "just want to get it over with" and those who want something more. Admittedly, the scheme allowing a defendant in nonauto cases to unilaterally foreclose a full-scale tort claim by making an early offer (except where the defendant has acted egregiously) is less satisfactory in denying at least some accident victims a chance at what they may want most from legal proceedings. At any rate, the early-offer plans seem philosophically to fit more with the no-fault innovators than with those who have no different system in mind but rather focus their reform suggestions on incremental changes in tort rules themselves.

Such tinkerers are a disparate group. They include most of the business and professional groups hostile to tort, as well as some of the provictim advocates. In the past decade, tinkerers have by and large succeeded in enacting relatively minor reforms, making it harder for plaintiffs to win tort suits or to win as much if they do succeed. Four reforms seem worthy of mention because they purport at least to preserve the strengths or ameliorate weaknesses in the tort system.

First, many states—following some of the reformers cited in this chapter—have abolished, for at least some categories of cases (medical malpractice, for example), the "collateral source rule." That rule traditionally permitted a plaintiff to be paid twice for some of his expenses—once by, say, a first-party health insurance plan to which he belonged, such as Blue Cross, and again by the tort defendant. Although there were understandable reasons for this rule—having much to do with courts' reluctance to reward defendants for plaintiffs' own insurance coverage—its abolition grew increasingly sensible, especially compared with double payment for a single loss, and especially as it became ever more apparent that liability insurance returned many fewer cents in benefits per premium dollar than did first-party insurance. Tort law's compensation goals are, after all, fully served when the plaintiff's real losses are compensated once from whatever source. Admittedly, theoretically at least, abandoning the collateral source rule reduces the deterrent pressure on careless actors below the "just right" level. In practice, however, the sizable costs of defending a tort suit, including the risk of losing, seem to ensure that any reductions in deterrent pressure from abolition of the collateral source rule will be worth it.

The second area of tinkering, and probably the more critical, because more significantly controversial, has been with respect to limits on damages for intangible injuries, such as punitive damages or for pain and suffering. Punitive damages over and above a claimant's medical and wage losses are assessable in a civil case, as the name indicates, against a defendant guilty of egregious misconduct. Whether punitive damages ought to be awarded in civil cases at all and if so when, for how much, and to whom (the state? the victim?) is being rigorously contested in the press, law reviews, courts, and legislatures. The last have imposed caps on punitive awards in many states. A skeptic might ask, though, why punitive damages are deemed so significant if Massachusetts and Washington State disallow them altogether as a practical matter but still essentially face all tort law's problems.

Much more significant, actuarially and otherwise, are damages for pain and suffering. These damages for psychic harm have also been a target of many reform proposals. Some reformers would excise them completely from tort or alternative compensation systems. Others would cap damages—in fact, caps on nonpecuniary damages have been among the favorite piecemeal reforms with state legislatures for the last decade. It should be noted again that the two "tinkering" reforms mentioned so far—like all those proposed by sellers of goods and services and their insurers, including the reforms proposed in the GOP's Contract with America—are one sided. Unlike the auto choice and early-offer proposals, they either (1) make it harder for claimants to recover, or (2) award them less when they do so, with no corollary advantage to those injured by products or services. Such one-sided reforms are an easy target for plaintiffs' lawyers, who successfully tar them as antipopulist. Workers' compensation and no-fault insurance, on the other hand, reduce payment (for example, not paying for pain and suffering) but make it more readily available (paying regardless of fault).

According to tort law's adherents, those who would abolish noneconomic damages—including those who support no-fault plans—are asserting that people should be afforded money to make up for ravaged pocketbooks but not for the psychic losses from ravaged lives. This distinction overlooks the reality—as even little Elissa Young knew—that although life with less money is infinitely preferable to life without a person we love, a person will suffer not only monetarily but psychologically: tort law acknowledges and compensates monetary cum psychological injuries, confident that the courts can calculate—or at least approximate—such compensation.

Courts might arguably have similar confidence with respect to psychological injuries that do not result in loss of money if they adopted uniform scales for nonpecuniary injuries which various experts have proposed or are working on.[17] Such scales would arguably allow the law to assess more equitably the nonpecuniary loss component of a tort award. And yet, critics observe, the intractability of designing a scale or schedule of payment for psychic losses has long plagued workers' compensation. Indeed, one of the key sources of that system's skyrocketing costs, in addition to payment and administration of claims (including legal fees), has been the jockeying of lawyers on both sides to manipulate such inherently amorphous items of loss represented by schedules of psychic detriment.

But if uniform scales could be used to determine the amounts to be awarded for certain kinds of injuries, the regressiveness of the tort system—which continues to be one of its most intractable problems—could be alleviated. As we have discussed, making the mail clerk in Howard Young's law firm pay the same amount for "tort insurance" as Howard seems unfair when the former's much lower salary qualifies him for about one-tenth of Howard's potential award. Payment for noneconomic loss, particularly if such injuries were compensated on a schedule, would ameliorate that injustice because the two persons would be receiving equal amounts for at least part of their injuries (admittedly not for wage loss). On the other hand, scheduling of such benefits manifestly lessens the individualized justice of which tort law's adherents boast. Is the psychic loss of a finger to a pianist to be equated to a digital loss of a person rarely making specialized use of his hand?

At any rate, tort law's adherents view the payment for noneconomic loss as buttressing the strength of the tort system as a source of meaning for the victims of accidents. The provision of damages for psychic harms honors the victim's injury. It respects the whole of his experience (though admittedly much less so if the damages would be uniformly scheduled). If he is to recover damages for what he feels and has felt, then the tort plaintiff must be permitted to tell that part of his story which may be most important to him. Certainly what was most relevant about this accident to all of the Youngs was its wrecking-ball effect on their emotional lives—Howard's humiliation, the children's sense of rejection, Nicole's loss of love and support. If the system denies to all of them the ability to force society to confront and respect the essence of their injury, it will have lost, the argument goes, one of its major potential benefits.

On the other hand, advocates of no-fault schemes argue that with limited funds to go around (which will always be the case), it is better to use those precious dollars to pay more people their actual economic losses (in the form of medical costs and lost wages) than to pay some, but not all, for both economic and noneconomic losses—especially given the transaction costs involved in determining the economic value of noneconomic loss. After all, the argument goes, forms of first-party insurance (like health insurance or disability insurance covering wages) don't normally offer to pay for noneconomic psychic losses. This apparently stems from the reluctance of insureds, when buying insurance for themselves, to pay for it. If so, tort critics ask, why force people to buy such coverage (indirectly in the cost of goods and services) in the form of tort liability insurance?[18] Critics of payment for pain and suffering also point out that such damages, according to a leading authority on the subject, really serve only as a rough means of paying the plaintiff's attorney fee.[19] So why not, they ask, just simplify the system to both lessen the need for attorneys and eliminate damages for pain and suffering?

Another suggested reform—also mostly incremental—is offered by the executive editor of the recent American Law Institute's study of enterprise liability, Paul Weiler. Having immersed himself, with a team of eminent torts scholars, in the intricacies of medical malpractice and products liability cases, Professor Weiler produced a series of suggestions, including the big step of experimentation with no-fault systems for medical malpractice. But Weiler himself recognized some of the difficulties with such a huge systemic change in the medical injury area. So he also recommended that, quite apart from such a radical no-fault change, hospitals and HMOs be made primarily liable for all accidental injuries inflicted on patients by the malpractice of anyone affiliated with the institution, displacing the liability of individual doctors or other health care providers.[20] In some respects, this proposal mirrors the evolving willingness of tort law over the decades to find institutions liable for the actions of individuals with whom they have significant relationships and opportunity to control. (After an early embrace of this idea of "enterprise liability," the Clinton Health Care Task Force later backed away from it.)

Weiler's proposal addresses both the strengths and weaknesses in tort law. To maximize the deterrent effects of tort law's liability rulings, it would direct them at entities that have the sophistication to better understand what the liability ruling means and the power to take institutional steps (training, new procedures, checklists, communication methods) to reduce the chance of similar accidents happening again. Weiler's proposal, later fleshed out with the help of University of Virginia law professor Kenneth Abraham, seeks to reduce the administrative costs of present medical malpractice lawsuits that entail multiple defendant health care providers, each represented by an expensive defense lawyer. Finally, it seeks to ameliorate the emotional trauma of the tort system for individual doctors by rechanneling the system toward institutional parties and tries to change tort rules in ways that will reduce their trauma—trauma entirely over and above the financial costs of litigation.[21]

A third type of reform, the class action, started out by "tinkering" with the number of parties allowed in a case and trying to curb transaction costs by merging many potential litigants into one action. This innovation—which has grown way beyond "tinkering"—was a response of the courts to the problem of a large number of plaintiffs injured in the same kind of adverse event—for example, mass (often toxic) tort cases for, say, workers exposed to asbestos dust or women with silicone breast implants. These sort of cases involved so many different defendants and plaintiffs that judges felt a need to innovate rather than risk having masses of related claims that would take far more than their judicial lifetimes to resolve. Some advantages seen as stemming from this sort of reform were a uniformity of discovery documents applicable to many cases of a similar type, computerized claims analysis, routinized payment, and the like.

This book has not focused on such mass or toxic tort cases but on the relatively much more common individual traumatic injuries. In thinking about tort reform, a basic question is that if tort law cannot deal effectively with relatively simple individual accidents arising from automobiles, subways, medical malpractice, or malfunctioning products, how can it hope to solve the infinitely more complex problems stemming from indirect illnesses from, say, toxic chemicals? But paradoxically, real tort reform of products liability law, with automatic payment only for economic losses, may in fact be first applied in mass or toxic cases because traditional tort law based on fault has broken down there most of all. So far, though, there are few signs of such a breakthrough.

The rampant complexities of mass or toxic tort cases have been well treated in a piece by Professor Brickman.[22] Class actions can result, for example, in vigorous debate about what illness or injury, if any, was caused over a long period of time by what chemical or other product component, and what damages and even what jurisdiction's law apply to far-flung and disparate claimants and defendants. Thus such cases can see federal law flouting state law and vice versa as courts see themselves increasingly overwhelmed by even a few such cases of millions of persons occupationally exposed to asbestos, or more than a million women receiving breast implants, or Vietnam veterans exposed to Agent Orange. Federal court procedural rules make all qualifying persons a party to the class action unless a potential plaintiff elects to opt out of the class. This has exponentially increased the size of classes and spawned the class action lawyer in what has become a billion dollar industry. Although the plaintiff initially used to gain class certification must have suffered an injury, those joining the class afterward require only the possibility of having suffered adverse effects. For example, thousands of uninjured plaintiffs have later joined in a class of those injured by asbestos, though having no signs of impairment. This can force the defendant to compensate many people who have never been injured as well as those class members who have actually suffered injury. Thus, in its own way the class action can mimic the seemingly arbitrary and unjust over- and undercompensation scheme one finds in the normal tort system as applied to, say, auto accidents.

Class actions can also mean huge conflicts of interest, as well as denial of due process to future claimants. Lawyers supposedly representing a whole class of claimants may be tempted to enter into side settlements that favor their current clients over future ones. Future claimants may be denied due process rights of notice and opportunity to participate. Even more infuriating to the public are settlements whereby claimants' counsel walk away with millions of dollars in fees while their clients receive derisory compensation in scrip for free car safety inspections or discounts on the future purchase of the offending seller's product, ranging from $400 in nontransferable coupons good for a year on a new Ford to a deduction from an airline fare to a free box of Cheerios.[23] Critics see such settlements as evidence of collusion between claimants' lawyers and large corporate defendants.

On the other hand, by no means do all the abuses adversely affect only claimants. As Professor Brickman points out, there are fears concerning the fairness and even the constitutionality of class actions—of their "strong-arming defendants into settlement." He points to one court as long ago as 1973 that spoke of the blackmail-like effect of class certifications on defendants who face, as the court put it, "the huge and unavoidable expense of producing witnesses and documents pursuant to . . . [pretrial] orders . . . [which] have brought such pressure on defendants as to induce settlement in large amounts as the alternative to complete ruin and disaster."[24] But logistical burdens are not the only risk facing defendants against whom a class is certified. Even if a defendant has won the great bulk of individual cases resolved up to that point, and even if the odds are very high that such early successes will continue, a defendant risks having to pay not only a single case's damages but much, much more because of the all-or-nothing cumulation of multiple claims.

Furthermore, as we have seen, the damage figures are from an indefinitely large pool of injured and allegedly injured claimants rather than only those actually choosing up to that point to sue. In addition, class actions in tort cases commonly include claims for punitive damages, which juries often compute by multiplying the damages assessed for actual losses.

As Professor Brickman puts it:

> The result is the emergence of what might be called the bet-your-company class action. The long-shot risk of an adverse verdict, which hovers in the background even in a case strongly favoring the defendant, takes on qualitatively new menace once the stakes reach this level. Even if one expects that appellate courts would find some grounds on which to reverse any such outcome—hardly a safe assumption—the procedure for securing such appeal underscores the aggregated action's formidable threat value. The usual rule is that a losing defendant asking to stay the execution of a judgment while it appeals must post a bond in at least the amount of the judgment. In the run of individual cases this may pose no great hardship, but in mass personal injury cases the verdict can easily exceed the company's cash on hand or even its net worth. The moment such a verdict is handed down banks would be likely to cut off a defendant's lines of credit, plunging it into bankruptcy even if it had excellent chances of getting the verdict reversed at the appellate level.

Furthermore, as Brickman points out, because a certification ruling in itself is often not considered a final court order, it is not immediately appealable. Rather, the defendant must go to trial, able only to raise the certification issue on an appeal based on the merits of the whole case. But this is precisely the point when the requirement of posting a bond can make an appeal such a disaster. The result: a defendant knows that it must settle a mass-tort case before it reaches that point. Thus certification issues are likely not to reach an appellate court.

Brickman goes on to observe that at this point an "even more ominous dynamic comes into play." Defendants who settle do not have a choice as to which part of the class to settle with: "[T]hey must settle with all, including—often—claimants without any discernible injury," with their opposing lawyers free to recruit more class members. This means extortionate demands reinforced by lawyer's fees for huge numbers of claimants amounting to tens, even hundreds of millions of dollars. So even if class actions began with a group of genuinely injured parties with arguably valid cases, the litigation expands, in Brickman's phrase, by "concentric rings to pull in ever-larger numbers who display either no symptoms at all or unverifiable symptoms and sometimes scant evidence of exposure to the product or activity in question."[25]

It was the fear of the dynamics of all this that recently caused Congress—with many Democrats joining Republicans—to override a veto by President Clinton of legislation aimed at class actions in another similar area of law—one occurring after a drop in a company's stock prices. This override, it should be noted, was bitterly denounced by claimants' lawyers and consumer groups as insulating wrongdoers from responsibility. Regardless of the merits of Clinton's veto in this instance or the abuse of class actions, it is certainly the case that the costs to claimants of pursuing individual actions have been so prohibitive that alleged wrongdoers without the threat of class actions have often been able to escape liability with relative impunity. Witness the phenomenon through the years of tobacco companies vastly outspending catastrophically affected claimants and their lawyers and thus driving them from the field—that is, until class actions threatened to level the playing field, and maybe then some.

So which is worse? A whip hand for defendants without class actions or a whip hand for claimants with them?

The latter, according to an opinion by the controversial but brilliant American jurist Richard Posner. Writing for a divided federal appellate court, Judge Posner decertified a class for hemophiliacs who were infected with HIV through contaminated blood products in the early years of the AIDS epidemic. He questioned the constitutionality and the fairness in letting "[o]ne jury, consisting of six persons . . . hold the fate of an industry in the palm of its hand."[26] (Other courts seem to be similarly backing off their enthusiasm for class actions.)

It is bad enough, argue tort law's adherents, that common law rights should be fundamentally altered by legislatures. It is much worse, in the eyes of not only tort law's adherents but others, that rights on both sides should be arbitrarily—often covertly—varied or even abolished by the whim of judges desperate to lighten their dockets, or, worse yet, by nontrial procedures run by those to whom judges delegate the task, whether trustees supervising available funds, or other court-appointed surrogates, or even selected partisans. But tort foes counter that it was the manifest inadequacy of individualized tort law that sent harassed courts to these radically altered mass remedies in the first place. On the other hand, if the rules are to be radically altered, ought it be by courts? Well, if legislatures won't act—perhaps because the problems of mass torts are especially seen as legislatively insoluble—what are the (overwhelmed and understaffed) courts to do? Some, including Judge Posner, would say, buckle down and prepare to try the cases in the old-fashioned way—one-by-one. That, they say, would result in massive out-of-court individualized settlements for almost all cases as the expense, delays, and fortuities become apparent to litigants on both sides. But even if so, wouldn't defendants often be handed back that whip hand they often wield in dealing with individual claimants? More than anything, according to some observers, that courts have become so ineptly mired in dealing with mass and toxic tort cases starkly illustrates how difficult it is to apply simple rules of, say, right and wrong—in other words, standards based on fault—in a modern technological age. But if the old fault-based rules of culpability and causation are judged to be failing, what manageable new ones will be better?

All this necessarily rather cursory treatment of reforms—whether "tinkering" or more sweeping—that have emanated from reams of careful analysis by scholars and distinguished groups of legal specialists and have occasioned passionate and expensive battles in legislative hallways across the nation may suggest to some a lack of respect for the detailed procedures that occupy the time and attention of P. J. Cowcroft, Judge Constance Small, and their legal colleagues everywhere. Not necessarily so. Rather, it can be seen as reflecting the variety of perspectives on the tort system that we have invited the reader of this book to share. Those perspectives look at what tort law tries to do and might in the future do for society. They evaluate the particulars of tort law and how those particulars contribute to or detract from what it might do for us.

It is late on a summer night at the two-bedroom tract home of Howard and Nicole Young. A box fan pulls strands of heavy ninety-degree air out of their bedroom. Seven-year-old Laura and her teenage sister, Elissa, sleep damp and uncovered in their bedroom's bunk beds. Howard snores fitfully, twisted in the awkward ball that sleep choreographs. Under a dim lamp, in the bed next to Howard's, Nicole darns Laura's sock.

Each has taken a journey to be wished on no one. They never wanted to see tort law at first hand. The readers of this book have seen how tort law can change people's lives. Does it change them sufficiently for the good, especially when compared to alternatives? That question is being vigorously disputed across the land. We can only hope the reader is now in a better position to help society decide.

Table A.1. Estimated 1996 Savings from an Auto-Choice Plan (in billions)

	Private	Commercial	Total
Total Auto Insurance Premiums	$110.7	$25.0	$135.7
Total Available Savings if 100% Switch	$ 31.7	$ 8.3	$ 40.0
Savings (%)	28.6%	33.3%	N/A
Savings for Low Income Drivers	44.9%	N/A	N/A

Source: Improving the American Legal System: The Economic Benefit of Tort Reform, Joint Economic Committee (JEC), United States Congress 5–6 (March 1996), based on data from J. O'Connell et al., "The Comparative Cost of Consumer Choice for Auto Insurance in All Fifty States," 55 *Md. L. Rev.* 160, 172–73 (1996), supplemented by updated information of JEC staff.

Table A.2. State-by-State 1996 Savings from Auto Choice

State	Proportional Savings			Average Private Passenger Premium		
	Total Savings (millions)*	All Private Drivers*	Low-Income Drivers*	Est. 1996 Average Premium	Average Savings under Auto Choice*	Average Premium under Auto Choice
All U.S.	$40,037	28.6%	44.9%	$773	$221	$551
Alabama	312	16.8	31.5	631	106	525
Alaska	37	12.1	19.3	913	110	803
Arizona	777	34.8	49.4	878	306	573
Arkansas	337	27.9	45.9	691	193	498
California	5,260	33.0	50.5	884	292	592
Colorado	672	30.6	45.8	891	273	619
Connecticut	987	39.2	54.6	924	362	562
Delaware	148	28.9	39.7	874	253	622
Florida	2,220	27.1	37.6	668	181	487
Georgia	834	20.9	36.6	712	149	563
Hawaii	345	40.6	51.7	1,081	439	642
Idaho	145	27.8	44.8	578	161	417
Illinois	1,393	24.2	41.8	679	164	514
Indiana	763	26.1	41.9	620	162	458
Iowa	321	24.7	42.3	521	129	393
Kansas	87	7.1	12.5	638	45	593
Kentucky	61	3.5	5.3	700	25	675
Louisiana	1,015	44.0	61.8	927	407	520
Maine	180	31.3	49.8	538	168	370
Maryland	1,007	34.6	49.7	775	268	507
Massachusetts	1,731	39.3	52.3	1,093	430	663
Michigan	890	15.7	27.7	815	128	687
Minnesota	785	31.3	46.0	740	232	508
Mississippi	254	21.4	37.3	703	151	552
Missouri	679	25.9	42.4	680	176	504
Montana	142	34.3	57.4	653	224	429

(continued)

| State | Proportional Savings | | | Average Private Passenger Premium | | |
	Total Savings (millions)*	All Private Drivers*	Low-Income Drivers*	Est. 1996 Average Premium	Average Savings under Auto Choice*	Average Premium under Auto Choice
Nebraska	$198	24.7%	43.1%	$607	$150	$457
Nevada	310	35.5	51.1	975	346	628
New Hampshire	144	21.7	34.8	685	149	536
New Jersey	2,346	36.1	53.0	1,093	395	698
New Mexico	272	33.1	51.2	870	288	582
New York	3,877	35.3	52.4	1,115	393	722
North Carolina	1,088	30.8	44.6	554	170	383
North Dakota	−17	−6.1	−11.2	507	−31	538
Ohio	1,294	26.5	42.3	577	153	424
Oklahoma	428	27.8	45.7	669	186	483
Oregon	402	25.0	36.5	659	165	494
Pennsylvania	1,994	29.7	43.2	744	221	523
Rhode Island	156	23.3	32.6	1,103	256	846
South Carolina	556	30.6	45.0	708	217	491
South Dakota	112	34.9	59.2	595	207	387
Tennessee	452	19.4	33.6	595	116	479
Texas	2,920	32.1	47.1	908	292	617
Utah	217	27.7	44.4	708	196	512
Vermont	50	17.2	30.1	601	103	498
Virginia	896	29.5	42.9	578	170	408
Washington	951	35.4	50.2	793	281	512
West Virginia	334	36.3	56.0	807	293	514
Wisconsin	704	30.9	50.7	569	176	393
Wyoming	52	24.1	45.6	609	147	462

Source: Improving the American Legal System: The Economic Benefit of Tort Reform, Joint Economic Committee (JEC), United States Congress at 6 (March 1996).

*Assumes 100% switch (percentage savings vary little with proportion of those who switch). Based on state laws as of 1988.

Introduction

1. *The Case of the Thorns,* Year Book 6, Edition 4, 7a, pl. 18 (1466).

2. The term *accident* will be used throughout the book to describe the typical mode of injury that may make people tort "victims." Although that term is meant to include situations in which one person intentionally injures another, such intentional injuries make up a small and generally simpler part of tort litigation in the United States. Therefore, they do not demand much specific attention in the context of the world of accidents that underlies most tort law.

CHAPTER 1: *How Tort Law Works*

1. Howard Young and his family and the events described herein are creations of the authors. They do not exist precisely as described. The events were suggested to the authors by two New York City cases involving intoxicated persons struck by subway trains. The cases received substantial publicity in late 1990 and early 1991. The people and their reactions were suggested by the authors' readings about thousands of tort cases. The processes that Howard Young and his family—and the actors they bring into the tort system—will face in the subsequent pages of this chapter represent fairly the realities of the torts process as we understand them.

2. Only about 10 percent of Americans are covered by long-term disability insurance. American Law Institute, Reporters' Study, 1 *Enterprise Responsibility for Personal Injury* (Philadelphia: The Institute, 1991) 157–58 [hereinafter ALI Study]. One estimate concludes that only about 20 percent of employed Americans have private insurance that would partially replace wages lost due to long-term disabilities. See P. Danzon, "Tort Reform and

the Role of Government in Private Insurance Markets," 13 *J. Leg. Stud.* 517, 523 (1984). Although more persons have some insurance against short-term disabilities—less than two years—three-quarters of the population does not. ALI Study, at 157.

3. The authors use the pronouns *he/his/him* and *she/her* throughout the book based on the gender of the fictional character who plays that role in this opening chapter's story of Howard Young's accident. For example, unless referring to a particular person, the masculine pronoun is used for a tort plaintiff, and the feminine for a plaintiff's lawyer, because Howard Young and P. J. Cowcroft are of those respective genders.

4. See R. Abel, "The Real Tort Crisis: Too Few Claims," 48 *Ohio St. L.J.* 443, 448–51; D. Harris et al., *Compensation and Support for Illness and Injury* (Oxford: Clarendon, 1984) ch. 2 [hereinafter Compensation and Support]. For information from a recent extensive study, indicating that only one claim for compensation arises from every eight instances of hospital injury due to medical negligence, see Harvard Medical Practice Study, *Patients, Doctors, and Lawyers: Medical Injury, Malpractice Litigation, and Patient Compensation in New York* (Cambridge: Harvard University Press, 1990) ch. 7; see also P. Danzon, *Medical Malpractice: Theory, Evidence, and Public Policy* (Cambridge: Harvard University Press, 1985) 19–21, 23.

5. This underlying premise assumes a situation in which a defendant (or defendants) is judged fully responsible for the plaintiff's injuries and those injuries are the sort that tort law does not exclude from compensation. In the Youngs' case, Howard clearly would be judged partially responsible, perhaps primarily responsible, for his own injuries. As a result, in the state that we here hypothesize, he would not be paid full compensation. Such issues in tort law, including whether the emotional and psychological injuries suffered by Nicole, Elissa, and Laura would be compensable injuries, are dealt with more fully in subsequent chapters.

6. It is increasingly common for settlement payments to a successful plaintiff in a tort suit to be "structured" so that he is paid periodically certain amounts at set times in the future, rather than one large sum all at once.

7. K. Freifeld, "Court KOs $1.87M TA Award, Orders New Trial," *Newsday,* Feb. 15, 1991.

8. I. Wilkerson, "Tylenol Maker Settles in Tampering Deaths," *New York Times,* May 14, 1991.

9. A. Alschuler, Foreword: "The Vanishing Civil Jury," *U. Chi. Legal Forum* 1, 6 (1990).

10. See J. Kakalik and N. Pace, *Costs and Compensation Paid in Tort Litigation* (Santa Monica, Calif.: RAND Institute for Civil Justice, 1986) 70. Various studies in the past decade have estimated the percentage of total expenses in tort litigation that are paid out as compensation to injured plaintiffs. For medical malpractice, products liability, and some toxic tort cases, the percentage drops lower than the 46 cents on the dollar figure cited, down toward 37–40 cents on the dollar. See S. Sugarman, *Doing Away with Personal Injury Law* (New York: Quorum, 1989) 23–24.

11. See M. Green, "The Inability of Offensive Collateral Estoppel to Fulfill Its Promise: An Examination of Estoppel in Asbestos Litigation," 70 *Iowa L. Rev.* 141, 221–23, 228–35 (1984).

12. P. H. Schuck, "Scheduled Damages and Insurance Contracts for Future Services: A Comment on Blumstein, Bovbjerg, and Sloan," 8 *Yale J. on Reg.* 213, 215–16 (1991).

13. C. Anderson, "$9 Million Award Against Transit Authority Upset," *New York L.J.*, Dec. 12, 1990, at 1.

CHAPTER 2: *Legal Rules That Bend, Not Break*

1. See, e.g., National Center for State Courts, State Court Caseload Statistics in 1989, at 3 (1991) (447,374 tort cases filed in state courts in 1989, an increase of 26.7 percent over filings in 1984); M. Galanter et al., "A Transformation of American Business Disputing? Some Preliminary Observations," Inst. for Legal Studies, Working Paper No. DPRP 10-3 (1991) (reporting on increases in tort filings in federal court from 1960 to 1988). J. O'Connell, "Blending Reform of Tort Liability and Health Insurance: A Necessary Mix," 79 *Cornell L. Rev.* 1303 (1994).

2. See, e.g., S. Sugarman, *Doing Away with Personal Injury Law* (New York: Quorum, 1989); Peter Huber, *Liability: The Legal Revolution and Its Consequences* (New York: Basic, 1988); P. Bell, "Analyzing Tort Law: The Flawed Promise of Neocontract," 74 *Minn. L. Rev.* 1177, 1185–91 (1990) (describing proponents of various contract-oriented approaches).

3. See, e.g., C. Gregory, "Trespass, to Negligence, to Absolute Liability," 37 *Va. L. Rev.* 359 (1951); M. Horwitz, *The Transformation of American Law, 1780–1860* (Cambridge: Harvard Univ. Press, 1977) at 67–108; G. Schwartz, "Tort Law and the Economy in Nineteenth Century America: A Reinterpretation," 90 *Yale L.J.* 1717 (1981); R. Rabin, "The Historical Development of the Fault Principle: A Reinterpretation," 15 *Ga. L. Rev.* 925 (1981).

4. The discussion of that case was so widespread among print and broadcast media that the McDonald's scalding coffee case seems to have taken a central place in the lore of what tort law is all about in this country. For a brief, reasonably balanced discussion of the case, see "Is Lawsuit Reform Good for Consumers?" *Consumer Reports,* May 1995, at 312.

5. For the strongest advocacy of this position, see Huber, *supra* note 2.

6. For a good summary of the major strands of judicial decisions on this issue, see *Smith v. Eli Lilly Co.,* 137 Ill.2d 222, 560 N.E.2d 324 (Ill. 1990).

7. New York's highest court did that in *Hymowitz v. Eli Lilly and Co.,* 73 N.Y.2d 487, 539 N.E.2d 1069 (N.Y. 1989).

8. See particularly D. Rosenberg, "The Causal Connection in Mass Exposure Cases: A 'Public Law' Vision of the Tort System," 97 *Harv. L. Rev.* 851 (1984); American Law Institute, Reporters' Study, 2 *Enterprise Responsibility for Personal Injury* (Philadelphia: The Institute, 1991) 369–81 [hereinafter ALI Study].

9. For an argument against this philosophy see L. Bender, "A Lawyer's Primer on Feminist Theory and Tort," 38 *J. Legal Ed.* 3 (1988).

10. See, e.g., ALI Study, *supra* note 8, at 199–230. But for arguments opposing elimination or arbitrary reductions in payment for pain and suffering, see S. P. Croley and J. D. Hanson, *The Nonpecuniary Costs of Accidents,* 108 *Harv. L. Rev.* 1785 (1995).

CHAPTER 3: *Helping the Needy or Greedy?*

1. See, e.g., American Law Institute, Reporters' Study, 1 *Enterprise Responsibility for Personal Injury* (Philadelphia: The Institute, 1991) 59–66 [hereinafter ALI Study]; M. Galanter, "The Day After the Litigation Explosion," 46 *Md. L. Rev.* 3 (1986). For an index and a complete table of contents to the ALI study, both of which the study lacks, see J. O'Connell and A. S. Glovsky, "An Index to the ALI Reporters' Study on Enterprise Responsibility for Personal Injury," 31 *San Diego L. Rev.* 665 (1994). Some of the most extreme increases in the frequency of tort claims and in the average amount paid out for those claims have come in the area of medical negligence. Even there, spending for malpractice insurance has gone up only slightly faster than spending on health care generally. 1 ALI Study, at 286–87.

2. See, e.g., ALI Study, *supra* note 1, at 55–56; *Medical Economics,* Nov. 18, 1991, at 188 (average medical malpractice premiums declining for most expensive specialties during the 1989–91 period).

3. J. O'Connell, "Blending Reform of Tort Liability and Health Insurance: A Necessary Mix," 79 *Cornell L. Rev.* 1303 (1994), reporting on percentages of all sources of compensation in 1960, 1982, 1984, 1988, and 1990; D. Hensler et al., RAND Institute for Civil Justice, *Compensation for Accidental Injuries in the United States* (Santa Monica, Calif.: RAND Institute for Civil Justice, 1991) 107–8 [hereinafter ICJ Study].

4. See ALI Study, *supra* note 1, at 106 n. 4.

5. *Family* in this context would mean whatever group of persons the injured plaintiff was supporting in full or in part with his earnings.

6. J. Keynes, *Essays in Persuasion* (New York: Harcourt Brace, 1932) 363; also quoted in J. Galbraith, *The Affluent Society* (Boston: Houghton Mifflin, 1969) 151.

7. For a good presentation of most of these criticisms, see S. Sugarman, *Doing Away with Personal Injury Law* (New York: Quorum, 1989) 35–41.

8. ICJ Study, *supra* note 3, at 23.

9. Harvard Medical Practice Study, *Patients, Doctors, and Lawyers: Medical Injury, Malpractice Litigation, and Patient Compensation in New York* (Cambridge: Harvard University Press, 1990) ch. 7.

10. ICJ Study, *supra* note 3, at 121–28.

11. See, e.g., Sugarman, *supra* note 7, at 129–33.

12. See, e.g., O'Connell, *supra* note 3; ICJ Study, *supra* note 3, at 175.

13. ALI Study, *supra* note 1, at 59.

14. For a thorough discussion of the weaknesses of the workers' compensation system in compensating particular categories of injuries, see ALI Study, *supra* note 1, at 113–17.

15. ALI Study, *supra* note 1, at 154–55.

16. *Id.* at 181–202.

17. For a more detailed discussion of the critics' arguments presented in this paragraph and of the possible rejoinders to such criticism, see P. Bell, "Analyzing Tort Law: The Flawed Promise of Neocontract," 74 *Minn. L. Rev.* 1177, 1231–37 (1990).

18. See, e.g., J. O'Connell and B. Kelly, *The Blame Game* (Lexington, Mass: Lexington, 1987) ch. 6; H. Ross, *Settled Out of Court* (Chicago: Aldine, 1970) 118; M. Mayer, *The Lawyers* (New York: Harper and Row, 1967) 263.

19. J. O'Connell, *The Injury Industry* (New York: Commerce Clearing House, 1971) 31–35.

CHAPTER 4: *Making a Safer World*

1. This has been the view of most scholars and judges. See G. White, *Tort Law in America: An Intellectual History* (New York: Oxford University Press, 1980) 146–47 (describing intellectual attitudes during the past century); see also W. Landes and R. Posner, *The Economic Structure of Tort Law* (Cambridge: Harvard University Press, 1987).

2. On deterrence see, e.g., P. Bell, "Legislative Intrusions into the Common Law of Medical Malpractice: Thoughts About the Deterrent Effect of Tort Liability," 35 *Syr. L. Rev.* 939, 979–80 (1984). Much of the research about the deterrent effects of legal sanctions has focused on criminal sanctions.

3. See "Obvious Solution," *Syracuse New Times,* April 1, 1992 (reporting on a British Medical Journal article in which a team of Welsh doctors recommended solving the problem of payouts for broken-glass bar fights, which approached $1.8 million annually, by switching to the use of tempered glass beer mugs, which disintegrated into tiny cubes on impact).

4. See, e.g., Associated Press, "New Whooping Cough Vaccine Under Study," *New York Times,* Oct. 31, 1989.

5. Several works have challenged the conventional wisdom that tort law deters actors from unreasonably unsafe behavior. See, e.g., S. Sugarman, *Doing Away with Personal Injury Law* (New York: Quorum, 1989) 3–34, 144–48; American Law Institute, *Reporters' Study,* 1 *Enterprise Responsibility for Personal Injury* (Philadelphia: The Institute, 1991) 30–33, 263–64, 295–98, 357–60, 376–81, 398–402, 413–18, 428–31 [hereinafter ALI Study]; P. Huber and R. Litan, eds., *The Liability Maze: The Impact of Liability Law on Safety and Innovation* (Washington, D.C.: Brookings Institution, 1991); G. Blackmon and R. Zeckhauser, "State Tort Reform Legislation: Assessing Our Control of Risks," in *Tort Law and the Public Interest* (New York: Norton, 1991) 272, 288–93 (P. H. Schuck, ed.). For a thorough and objective attempt to appraise the efficacy of tort law and alternatives thereto, including effects on deterrence, see D. Dewees, D. Duff, and M. Trebilcock, *Exploring the Domain of Accident Law: Taking the Facts Seriously* (New York: Oxford University Press, 1996) [hereinafter Dewees et al.]; On deterrence especially, see G. Schwartz, "Reality in the Economic Analysis of Tort Law: Does Tort Law Really Deter?" 42 *UCLA L. Rev.* 377, 393–97 (1994).

6. See G. Priest, "The Current Insurance Crisis and Modern Tort Law," 96 *Yale L.J.* 1521, 1527 n. 34, 1570 n. 193 (1987).

7. See, e.g., G. Schwartz, "The Ethics and Economics of Tort Liability Insurance," 75 *Corn. L. Rev.* 313, 342–43 (1990).

8. See D. Nye, D. Gifford, B. Webb, and M. Dewar, "The Causes of the Malpractice Crisis: An Analysis of Claims, Data, and Insurance Company Finances," 76 *Georgetown L.J.* 1495, 1558 (1988).

9. For further elaboration of this aspect of countertheory, see W. Olson, "Overdeterrence and the Problem of Comparative Risk," in *New Directions in Liability Law* (New York: The Academy of Political Science, 1988) 42 (W. Olson, ed.); P. Huber, *Liability: The Legal Revolution and Its Consequences* (New York: Basic, 1988).

10. For a recent summary of evidence about defensive medicine, see P. Weiler, *Medical Malpractice on Trial* (Cambridge: Harvard University Press, 1991) 85–90.

11. *The Liability Maze: The Impact of Liability Law on Safety and Innovation* (Washington, D.C.: Brookings Institution, 1991) (P. W. Huber and R. E. Litan, eds.).

12. M. Geyelin, "Tort Bar's Scourge: Star of Legal Reform Kindles Controversy but Collects Critics," *Wall Street Journal,* Oct. 16, 1992.

13. ALI Study, *supra* note 5, at 32, 359–60, 376–80 (concluding that there is evidence of at least some deterrent value in motor vehicle and medical malpractice litigation). See Schwartz, *supra* note 5. See also Sugarman, *supra* note 5, at 21–23 (concluding that deterrence theorists have no convincing support for their position); D. Dewees et al., *supra* note 5, passim.

14. ALI Study, *supra* note 5.

15. Weiler, *supra* note 10, at 91.

16. ALI Study, *supra* note 5, at 245. For an illustration of equally lax enforcement from the Food and Drug Administration, usually regarded as one of the most conscientious and effective regulatory agencies, see R. Abel, "The Real Tort Crisis: Too Few Claims," 48 *Ohio St. L.J.* 443, 458–59 (1987) (the FDA inspected a very low percentage of imported fruits and vegetables for contamination; of 164 lots of adulterated food it did identify, damages were imposed in only eight cases).

17. ALI Study, *supra* note 5, at 244.

18. See also C. Gorman, "Can Drug Firms Be Trusted?" *Time,* Feb. 10, 1992, at 43.

19. Schwartz, *supra* note 5.

CHAPTER 5: *Flawed Transactions*

1. The $300 billion figure comes from former Vice President Dan Quayle in the August 1991 report from the President's Council on Competitiveness, titled Agenda for Civil Justice Reform in America. Although the report made no effort to explain how the vice president arrived at that figure, some critics of the tort system have offered after-the-fact explanations for why that might be a reasonable guess. See, e.g., W. Olson, "Slowing the Recovery: Too Many Lawsuits," *San Diego Union-Tribune,* May 3, 1992. The $152 billion figure, estimated for 1994, is from an actuarial consulting firm. Tillinghast, *Tort Cost Trends: An International Perspective* (Weatogue, Conn.: Tillinghast-Towers Perrin, 1995) 3. This study purported to measure the "direct" costs of the tort system by looking at liability insurance costs nationally. See also L. Spencer, "The Tort Tax," *Forbes,* Feb. 17, 1992, at 40. Using a similar methodology, the American Law Institute's Reporters in 1991 estimated "very roughly" that the entire tort system probably costs $100 billion annually. American Law Institute, Reporters' Study, 1 *Enterprise Responsibility for Personal Injury* (Philadelphia: The Institute, 1991) 57 [hereinafter ALI Study]. A $16–19 billion figure comes from a study done by the RAND Corporation's Institute for Civil Justice in 1985. But unlike the Tillinghast and ALI figures, that represents only the costs of the operation of the tort system, exclusive of the compensation paid to injured persons. J. Kakalik and N. Pace, *Costs and Compensation Paid in Tort Litigation* (Santa Monica, Calif.: RAND Institute for Civil Justice, 1986) vii. For more on the costs of the tort system, see G. Schwartz, "Reality in the Economic Analysis of Tort Law: Does Tort Law Really Deter?" 42 *U.C.L.A. L. Rev.* 377, 432–43 (1994).

2. The data in this section come from studies done by the RAND Corporation in the 1980s. Those studies are summarized best in two RAND publications: Kakalik and Pace, *supra* note 1, xiii, and D. R. Hensler et al., *Trends in Tort Litigation* 27 (Santa Monica, Calif.: RAND Institute for Civil Justice, 1987). Where the figures in the text do not add up to $1.00 or 100 percent, it is because RAND's figures were rounded off.

3. U.S. Dept. of Transportation, 1 *Economic Consequences of Automobile Accident Injuries Report of the Westat Research Corp.* (1970) 146–47 (Table 15FS).

4. See P. Weiler, *Medical Malpractice on Trial* (Cambridge: Harvard University Press, 1991) 53–54, explaining the unequal burden delay imposes on

seriously injured persons as the impetus for settlements that tend to leave those persons substantially undercompensated. Weiler refers to a GAO study in which persons most severely injured by medical malpractice settled their cases for an average total compensation of $400,000, though their economic loss alone was estimated at $1.7 million on average. This undercompensation of serious losses by the tort system is a well-documented phenomenon. See, e.g., M. Saks, "Do We Really Know Anything About the Behavior of the Tort Litigation System—and Why Not?" 140 *U. Pa. L. Rev.* 1147, 1216–20 (1992).

In medical malpractice suits, Weiler notes, it typically takes three years from the time of injury before the tort system provides compensation to injured patients. Weiler, *supra,* at 52. For the study showing delays inherent in automobile accident tort litigation, see ALI Study, *supra* note 1, at 368.

5. See S. Sugarman, *Doing Away with Personal Injury Law* (New York: Quorum, 1989) 51, n. 24 (citing G. Priest, "The Current Insurance Crisis and Modern Tort Law," 96 *Yale L.J.* 1521, 1560 (1987). Paul Weiler has estimated the administrative costs of the workers' compensation systems at a slightly lower 15–20 percent of overall expenditures. P. Weiler, *supra* note 4, at 229, n. 38. It is not clear from these sources whether the figure for workers' compensation costs including a claimant's costs in obtaining the award, particularly with respect to legal fees and expenses, includes the parties' time.

6. See, inter alia, R. Keeton and J. O'Connell, *Basic Protection for the Traffic Victim: A Blueprint for Reforming Automobile Insurance* (Boston: Little, Brown, 1965); J. O'Connell, "A 'Neo No-Fault' Contract in Lieu of Tort: Preaccident Guarantees of Postaccident Settlement Offers," 73 *Calif. L. Rev.* 898 (1985); J. O'Connell and C. Kelly, *The Blame Game* (Lexington, Mass.: Lexington, 1987) ch. 12.

7. See, e.g., the treatment in W. Prosser, J. Wade, and V. Schwartz, *Cases and Materials on Torts* (Brooklyn: Foundation, 1988) 202–9 (8th ed.) of the United States Supreme Court's hasty retreat from an opinion by Holmes that set down clear rules of improper conduct for vehicles approaching railroad crossings. Faced with a case in which unusual circumstances made it arguably reasonable for a driver to do what generally was unreasonable at a railroad crossing, the Court by an opinion by Cardozo rescinded a rule it had put into place with great confidence only seven years previously. Pokara v. Wabash Ry., 292 U.S. 580 (1934), overruling Baltimore & Ohio R.R. v.

Goodman, 275 U.S. 66 (1927). See Prosser et al. *supra* for other examples of this phenomenon of courts having to back off.

8. For such a response, from the perspective more of injurers and injury-free consumers than of the injured, see P. Huber, *Liability: The Legal Revolution* (New York: Basic, 1988), and W. Olson, *The Litigation Explosion* (New York: Thomas Talley–Dutton, 1991). For a more comprehensive study, see D. Dewees, D. Duff, and M. Trebilcock, *Exploring the Domain of Accident Law: Taking the Facts Seriously* (New York: Oxford University Press, 1996).

9. Another example of the public policy response is Sugarman, *supra* note 5.

10. The insiders' response predictably has come from judges as much as from scholars. Their tinkering has been most prominent with respect to the tidal wave of asbestos cases that struck the courts in the 1980s and with regard to other mass toxic tort cases. To gain a sense of some of these efforts, see American Law Institute, Reporters' Study, 2 *Enterprise Responsibility for Personal Injury* (Philadelphia: The Institute, 1991) 402–39; Symposium, "Claims Resolution Facilities and the Mass Settlement of Mass Torts," 53 *L. & Contemp. Pblms.* 1–198 (F. E. McGovern, ed., 1990); M. Saks and P. Blanck, "Justice Improved: The Unrecognized Benefits of Aggregation and Sampling in the Trial of Mass Torts," 44 *Stan. L. Rev.* 815, 816–26 (1992). It is probably too artificial to characterize all "insider responses" as tinkering with a given framework in an attempt at streamlining. These responses were classed in a category together to capture a kind of thinking: that which was concerned above all with getting tort claims processed, quickly and cheaply, usually in settings in which court logjams had already occurred. Of course, even those persons most focused on claims processing were concerned, in "tinkering," with sustaining the values that they felt the tort system was trying to serve.

11. R. MacCoun et al., *Alternative Adjudication: An Evaluation of the New Jersey Automobile Arbitration Program* (Santa Monica, Calif.: RAND Institute for Civil Justice, 1988) 41–42. For descriptions and somewhat positive assessments of the cost-reducing effects of the two variants on traditional tort procedure, see A. Levin and D. Colliers, "Containing the Cost of Litigation," 37 *Rutgers L. Rev.* 219 (1984–85); R. Peckham, "A Judicial Response to the Cost of Litigation: Case Management, 2-Stage Discovery Planning and Alternative Dispute Resolution," 37 *Rutgers L. Rev.* 253 (1984–85).

12. Plaintiff pressure may be a significant missing element in many tort cases. In the asbestos litigation, plaintiffs were notoriously passive in their

interactions with their attorneys in the face of unconscionable delays in the resolution of their claims—unconscionable in the sense that some clients' physical condition deteriorated drastically, with some dying during the litigation. D. Hensler et al., *Asbestos in the Courts: The Challenge of Mass Toxic Torts* (Santa Monica, Calif.: RAND Institute for Civil Justice, 1985) 83.

CHAPTER 6: *Just Proceedings?*

1. See, e.g., J. Coleman, "Moral Theories of Torts: Their Scope and Limits," 1 *Law & Phil.* 371 (1982) (part 1), 2 *Law and Phil.* 5 (1983) (part 2); G. Fletcher, "Fairness and Utility in Tort Theory," 85 *Harv. L. Rev.* 537 (1972); E. Weinrib, "Understanding Tort Law," 23 *Val. U. L. Rev.* 485 (1989); R. Wright, "Allocating Liability Among Multiple Responsible Causes: A Principled Defense of Joint and Several Liability for Actual Harm and Risk Exposure," 21 *U.C. Davis L. Rev.* 1141, 1179–94 (1988).

2. See American Law Institute, Reporters' Study, 1 *Enterprise Responsibility for Personal Injury* (Philadelphia: The Institute, 1991) 24–25 [hereinafter ALI study].

3. See, e.g., J. O'Connell, *The Lawsuit Lottery* (New York: Free Press, 1979) 8.

4. See, e.g., D. Owen, "The Moral Foundations of Products Liability Law: Toward First Principles," 68 *Notre Dame L. Rev.* 427 (1993) (concluding that the principles of moral and political philosophy relevant to issues of tort theory are so many, varied, and complex that they cannot be reduced to a single, exclusive metatheory); S. Sugarman, *Doing Away with Tort Law* (New York: Quorum, 1990) 57–62 (discussing major theorists who write about justice in tort law, and concluding "we have no clear and convincing theory of corrective justice"); C. Wells, "Tort Law as Corrective Justice: A Pragmatic Justification for Jury Adjudication," 88 *Mich. L. Rev.* 2348, 2364–76 (1990).

5. See Owen, *supra* note 4, at 434–35: "Yet conventional corrective justice models cannot alone provide a moral justification for products liability law that is at all complete. Their formal abstraction may dazzle the intellect but fails to help determine whether a harmful act was also 'wrongful,' thus leaving corrective justice drained of a substantive core to help resolve the fundamental moral questions of accountability for products accidents."

6. A brief introduction to these varying philosophical approaches can be found in Owen, *supra* note 4.

7. See, e.g., L. Bender, "A Lawyer's Primer on Feminist Theory and Torts," 38 *J. Legal Educ.* 3, 31–36 (1988); E. Weinrib, "Liberty, Community, and Corrective Justice," 1 *Can. J. Law & Juris.* 1 (1988) (pointing to tort law's rules in these "failure to act" cases as evidence it rejects communitarian and natural law theories of justice).

8. See Owen, *supra* note 4 (disagreeing, very respectfully, with the conclusions of John Attanasio in "The Principle of Aggregate Autonomy and the Calabresian Approach to Products Liability," 74 *Va. L. Rev.* 677 [1988]). See also Wells, *supra* note 4, at 2375 (emphasizing the extent to which the values identified as at the core of carefully constructed theories of justice could be related to legal rules in ways quite different from, but equally plausible to, those favored by others articulating those theories of justice).

9. M. Saks, "Do We Really Know Anything About the Behavior of the Tort Litigation System—and Why Not?" 140 *U. Pa. L. Rev.* 1147, 1235–39 (1992).

10. For a much more elaborate introduction to this idea about justice, see R. C. Solomon, *A Passion for Justice* (Lanham, Md.: Rowman and Littlefield, 1995). Solomon, a University of Texas philosophy professor, author, and ethics consultant, postulates that people develop their senses of justice out of caring about increasingly large circles of others. His book argues that this expansion of caring will lead inevitably to more justice being done.

11. M. Saks and P. Blanck, "Justice Improved: The Unrecognized Benefits of Aggregation and Sampling in the Trial of Mass Torts," 44 *Stan. L. Rev.* 815, 834 (1992).

12. For cogent criticisms of the tort system, see ALI Study *supra* note 2, e.g., vol. 1 at 33, 51–52, 86–94, 102, 445; vol. 2, at 3–7.

13. P. Huber, "Safety and the Second Best: The Hazards of Public Risk Management in the Courts," 85 *Colum. L. Rev.* 277, 306–8, 311, 318 (1985); P. Huber, *Liability: The Legal Revolution and Its Consequences* (New York: Basic, 1988).

14. E. Griswold, *1962–63 Harvard Law School Dean's Report* 5–6. But for a vigorous defense of jury performance in medical malpractice cases as to both liability and damages, see N. Vidmar, *Medical Malpractice and the American Jury: Confronting the Myths About Jury Competence, Deep Pockets, and Outrageous Damage Awards* (Ann Arbor: University of Michigan Press, 1995).

CHAPTER 7: *Human Transactions*

1. References here and in many other parts of this chapter to the experiences and attitudes of tort plaintiffs who brought suits against defendants who abused them sexually are drawn from two recent articles: B. Feldthusen, "The Civil Action for Sexual Battery: Therapeutic Jurisprudence?" 25 *Ottawa L. Rev.* 203 (1994); and B. Feldthusen, "Discriminatory Damage Quantification in Civil Actions for Sexual Battery," 44 *Univ. of Toronto L.J.* 133 (1994). The author's information about these experiences and attitudes is drawn primarily from case reports and press accounts of tort suits by survivors of sexual abuse.

2. See, for example, N. Weston, "The Metaphysics of Modern Tort Theory," 28 *Val. L. Rev.* 919 (1994) (discussing the tendencies of individuals and American society to seek "relentlessly" to control and manage our accidents, to rationalize them and so to subject them to our calculative reason); H. Gans, *Middle American Individualism* (New York: Free Press, 1988). Novelist Russell Banks presents vivid descriptions of the differing reactions to tort litigation of persons with "shit happens" philosophies and those with more common "control-over-my-world" philosophies in *The Sweet Hereafter* (New York: Harper Collins, 1991).

3. G. James, "Groping for Answers in Tailgate Shooting," *New York Times,* December 31, 1992.

4. See K. Bumiller, *The Civil Rights Society* (Baltimore: Johns Hopkins University Press, 1988) 60.

5. As to the role of the tort lawsuit in dealing with victims' anger and providing vengeance and vindication, see the following works: J. Hampton, "A New Theory of Retribution," in *Liability and Responsibility: Essays in Law and Morals* (New York: Cambridge University Press, 1991) 377 (R. Frey and C. Morris, eds.); J. G. Murphy, "Retributive Hatred: An Essay on Criminal Liability and the Emotions," in the same book at 351; Bumiller, *supra* note 4, at 77–82; B. Bettelheim, *Surviving and Other Essays* (New York: Knopf, 1979) 19–36; Feldthusen, "Civil Action," *supra* note 1; S. Jacoby, *Wild Justice: The Evolution of Revenge* (New York: Harper and Row, 1983) 43; and R. Abel, "The Real Tort Crisis: Too Few Claims," 48 *Ohio St. L.J.* 443 (1987).

6. On the social educative function of tort lawsuits, see B. Yngvesson, "Inventing Law in Local Settings: Rethinking Popular Legal Culture," 98 *Yale L.J.* 1689 (1989) (law *creates* the social world by "naming" it); K. Bumiller,

"Speaking of Silence: The Civil Rights Society: The Social Construction of Victims," 43 *U. Miami L. Rev.* 493 (1988) (book review) (transformative power of injury claims with respect to people's understanding of their and others' lives); D. Harris et al., *Compensation and Support for Illness and Injury* (Oxford: Clarendon, 1984) 146 (chance that blame will be applied will influence people's interpretations of an event; tort law affects people's perceptions of causes of accidents); M. Minow, "Words and the Door To the Land of Change: Law, Language, and Family Violence," 43 *Vand. L. Rev.* 1665 (1990) (importance of storytelling to the reconstruction of dominant understandings); H. Fechner, "Toward an Expanded Conception of Law Reform: Sexual Harassment Law and the Reconstruction of Facts," 23 *U. Mich. J.L. Ref.* 475 (1990) (telling personal stories opens up the perspectives of judges and other dominant groups to other views of reality); Weston, *supra* note 2 (tort law as the place society looks for explanations of accidents consistent with a view of humans in charge of their lives). But see J. O'Connell and C. Kelly, *The Blame Game* (Lexington, Mass.: Lexington, 1987) Injuries, Insurance, and Injustice, chs. 1, 5 (indicating dissatisfactions for even successful tort litigants); J. O'Connell and R. Simon, "Payment for Pain and Suffering: Who Wants What, When and Why," 1972 *U. Ill. L. Forum* 1, 25–34 (showing little interest in or satisfaction from blaming after auto accidents).

7. For a view in one particular context of ways in which tort lawsuits can assist in the formation and success of broader political efforts, see R. Austin, "Employer Abuse, Worker Resistance, and the Tort of Intentional Infliction of Emotional Distress," 41 *Stan. L. Rev.* 1 (1988). In an article concerning the failed tobacco litigation, Robert L. Rabin observed that tort law has been most effective when it crystallizes an unsatisfied demand for political action. R. Rabin, "A Sociolegal History of the Tobacco Tort Litigation," 44 *Stan. L. Rev.* 853, 878 (1992).

8. For a discussion of these "denunciation" benefits that citizens derive from judicial determinations of wrongdoing and subsequent punishment of wrongdoers, see N. Walker, *Punishment, Danger, and Stigma: The Morality of Criminal Justice* (Oxford: B. Blackwell, 1980) 22–42.

9. A considerable body of literature discusses the stigma often associated with filing a tort lawsuit and some of the reasons—particularly cultural reasons—underlying that stigmatization of the plaintiffs. See, for example, D. Engel, "The Oven Bird's Song: Insiders, Outsiders, and Personal Injuries in an American Community," 18 *Law and Society Rev.* 551 (1984); R. Hay-

den, *The Cultural Logic of a Political Crisis: Common Sense, Hegemony, and the Great American Liability Insurance Famine of 1986* (Madison: Institute for Legal Studies, University of Wisconsin–Madison Law School, 1988) (Disputes Processing Research Program Working Paper 9-8); Abel, *supra* note 5.

10. O'Connell and Kelly, *supra* note 6 at 133–34.

11. M. Rozen, "Hairpiece v. Fat Boy," *American Lawyer,* Oct. 18, 1992, at 82.

12. Recent research has raised the possibility that a lawsuit actually enhances the duration and intensity of the physical pain experienced by accident victims. See E. Rosenthal, "Chronic Pain Fells Many Yet Lacks Clear Cause," *New York Times,* Dec. 29, 1992. More scientific studies of tort claims involving the survivors of those killed by others' wrongdoing recognizes both potential benefits and detriments of tort litigation in the grieving process. See P. Rosenblatt, "Grief and Involvement in Wrongful Death Litigation," 7 *Law and Human Behavior* 351 (1983).

13. For a discussion focusing on the psychological reactions of doctors to tort lawsuits, see P. Bell, "Legislative Intrusions into the Common Law of Medical Malpractice: Thoughts About the Deterrent Effects of Tort Liability," 35 *Syr. L. Rev.* 939 (1984). Recently, a Syracuse doctor, sued in a well-publicized trial for sexually harassing one of his employees, killed himself after he won the suit. *Syracuse Post-Standard,* December 28, 1992.

14. For a sense of findings about the extent to which litigants feel they are exercising control of their own lawsuits, see D. Hensler, "Resolving Mass Toxic Torts: Myths and Realities," 1989 *U. Ill. L. Rev.* 89, 92–95 (reporting that clients in "mass" tort lawsuits often said they had little control over the progress or outcomes of their lawsuits). But see E. Lind et al., *The Perception of Justice: Tort Litigant's Views of Trial, Court-Annexed Arbitration, and Judicial Settlement Conferences* (Santa Monica, Calif.: RAND Institute for Civil Justice, 1989) 74 (their study showed that litigants had higher levels of perceived control and participation in tort trials than literature suggested). It is worth noting both that "mass torts," in which a lawyer may have many similarly situated clients, may be especially prone to a lawyer's disengagement from the client. Similarly, there is no question that many plaintiffs' lawyers do a woeful job of keeping their clients informed and involved in the progress of their cases. See Feldthusen, "Civil Action," *supra* note 1 (emphasizing that the potential for client control in sexual battery cases depends to a considerable extent on the skills of the client's lawyer).

15. See, e.g., J. Lemieux, "Settlement Money in '89 School Bus Accident Tears Town Apart," *Los Angeles Times,* Jan. 2, 1994.

16. For a more detailed discussion of the differences between victims' experiences of criminal and tort proceedings in sexual abuse cases, see Feldthusen, "Civil Action," *supra* note 1.

17. S. Carroll, A. Abrahamse, and M. Vaiana, *The Costs of Excess Medical Claims for Automobile Personal Injuries* (Santa Monica, Calif.: RAND Institute for Civil Justice, 1995). U.S. Dept. of Justice, Federal Bureau of Investigation, Press Release, May 24, 1995.

18. A. Haggerty, "Insurer Gears up to Brake Phony Auto Accident Scams," *National Underwriter, Property and Casualty Ed.,* July 27, 1984, at 3.

19. P. Kerr, " 'Ghost Riders' Are Target of an Insurance Sting," *New York Times,* Aug. 18, 1993.

20. W. Glaberson, "Trial Takes Hard Look at a Personal Injury Law Firm," *New York Times,* Nov. 20, 1990.

21. T. Noah, "Review of A Civil Action by Jonathan Harr," *Washington Monthly* 50, 51 (Sept. 1995).

CHAPTER 8: *Context*

1. For fuller flavor of the psychological burdens medical professionals carry as a result of the tort system, see F. Hubbard, "The Physicians' Point of View Concerning Medical Malpractice: A Sociological Perspective on the Symbolic Importance of 'Tort Reform,' " 23 *Ga. L. Rev.* 295 (1989).

2. For a recent compilation of empirical evidence relevant to whether the tort system is biased against defendants see M. Saks, "Do We Really Know Anything About the Behavior of the Tort Litigation System—and Why Not?" 140 *U. Pa. L. Rev.* 1147, 1235–39 (1992) (summing up that in light of extensive evidence, "it is hard to avoid the unexpected conclusion that juries are one of society's most reliable decision-making institutions").

3. See Saks, *supra* note 2.

4. For work dealing with American attitudes toward torts claims generally by anthropologists, see R. Hayden, *The Cultural Logic of a Political Crisis: Common Sense, Hegemony, and the Great American Liability Insurance Famine of 1986* (Madison: Institute for Legal Studies, University of Wisconsin–Madison Law School, 1988) Working Paper 9-8; D. Engel, "The Oven Bird's Song: Insiders, Outsiders, and Personal Injuries in an American Community," 18 *Law and Society Rev.* 551 (1984).

5. W. E. Roman, "Lobby Effort to Curb Litigation Turns to States for Tort Reform," *Washington Times,* Feb. 4, 1993. The article reported a Texas poll in which 70 percent of respondents said that tort lawsuit abuse affected them as individuals.

6. *Id.*

7. C. Wasilewski, "Tort Reform: Courting Public Opinion," 87 Best's Review—Property-Casualty Insurance Edition, at 14 (June 1986).

8. P. Brimelow and L. Spencer, "The Best Paid Lawyers in America," *Forbes,* Oct. 16, 1989, at 197; "The Top Trial Lawyers," *Forbes,* Nov. 6, 1995, at 160.

9. The American Tort Reform Association, *Campaign Contributions to Congressional Candidates by the Plaintiffs' Lawyer Industry,* 1989–94 (April 1995). See also G. Simpson, "Trial Lawyers, After Flirting with GOP, Are Back at Democratic Party's Table," *Wall Street Journal,* July 16, 1996.

10. For a discussion of the Illinois contributions and reactions thereto, see R. Pearson and W. Grady, "Lawyer-Doctor Battle Helps Politicians," *Chicago Tribune,* Feb. 13, 1993.

11. For examples of some of the Republican efforts to campaign on tort-reform grounds, primarily by tying the Democrats and Bill Clinton to plaintiffs' lawyers, see: D. Frantz, "Trial Lawyers, Their Money, and Their Influence Have Become Issues in the Campaign," *New York Times,* Oct. 13, 1996. G. Rushford, "Tort Reform Advocates Fear Bush Will Scare Allies," *New Jersey Law Journal,* Sept. 7, 1992, at 4; M. Geyelin, "Knock at Clinton Puzzles Legal Reformers," *Wall Street Journal,* Sept. 8, 1992; D. Johnston, "The New Presidency: The Justice Department; Part of Attorney General–Designate's Record Disturbs Some Clinton Backers," *New York Times,* Jan. 13, 1993; J. Davidson, "Stage Is Set for Another Round in Fight Over Bill to Revise Product-Liability Law," *Wall Street Journal,* Sept. 2, 1992 (Bush: "[M]y opponent's campaign is being backed by every trial lawyer who ever wore a tasseled loafer").

12. Editorial, "Tort Song Tragedy," *Wall Street Journal,* Sept. 18, 1992. See also Editorial, "Litigation Liberalism," *Wall Street Journal,* May 12, 1992 ("[T]he plaintiffs' bar, especially the Association of Trial Lawyers of America [ATLA], has become the most important single fund-raising source for liberal Democrats").

13. See, with respect to juror attitudes, V. Hans and W. Lofquist, "Jurors' Judgments of Business Liability in Tort Cases: Implications for the Litigation Explosion Debate," 26 *L. & Soc. Rev.* 85 (1992). With regard to trends

in judicial decisions which favor defendants, particularly in products liability suits, see G. Schwartz, "Product Liability Reform by the Judiciary," 27 *Gonzaga L. Rev.* 303 (1991/92); J. Henderson and T. Eisenberg, "Inside the Quiet Revolution in Products Liability," 39 *U.C.L.A. L. Rev.* 731 (1992).

14. See J. O'Connell and M. Horowitz, "The Lawyer Will See You Now: Health Reform's Tort Crisis," *The Washington Post,* June 13, 1993; J. O'Connell, "Blending Reform of Tort Liability and Health Insurance: A Necessary Mix," 79 *Cornell L. Rev.* 1303 (1994).

CHAPTER 9: *Changes*

1. See, e.g., J. O'Connell and C. Kelly, *The Blame Game: Injuries, Insurance, and Injustice* (Lexington, Mass.: Lexington, 1989) chs. 11–12.

2. For examples of no-fault proposals, see, e.g., P. Weiler, *Medical Malpractice on Trial* (Cambridge: Harvard University Press, 1991); S. Sugarman, *Doing Away with Personal Injury Law* (New York: Quorum, 1989); J. O'Connell et al., "Tort Law: No-Fault Auto Insurance Symposium," 26 *San Diego L. Rev.* 977 (1989).

3. For an overview of the New Zealand system, see R. Mahoney, "New Zealand's Accident Compensation Scheme: A Reassessment," 40 *Am. J. Comp. Law* 159 (1992).

4. See Sugarman, *supra* note 2.

5. For a discussion of the types of automobile no-fault plans, locating them in the no-fault world, see B. Chapman and M. Trebilcock, "Making Hard Social Choices: Lessons from the Auto Accident Compensation Debate," 44 *Rutgers L. Rev.* 797 (1992). For an overview of workers' compensation plans, see M. Franklin and R. Rabin, *Tort Law and Alternatives: Cases and Materials* 720–44 (5th ed. 1992).

6. See Chapman and Trebilcock, *supra* note 5, at 818, n. 62. While studies of Quebec's pure no-fault system indicated that there might be cost savings in the 10–24 percent range, other studies put the savings at 5 percent, and some U.S. studies put the expected administrative savings somewhat higher. A recent RAND study postulated that a no-fault system that banned all noneconomic damages would reduce transaction costs 80 percent. S. Carroll and J. Kakalik, *No-Fault Automobile Insurance: A Policy Perspective* (Santa Monica, Calif.: RAND, 1991).

7. Tort law has accepted strict liability—liability without proof that neither the defendant nor its product was faulty—in a small group of situations

in which a defendant's actions injured someone while the defendant was engaged in an "abnormally dangerous activity." Such activities traditionally have been those—like blasting—in which only a few people engage and which pose, even when properly conducted, a very high risk that someone will get hurt. See Restatement, 2d, Torts, §§519, 520 (1965).

8. See Report of the U.S. National Commission on State Workmen's Compensation Law, Washington, D.C. (1972).

9. For a fuller discussion of these political struggles and the evidence questioning the adequacy of workers' compensation benefits antedating those struggles, see M. Feldman, "The Intellectual Ordering of Contemporary Tort Law," 51 *Md. L. Rev.* 980 (1992).

10. See R. Mahoney, "New Zealand's Accident Compensation Scheme: A Reassessment," 40 *Am. J. Comp. Law* 159 (1992) (New Zealand cutbacks); L. Mazzuca, "Shot Through with Problems," Crain Communications Inc., *Business Insurance,* Aug. 24, 1992, at 1.

11. See, e.g., *Morris v. Savoy,* 61 Ohio St. 3d 684, 576 N.E.2d 765 (1991) (ruling unconstitutional the Ohio legislature's $200,000 cap on nonpecuniary damages in medical malpractice actions).

12. Improving the American Legal System: The Economic Benefits of Tort Reform, Joint Economic Committee (JEC), United States Congress 5–6 (March 1996); J. O'Connell et al., "The Comparative Cost of Consumer Choice for Auto Insurance in All Fifty States," 55 *Md. L. Rev.* 160 (1996).

13. But see P. Weiler et al., *A Measure of Malpractice* (Cambridge: Harvard University Press, 1993), 76–109, 144–52.

14. Incorporated by S. 1861, 104th Cong., 2d Sess., sponsored by Sen. McConnell (R.-Ky.) and Sen. Dole (R.-Kan.).

15. P. Passell, "Windfall Fees in Injury Cases Under Assault," *New York Times,* Feb. 11, 1994. L. Brickman, M. Horowitz, and J. O'Connell, *Rethinking Contingency Fees* (Washington, D.C.: Manhattan Institute, 1994); M. Horowitz, "Making Ethics Real, Making Ethics Work: A Proposal for Contingency Fee Reform," 14 *Emory L. Rev.* 174 (1995).

16. E.g., E. A. Lind et al., *The Perception of Justice: Tort Litigant's View of Trials, Court Annexed Arbitration, and Judicial Settlement Conferences* (Santa Monica, Calif.: RAND Institute for Civil Justice, 1989); E. A. Lind and T. Tyler, *The Social Psychology of Procedural Justice* (Santa Monica, Calif.: RAND Institute for Civil Justice, 1988).

17. See, e.g., J. Blumstein et al., "Beyond Tort Reform: Developing Better Tools for Personal Injury," 8 *Yale J. on Reg.* 171 (1991); David Baldus of

the University of Iowa Law School has been working for some years with the National Center on State Courts to develop more workable guidelines for appellate courts to promulgate and use in making noneconomic injury awards more uniform and systematic.

18. But see S. Croly and J. Hanson, "The Nonpecuniary Costs of Accidents: Pain-and-Suffering Damages in Tort Cases," 108 *Harv. L. Rev.* 1785 (1995).

19. C. Wolfram, *Modern Legal Ethics* (St. Paul, Minn.: West, 1986) 528.

20. P. Weiler, *Medical Malpractice on Trial* (Cambridge: Harvard University Press, 1991) 122–32.

21. For further understanding of the negative experience of the lawsuit and the threat of such lawsuits in the medical area, see F. Hubbard, "The Physicians' Point of View Concerning Medical Malpractice: A Sociological Perspective on the Symbolic Importance of 'Tort Reform'," 23 *Ga. L. Rev.* 295 (1989); P. Bell, "Legislative Intrusions into the Common Law of Medical Malpractice: Thoughts About the Deterrent Effect of Tort Liability," 35 *Syr. L. Rev.* 939 (1984).

22. L. Brickman, "Class Action Reforming," *Manhattan Institute Research Memorandum,* Oct. 1995.

23. B. Meier, "Fistfuls of Coupons: Millions for Class-Action Lawyers Scrip for Plaintiffs," *New York Times,* May 26, 1965; for a symposium on the problems of individualized justice in mass torts actions, see R. Cramton, "Individualized Justice, Mass Torts, and 'Settlement Class Actions': An Introduction," 80 *Cornell L. Rev.* 811 (1995).

24. Brickman, *supra* note 22.

25. Brickman, *supra* note 22. On the frustratingly difficult problems of determining whether a product subject to mass tort litigation was defective or caused particular adverse results, see G. Kolata, "Will the Lawyers Kill Off Norplant?" *New York Times,* May 28, 1995; "A Case of Justice, or a Total Travesty: Researchers Say Bad Science Won the Day in Breast Implant Battle," *New York Times,* June 13, 1995. But see R. Gordon and L. Roth, "Dow Corning Created the Tort Monster," *Wall Street Journal,* June 6, 1995 (Letters to the Editor).

26. *In re Phone: Poulene Rorer Inc.,* 57 F. 3d 1293 (1995).

ronmental toxins, 38–39; market-share liability rules, 38; and failure to act, 40; unlimited, 43–44; costs of, 55, 83–84, 117; enterprise liability, 224. *See also* Products liability
Liability insurance: and deep pockets, 13–14; rates for, 47, 80–81, 178, 194, 210; and compensation, 55; and self-insurance, 80; and unclear communication of tort rules, 84; cost of, 136–37, 242n1; and businesses, 174; in Arkansas, 184; and health insurance, 190–91; inflationary effects on, 192; and contingency fees, 216–17; and collateral source rule, 220; and intangible harms, 223
Lieberman, Joseph, 212
Life insurance, 61, 106
Lobbyists, 23, 172–75, 178–86, 188–89, 196
Lost expectancy suffering, 53–54

McConnell, Mitch, 212, 219
Maine, 209
Malpractice. *See* Medical malpractice
Managed care organizations (MCOs), 191–94
Manhattan Institute, 189–90
Market regulation, and tort law, 70–75, 78, 82, 99
Market-share liability rules, 38
Massachusetts, 165, 221
Mass media, 138, 141
Mass tort cases, 113, 200, 224–25, 229, 249n14
MCOs (managed care organizations), 191–94
Medical expenses: as damages, 16; compensation for, 41, 53; as absolute needs, 57; and no-fault systems, 164, 202; padding of, 164–66
Medical malpractice: and tort law, xiii; claims of, 10, 58, 238n1; and

injuries, 26; and state legislatures, 28, 180–81; and tort reform, 28–29, 180–81, 200, 220; rates in suing and payout, 47; and compensation, 59, 133; and weak sanctions, 79; and unclear communication of tort rules, 83; and defensive medicine, 89, 92; and innovation, 93; and deterrence of unsafe behavior, 95, 100; and self-preservation instincts, 96; and morality, 98; transaction costs of, 103, 107, 237n10; defendants' stake in, 109; psychological costs of, 175; and cost control, 190–92; and managed care organizations, 192–94; and no-fault systems, 195, 202, 223–24; and delays, 243n4
Michigan, 164
Monsanto, 93
Morality, and deterrence of unsafe behavior, 98–99
Morgan, James, 154
Mosely, Shannon, 134
Moynihan, Daniel P., 212

Nader, Ralph, 178, 182, 185–86
National Association of Independent Insurers, 181
National Association of Manufacturers, 181
National Association of Mutual Insurance Companies, 181
National Insurance Consumer Organization, 182
Negligence: and reasonable care, 7, 29–31; and unreasonable behavior, 11; certainty of, 31; and strict liability, 31, 32; contributory negligence, 32–33, 34, 49, 150; and causation, 36–39
Neo-no-fault systems, 106, 210, 213–19
New Jersey, 113
New York, 28, 58, 164